perfect
fish & seafood

This is a Parragon Publishing book
This edition published in 2007

Parragon Publishing
Queen Street House
4 Queen Street
Bath BA1 1HE, UK

Copyright © Parragon 2007
Designed by Terry Jeavons & Company

ISBN 978-1-4054-7367-5

Printed in China

This book uses imperial, metric, and US cup measurements. Follow the same units of measurement throughout; do not mix imperial and metric. All spoon measurements are level, unless otherwise stated: teaspoons are assumed to be 5ml, and tablespoons are assumed to be 15ml. Unless otherwise stated, milk is assumed to be whole, eggs and individual fruits such as bananas are medium, and pepper is freshly ground black pepper.

Recipes using raw or very lightly cooked eggs should be avoided by infants, the elderly, pregnant women, convalescents, and anyone suffering from an illness. Pregnant and breast-feeding women are advised to avoid eating peanuts and peanut products.

perfect
fish&seafood

introduction

Fish has so many virtues that it is hard to know where to start listing them!

As a health food, fish is superb. It is high in first-class protein and low in salt. It contains vitamins, including A and D in oil-rich fish, and some of the B vitamins, as well as a whole range of minerals—iron, calcium, copper, magnesium, manganese, phosphorus, potassium, selenium, sodium, iodine, fluorine, and zinc. White fish is low in fat, and the fat in fresh oil-rich fish such as halibut, swordfish, salmon, scallops, and tuna contains high amounts of the polyunsaturated fats called omega-3 fatty acids. These fats are essential to health because they cannot be produced

by the human body, and research shows that they reduce cholesterol absorption and help to lower blood-cholesterol levels, preventing the arteries from clogging, and averting coronary heart diseases.

Omega-3 fatty acids are also believed to help in the prevention of cancers of the breast, prostate, and colon and reduce the inflammation associated with rheumatoid arthritis. They even improve brain function and decrease the risk of dementia, depression, and poor memory.

Fish is the perfect food for today's lifestyle—it is quick and easy to cook, and is both light and substantial. On top of all this, fish is good to eat! There is such an incredible variety of fish available, and so many interesting ways to cook it, that you might forget you are eating a highly nutritious superfood and simply focus on the delicious dishes that you can make with it. It can be cooked very simply—baked, roasted, broiled, grilled, pan-fried or stir-fried—or

added to risottos, paellas, pasta, soups, stews, elegant tarts or homely potato-topped pies. The list is endless.

Whether you are eating fish for the sake of your health, or because you love the taste and convenience of it, enjoy the fabulous recipes in this book!

soups & appetizers

Historically, a formal banquet always included a substantial fish course before the meat was served. Today, with our ever-changing lifestyles and appetites, we are more likely to choose a light, elegant appetizer. Soup is always a good choice, and Breton Fish Soup is a chic, creamy French recipe, while Mexican Fish & Roasted Tomato Soup will get the tastebuds tingling, and Thai Shrimp & Scallop Soup is stylish, yet incredibly quick to make.

Spanish tapas has become popular in recent years—you need to serve a good selection, so there are delicious recipes for Fresh Salmon in Mojo Sauce, Fish & Caper Croquettes, Tuna with Pimiento-stuffed Olives, Mussels with Herb & Garlic Butter, Lime-drizzled Shrimp, and Calamari. Japanese sushi is another trendy appetizer—if you've never made it before, Teriyaki Tuna Pressed Sushi with Green Bean Strips and Scattered Sushi with Shrimp, Crab & Avocado are easy to assemble.

For those occasions when you're out to impress with classic simplicity, serve Salmon Tartare or Gravlax, two dishes where the fish is slowly 'seasoned' rather than cooked, Potted Crab, Shrimp Cocktail, or Blinis, a Russian specialty of buckwheat pancakes topped with sour cream and smoked salmon. Gorgeous!

breton fish soup

ingredients

SERVES 4

2 tsp butter

1 large leek, thinly sliced

2 shallots, finely chopped

4 fl oz/125 ml/½ cup
    hard cider

10 fl oz/300 ml/1¼ cups fish
    stock

9 oz/250 g potatoes, diced

1 bay leaf

salt

4 tbsp all-purpose flour

7 fl oz/200 ml/scant 1 cup
    milk

7 fl oz/200 ml/scant 1 cup
    heavy cream

2 oz/55 g sorrel leaves

12 oz/350 g skinless
    monkfish or cod fillets, cut
    into 1-inch/2.5-cm pieces

method

1 Melt the butter in a large pan over medium-low heat. Add the leek and shallots, and cook, stirring frequently, for 5 minutes, or until they start to soften. Add the cider and bring to a boil.

2 Stir in the stock, potatoes, and bay leaf with a large pinch of salt (unless the stock is salty) and return to a boil. Reduce the heat, cover, and cook gently for 10 minutes.

3 Put the flour in a small bowl and very slowly whisk in a few tablespoons of the milk to make a thick paste. Stir in a little more milk to make a smooth liquid. Adjust the heat so that the soup bubbles gently. Stir in the flour mixture and cook, stirring frequently, for 5 minutes. Add the remaining milk and half the cream. Cook for an additional 10 minutes, or until the potatoes are tender.

4 Finely chop the sorrel and combine with the remaining cream. Stir into the soup and add the fish. Cook, stirring occasionally, for an additional 3 minutes, or until the monkfish stiffens or the cod just begins to flake. Taste the soup and adjust the seasoning, if necessary. Ladle into warmed bowls and serve.

fish & sweet potato soup

ingredients

SERVES 4

4 tbsp lemon juice

1 fresh red chile, seeded and
   finely sliced

pinch of nutmeg

9 oz/250 g white fish fillets,
   skinned, rinsed, and dried

1 tbsp vegetable oil

1 onion, chopped

4 scallions, chopped

2 garlic cloves, chopped

1 lb/450 g sweet potatoes,
   diced

32 fl oz/1 liter/4 cups
   vegetable stock

1 carrot, sliced

5^{1}/$_{2}$ oz/150 g white cabbage,
   shredded

2 celery stalks, sliced

salt and pepper

crusty bread, to serve

method

1 Put the lemon juice, chile, and nutmeg in a shallow, nonmetallic dish and mix together. Cut the fish fillets into chunks and add to the dish. Turn in the marinade until well coated. Cover with plastic wrap and let marinate in the refrigerator for 30 minutes.

2 Heat the oil in a large pan over medium heat. Add the onion and scallions and cook, stirring frequently, for 4 minutes. Add the garlic and cook, stirring, for 2 minutes.

3 Add the sweet potatoes, stock, salt, and pepper. Bring to a boil, then reduce the heat, cover, and let simmer for 10 minutes. Add the carrot, cabbage, and celery, season again, and let simmer for 8–10 minutes.

4 Let the soup cool slightly, then transfer to a blender or food processor and process until smooth, working in batches if necessary. Return to the pan. Add the fish and marinade and bring gently to a boil. Reduce the heat and let simmer for 10 minutes. Ladle the soup into bowls and serve with crusty bread.

mexican fish & roasted tomato soup

ingredients

SERVES 4

5 ripe tomatoes

5 garlic cloves, unpeeled

32 fl oz/1 liter/4 cups
    fish stock

1 lb 2 oz/500 g red snapper
    fillets, cut into chunks

2–3 tbsp olive oil

1 onion, chopped

2 fresh chiles, seeded and
    thinly sliced

lime wedges, to serve

method

1 Heat a dry, heavy-bottom skillet over high heat, add the tomatoes and garlic cloves, and cook, turning frequently, for 10–15 minutes until the skins are blackened and charred and the flesh is tender, or cook under a preheated hot broiler. Alternatively, put the tomatoes and garlic cloves in a roasting pan and bake in a preheated oven at 375–400°F/190–200°C for 40 minutes.

2 Let the tomatoes and garlic cool, then remove and discard the skins and coarsely chop the flesh, combining it with any juices from the pan. Set aside.

3 Heat the stock in a pan over medium heat until simmering, add the snapper, and cook just until opaque and slightly firm. Remove from the heat and set aside.

4 Heat the oil in a separate pan, add the onion and cook, stirring frequently, for 5 minutes until softened. Strain in the fish cooking liquid, then add the tomatoes and garlic and stir well. Bring to a boil, then reduce the heat and let simmer for 5 minutes to combine the flavors. Add the chiles.

5 Divide chunks of the poached fish among 4 soup bowls, ladle over the hot soup, and serve with lime wedges for squeezing over.

thai shrimp & scallop soup

ingredients

SERVES 4

32 fl oz/1 liter/4 cups
   fish stock
juice of $1/2$ lime
2 tbsp rice wine or sherry
1 leek, sliced
2 shallots, finely chopped
1 tbsp grated fresh gingerroot
1 fresh red chile, seeded and
   finely chopped
8 oz/225 g raw shrimp,
   shelled and deveined
8 oz/225 g live scallops,
   shucked and cleaned
$1^1/2$ tbsp chopped fresh
   flat-leaf parsley, plus extra
   to garnish
salt and pepper

method

1 Put the stock, lime juice, rice wine, leek, shallots, gingerroot, and chile in a large pan. Bring to a boil over high heat, then reduce the heat, cover, and let simmer for 10 minutes.

2 Add the shrimp, scallops, and parsley, season with salt and pepper, and cook for 1–2 minutes.

3 Remove the pan from the heat and ladle the soup into warmed serving bowls. Garnish with chopped parsley and serve.

crab & corn soup

ingredients

SERVES 4

4 oz/115 g fresh or frozen
    crabmeat

20 fl oz/625 ml/2$^{1}/_{2}$ cups
    water

15 oz/425 g canned
    cream-style corn, drained

$^{1}/_{2}$ tsp salt

pinch of pepper

2 tsp cornstarch, dissolved in
    2 tbsp water (optional)

1 egg, beaten

method

1 If using frozen crabmeat, blanch the flesh in boiling water for 30 seconds. Remove with a slotted spoon and set aside.

2 In a large pan, bring the water to a boil with the crab and corn and simmer for 2 minutes. Season with the salt and pepper. Stir in the cornstarch, if using, and continue stirring until the soup has thickened. Rapidly stir in the egg and serve.

salmon tartare

ingredients

SERVES 4

1 lb 2 oz/500 g salmon fillet,
   skinned

2 tbsp sea salt

1 tbsp superfine sugar

2 tbsp chopped fresh dill,
   plus extra sprigs to garnish

1 tbsp chopped fresh tarragon

1 tsp Dijon mustard

juice of 1 lemon

salt and pepper

topping

14 oz/400 g/1$\frac{3}{4}$ cups
   cream cheese

1 tbsp snipped fresh chives

pinch of paprika

method

1 Put the salmon in a shallow, nonmetallic dish. Combine the sea salt, sugar, and chopped dill in a small bowl, then rub the mixture into the fish until well coated. Season with pepper. Cover with plastic wrap and let chill in the refrigerator for at least 48 hours, turning the salmon once.

2 Put the tarragon in a bowl with the mustard, lemon juice, salt, and pepper. Remove the salmon from the refrigerator, chop into small pieces, and add to the bowl. Stir until the salmon is well coated.

3 To make the topping, put all the topping ingredients in a separate bowl and mix well together. Put a 4-inch/10-cm steel cooking ring or round cookie cutter on each of 4 small serving plates. Divide the salmon among the 4 steel rings so that each ring is half full. Level the surface of each one, then top with the cream cheese mixture. Smooth the surfaces, then carefully remove the steel rings. Garnish with dill sprigs and serve.

gravlax

ingredients

SERVES 8–12

2 salmon fillets, with skin on,
  about 1 lb/450 g each
6 tbsp coarsely chopped
  fresh dill
4 oz/115 g/³/₈ cup sea salt
1³/₄ oz/50 g/¹/₄ cup sugar
1 tbsp white peppercorns,
  coarsely crushed
12 slices brown bread,
  buttered, to serve
lemon slices and fresh dill
  sprigs, to garnish

method

1 Rinse the salmon fillets under cold running water and dry with paper towels. Put 1 fillet, skin-side down, in a nonmetallic dish.

2 Mix the dill, sea salt, sugar, and peppercorns together in a small bowl. Spread this mixture over the fillet in the dish and put the second fillet, skin-side up, on top. Put a plate, the same size as the fish, on top and weigh down with 3–4 food cans.

3 Let chill in the refrigerator for 2 days, turning the fish about every 12 hours and basting with any juices that come out of the fish.

4 Remove the salmon from the brine and thinly slice, without slicing the skin, as you would smoked salmon. Cut the buttered bread into triangles and serve with the salmon. Garnish with lemon slices and dill sprigs.

fresh salmon in mojo sauce

ingredients

SERVES 8

4 fresh salmon fillets,
 weighing about
 1 lb 10 oz/750 g in total
salt and pepper
3 tbsp olive oil
1 fresh flat-leaf parsley sprig,
 to garnish

mojo sauce

2 garlic cloves, peeled
2 tsp paprika
1 tsp ground cumin
5 tbsp extra-virgin olive oil
2 tbsp white wine vinegar
salt

method

1 To prepare the mojo sauce, put the garlic, paprika, and cumin in the bowl of a food processor and, using a pulsing action, blend for 1 minute to mix well together. With the motor still running, add 1 tablespoon of the olive oil, drop by drop, through the feeder tube. When it has been added, scrape down the sides of the bowl with a spatula, then very slowly continue to pour in the oil in a thin, steady stream, until all the oil has been added and the sauce has slightly thickened. Add the vinegar and blend for an additional 1 minute. Season the sauce with salt.

2 To prepare the salmon, remove the skin, cut each fillet in half widthwise, then cut lengthwise into 3/4-inch/2-cm-thick slices, discarding any bones. Season the pieces of fish with salt and pepper.

3 Heat the olive oil in a large, heavy-bottom skillet. When hot, add the pieces of fish and cook for about 10 minutes, depending on its thickness, turning occasionally until cooked and browned on both sides.

4 Transfer the salmon to a warmed serving dish, drizzle over some of the mojo sauce, and serve hot, garnished with parsley, and accompanied by the remaining sauce.

salmon & prawn spring rolls with plum sauce

ingredients

SERVES 4

4$\frac{1}{2}$ oz/125 g salmon fillet, skinned, boned and cut into $\frac{1}{8}$-inch/3-mm cubes

2$\frac{1}{4}$ oz/60 g bean sprouts

2$\frac{1}{4}$ oz/60 g Chinese cabbage, finely shredded

1 oz/25 g scallion, finely chopped

2$\frac{1}{4}$ oz/60 g red bell pepper, seeded and finely sliced into strips

$\frac{1}{4}$ tsp five-spice powder

2$\frac{1}{4}$ oz/60 g cooked shelled shrimp

4 spring roll wrappers, halved widthwise

vegetable oil spray

$\frac{1}{4}$ tsp sesame seeds

plum sauce

3$\frac{1}{2}$ fl oz/100 ml water

2 fl oz/50 ml orange juice

$\frac{1}{2}$ tsp chopped red chile

1 tsp grated gingerroot

7 oz/200 g red plums, pitted weight

1 tsp chopped scallion

1 tsp chopped fresh cilantro

$\frac{1}{4}$ tsp sesame oil

method

1 To make the sauce, put the water, orange juice, chile, gingerroot, and plums into a pan and bring to a boil. Reduce the heat, cover, and let simmer for 10 minutes. Remove from the heat, blend with a hand-held electric blender, or use a food processor, then stir in the scallion, cilantro, and sesame oil. Let cool.

2 Heat a nonstick wok over high heat, add the salmon, and stir-fry for 1 minute. Remove from the wok with a slotted spoon onto a plate. Using the cooking juices from the salmon, stir-fry the vegetables with the five-spice powder until just tender, drain in a colander, then stir in the cooked salmon and shrimp—the mixture should be quite dry to prevent the rolls from becoming soggy.

3 Divide the salmon and vegetable mixture into 8 portions. Spoon a portion along one short edge of each spring roll wrapper and roll up, tucking in the sides.

4 Lay the spring rolls on a nonstick cookie sheet and spray lightly with vegetable oil, sprinkle with sesame seeds and bake in a preheated oven for 12–15 minutes, or until golden brown. Serve the spring rolls with the cold plum sauce separately.

fish & caper croquettes

ingredients

MAKES 12

12 oz/350 g white fish fillets,
  such as cod, haddock or
  monkfish, skinned and
  boned
10 fl oz/300 ml/1^1/$_4$ cups milk
salt and pepper
4 tbsp olive oil or
  2 oz/55 g butter
2 oz/55 g/scant ^{1}/$_2$ cup
  all-purpose flour
4 tbsp capers,
  coarsely chopped
1 tsp paprika
1 garlic clove, crushed
1 tsp lemon juice
3 tbsp chopped fresh
  flat-leaf parsley, plus extra
  sprigs to garnish
1 egg, beaten
2 oz/55 g/1 cup fresh white
  bread crumbs
1 tbsp sesame seeds
corn oil, for deep-frying
lemon wedges, to garnish
mayonnaise, to serve

method

1 Put the fish fillets and milk in a large skillet and season with salt and pepper. Bring to a boil, lower the heat and cook, covered, for 8–10 minutes, or until the fish flakes easily. Remove and flake the fish, reserving the milk.

2 Heat the olive oil or butter in a pan. Stir in the flour to form a paste and cook gently, stirring, for 1 minute. Gradually stir in the reserved milk until smooth. Slowly bring to a boil, stirring, until the mixture thickens.

3 Remove from the heat, add the fish, and beat until smooth. Add the capers, paprika, garlic, lemon juice, and parsley, season again and mix well. Transfer to a dish, let cool, and chill, covered, for 2–3 hours.

4 Pour the beaten egg onto a plate. Combine the bread crumbs and sesame seeds on another plate. Divide the fish mixture into 12 portions and form each portion into a 3-inch/7.5-cm sausage shape. Dip each croquette in the beaten egg, then coat it in the bread crumb mixture. Let chill for 1 hour.

5 Heat the oil in a deep-fryer to 350–375°F/180–190°C. Cook the croquettes, in batches, for 3 minutes, or until golden brown and crispy. Drain well on paper towels.

6 Serve piping hot, garnished with lemon wedges and parsley sprigs, and accompanied by a bowl of mayonnaise for dipping.

fish cakes

ingredients

SERVES 4

1 lb/450 g skinned white fish
    fillets, cut into cubes

1 egg white

2 kaffir lime leaves, torn
    coarsely

1 tbsp Thai green curry paste

55 g/2 oz green beans,
    chopped finely

1 fresh red chile, seeded and
    chopped finely

bunch of fresh cilantro,
    chopped

vegetable or peanut oil for
    cooking

1 fresh green chile, seeded
    and sliced, to serve

dipping sauce

4 oz/115 g/generous 1/2 cup
    superfine sugar

2 fl oz/50 ml/1/4 cup white
    wine vinegar

1 small carrot, cut into thin
    sticks

2-inch/5-cm piece cucumber,
    peeled, seeded, and cut
    into thin sticks

method

1 Put the fish into a food processor with the egg white, lime leaves, and curry paste, and process until smooth. Scrape the mixture into a bowl and stir in the green beans, red chile, and cilantro.

2 With dampened hands, shape the mixture into small patties, about 2 inches across. Place them on a large plate in a single layer and let chill for 30 minutes.

3 Meanwhile, make the dipping sauce. Put the sugar in a pan with 1 1/2 tablespoons water and the vinegar and heat gently, stirring until the sugar has dissolved. Add the carrot and cucumber, then remove from the heat and let cool.

4 Heat the oil in a skillet and cook the fish cakes, in batches, until golden brown on both sides. Drain on paper towels and keep warm while you cook the remaining batches. If desired, reheat the dipping sauce. Serve the fish cakes immediately with warm or cold dipping sauce, topped with chile slices.

tuna with pimiento-stuffed olives

ingredients

SERVES 6

2 fresh tuna steaks, weighing about 9 oz/250 g in total and about 1 inch/2.5 cm thick

5 tbsp olive oil

3 tbsp red wine vinegar

4 sprigs of fresh thyme, plus extra to garnish

1 bay leaf

salt and pepper

2 tbsp all-purpose flour

1 onion, finely chopped

2 garlic cloves, finely chopped

3 oz/85 g/$1/2$ cup pimiento-stuffed green olives, sliced

method

1 Remove the skin from the tuna steaks, then cut the steaks in half along the grain of the fish. Cut each half into $1/2$-inch/1-cm-thick slices against the grain.

2 Put 3 tablespoons of the olive oil and the vinegar in a large, shallow, nonmetallic dish. Strip the leaves from the sprigs of thyme, add these to the dish with the bay leaf, and season with salt and pepper. Add the prepared strips of tuna, cover the dish, and let marinate in the refrigerator overnight.

3 Put the flour in a plastic bag. Remove the tuna strips from the marinade, reserving the marinade for later, add them to the bag of flour and toss well until lightly coated.

4 Heat the remaining olive oil in a large skillet. Add the onion and garlic and cook gently for 5–10 minutes, or until softened and golden brown. Add the tuna strips and cook for 2–5 minutes, turning several times, until the fish becomes opaque. Add the reserved marinade and olives to the skillet and cook for an additional 1–2 minutes, stirring, until the fish is tender and the sauce has thickened.

5 Serve the tuna and olives piping hot, garnished with thyme sprigs.

teriyaki tuna pressed sushi with green bean strips

ingredients

MAKES 15 PIECES

7 oz/200 g sushi-grade tuna
    or tuna fillet, thinly sliced
2 tbsp teriyaki sauce
1 tbsp oil
10 green beans, trimmed and
    cut in half
oil, for cooking
1 tsp toasted sesame seeds
2 tbsp Japanese mayonnaise
pickled ginger and wasabi
    paste, to serve

sushi rice

$4^{1}/_{2}$ oz/125 g/generous
    $^{1}/_{2}$ cup sushi rice, washed
    under cold running water
    until the water runs clear,
    then drained
$5^{1}/_{2}$ fl oz/160 ml/scant $^{3}/_{4}$ cup
    water
$^{1}/_{2}$ piece of kombu
1 tbsp sushi rice seasoning

method

1 Put the sushi rice in a pan with the water and kombu, cover, and bring rapidly to a boil. Remove the kombu, then re-cover, reduce the heat, and let simmer for 10 minutes. Turn off the heat and let the rice stand, covered, for 15 minutes. Put the hot rice in a large, very shallow bowl, pour the seasoning evenly over the surface, and mix it carefully into the rice with a spatula, using quick cutting strokes. Fan the rice with your hand to cool it.

2 Coat the tuna slices in the teriyaki sauce and cook in the oil in a skillet for 1 minute on each side, then cut them into thick strips. Blanch the green beans in boiling water for a minute, then cool under cold running water and drain.

3 Oil a 7-inch/18-cm loose-bottom square cake pan and line it with a piece of plastic wrap large enough to hang over the edges. Oil the plastic wrap and sprinkle in the sesame seeds. Pack the rice into the pan, spread over the mayonnaise, then arrange the tuna and beans in thick, diagonal strips. Cover with plastic wrap, put another pan on top, and weigh down.

4 Let chill for 15 minutes, then loosen the sides of the pan, and pull out the sushi. Cut into 15 pieces with a wet, sharp knife. Serve with pickled ginger and wasabi paste.

scattered sushi with shrimp, crab & avocado

ingredients

SERVES 4

6 large raw shrimp, shelled
and deveined, tails left on
1 tbsp oil
1 cooked prepared crab
double quantity freshly
cooked sushi rice
(see page 32)
juice and grated rind of 1
lemon
1 ripe avocado, cut into strips
$1/2$ cucumber, peeled and cut
into slices

method

1 Sauté the shrimp for 2 minutes on each side in the oil. Once they are cooked, let cool. Lift the crabmeat out of the shell.

2 Mix the sushi rice with the lemon juice and grated lemon rind.

3 Divide the rice among 4 wooden or ceramic bowls. Arrange the shrimp, crab, avocado, and cucumber on top of the rice.

seafood tempura

ingredients

SERVES 4

8 large raw shrimp, shelled
　and deveined
8 squid rings
5$\frac{1}{2}$ oz/150 g package
　tempura mix
4 live scallops, shucked
　and cleaned
7 oz/200 g firm white fish
　fillets, cut into strips
vegetable oil, for deep-frying
few drops sesame oil
shoyu (Japanese soy sauce),
　to serve

method

1 Make little cuts on the underside of the shrimp to keep them straight while they cook. Remove and discard any membranes from the squid rings.

2 Combine the tempura mix with the amount of water specified on the package instructions in a large bowl until you have a lumpy batter full of air bubbles. Do not try to make the batter smooth or it will be heavy, and use it straight away or it will settle. Drop all the seafood into the batter.

3 Heat the vegetable oil in a deep-fryer, large, heavy-bottom pan, or wok to 350–375°F/180–190°C, or until a cube of bread browns in 30 seconds. Add the sesame oil.

4 Deep-fry 2–3 tempura pieces at a time for 2–3 minutes until a very light golden color (if you deep-fry too many pieces at one time, the oil temperature will drop and the batter will be soggy). Remove with a slotted spoon and drain off as much oil as possible, then drain on paper towels for 30 seconds. Serve very hot with shoyu as a dipping sauce.

mussels with herb & garlic butter

ingredients

SERVES 8

1 lb 12 oz/800 g fresh mussels, in their shells

splash of dry white wine

1 bay leaf

3 oz/85 g butter

12 oz/350 g/generous 1/2 cup fresh white or brown bread crumbs

4 tbsp chopped fresh flat-leaf parsley, plus extra sprigs to garnish

2 tbsp snipped fresh chives

2 garlic cloves, finely chopped

salt and pepper

lemon wedges, to serve

method

1 Scrub the mussel shells under cold running water and pull off any beards. Discard any with broken shells. Tap the remaining mussels and discard any that refuse to close.

2 Put the mussels in a large pan and add the wine and the bay leaf. Cook, covered, over high heat for 5 minutes, shaking the pan occasionally, or until the mussels are opened. Drain the mussels and discard any that remain closed. Shell the mussels, reserving one half of each shell. Arrange the mussels, in their half shells, in a large, shallow, ovenproof serving dish.

3 Melt the butter and pour into a small bowl. Add the bread crumbs, parsley, chives, garlic, salt, and pepper and mix well together. Let stand until the butter has set slightly. Using your fingers or 2 teaspoons, take a large pinch of the herb and butter mixture and use to fill each mussel shell, pressing it down well.

4 To serve, bake the mussels in a preheated oven, 450°F/230°C, for 10 minutes, or until hot. Serve immediately, garnished with parsley sprigs, and accompanied by lemon wedges for squeezing over them.

potted crab

ingredients

SERVES 4–6

1 large cooked crab,
    prepared if possible
salt and pepper
whole nutmeg, for grating
2 pinches of cayenne pepper
juice of 1 lemon, or to taste
8 oz/225g lightly salted butter
buttered toast slices and
    lemon wedges, to serve

method

1 If the crab is not already prepared, pick out all the white and brown meat, taking great care to remove all the meat from the claws.

2 Mix the white and brown meat together in a bowl, but do not mash too smoothly. Season well with salt and pepper and add a good grating of nutmeg, the cayenne pepper, and lemon juice.

3 Melt half the butter in a pan over medium heat and carefully stir in the crabmeat. Turn the mixture out into 4–6 small soufflé dishes or ramekins.

4 Melt the remaining butter in a clean pan over medium heat, then continue heating for a few moments until it stops bubbling. Allow the sediment to settle, then carefully pour the clarified butter over the crab mixture. Cover and let chill in the refrigerator for at least 1 hour before serving with buttered toast and lemon wedges. The seal of clarified butter allows the potted crab to be kept for 1–2 days.

caribbean crab cakes

ingredients

MAKES 16

1 potato, peeled and
cut into chunks
pinch of salt
4 scallions, chopped
1 garlic clove, chopped
1 tbsp chopped fresh thyme
1 tbsp chopped fresh basil
1 tbsp chopped fresh cilantro
8 oz/225 g white crabmeat,
drained if canned and
thawed if frozen
$1/2$ tsp Dijon mustard
$1/2$ fresh green chile, seeded
and finely chopped
1 egg, lightly beaten
pepper
all-purpose flour, for dusting
sunflower oil, for pan-frying
lime wedges, to garnish
cherry tomatoes, to serve

method

1 Put the potato in a small pan and add water to cover and the salt. Bring to a boil, then reduce the heat, cover, and let simmer for 10–15 minutes, or until softened. Drain well, turn into a large bowl, and mash with a potato masher or fork until smooth.

2 Meanwhile, put the scallions, garlic, thyme, basil, and cilantro in a mortar and pound with a pestle until smooth. Add the herb paste to the mashed potato with the crabmeat, mustard, chile, egg, and pepper. Mix well, cover with plastic wrap, and let chill in the refrigerator for 30 minutes.

3 Sprinkle flour onto a large, flat plate. Shape spoonfuls of the crabmeat mixture into small balls with your hands, then flatten slightly and dust with flour, shaking off any excess. Heat the oil in a skillet over high heat, add the crab cakes, and cook in batches for 2–3 minutes on each side until golden. Remove with a slotted spoon and drain on paper towels. Set aside to cool to room temperature.

4 Arrange the crab cakes on a serving dish and garnish with lime wedges. Serve with a bowl of cherry tomatoes.

shrimp cocktail

ingredients

SERVES 4

$1/2$ iceberg lettuce, finely
   shredded
5 fl oz/150 ml/$2/3$ cup
   mayonnaise
2 tbsp light cream
2 tbsp tomato ketchup
few drops of Tabasco sauce,
   or to taste
juice of $1/2$ lemon, or to taste
salt and pepper
6 oz/175 g cooked shelled
   shrimp
paprika, for sprinkling
4 cooked shrimp, in their
   shells, and 4 lemon slices,
   to garnish
thin buttered brown bread
   slices (optional), to serve

method

1 Divide the lettuce among 4 small serving dishes (traditionally, stemmed glass ones, but any small dishes will be fine).

2 Mix the mayonnaise, cream, and tomato ketchup together in a bowl. Add the Tabasco sauce and lemon juice and season well with salt and pepper.

3 Divide the shelled shrimp equally among the dishes and pour over the dressing. Cover and let chill in the refrigerator for 30 minutes.

4 Sprinkle a little paprika over the cocktails and garnish each dish with a shrimp and a lemon slice. Serve the cocktails with slices of brown bread and butter.

lime-drizzled shrimp

ingredients

SERVES 6

4 limes

12 raw jumbo shrimp,
   in their shells

3 tbsp olive oil

2 garlic cloves, finely chopped

splash of fino sherry

salt and pepper

4 tbsp chopped fresh
   flat-leaf parsley

method

1 Grate the rind and squeeze the juice from 2 of the limes. Cut the remaining 2 limes into wedges and set aside for later.

2 To prepare the shrimp, remove the head and legs, leaving the shells and tails intact. Using a sharp knife, make a shallow slit along the back of each shrimp, then pull out the dark vein and discard. Rinse the shrimp under cold water and dry on paper towels.

3 Heat the olive oil in a large, heavy-bottom skillet, then add the garlic and cook for 30 seconds. Add the shrimp and cook for 5 minutes, stirring from time to time, or until they turn pink and start to curl. Mix in the lime rind, juice, and a splash of sherry to moisten, then stir well together.

4 Transfer the cooked shrimp to a serving dish, season with salt and pepper, and sprinkle with the parsley. Serve piping hot, accompanied by the reserved lime wedges for squeezing over the shrimp.

calamari

ingredients

SERVES 6

1 lb/450 g prepared squid
all-purpose flour, for coating
sunflower oil, for deep-frying
salt
lemon wedges, to garnish
garlic mayonnaise, to serve

method

1 Slice the squid into $1/2$-inch/1-cm rings and halve the tentacles if large. Rinse under cold running water and dry well with paper towels. Dust the squid rings with flour so that they are lightly coated.

2 Heat the oil in a deep-fat fryer, large, heavy-bottom pan, or wok to 350–375ºF/180–190ºC, or until a cube of bread browns in 30 seconds. Deep-fry the squid rings in small batches for 2–3 minutes, or until golden brown and crisp all over, turning several times (if you deep-fry too many squid rings at one time, the oil temperature will drop and they will be soggy). Do not overcook as the squid will become tough and rubbery rather than moist and tender.

3 Remove with a slotted spoon and drain well on paper towels. Keep warm in a low oven while you deep-fry the remaining squid rings.

4 Sprinkle the fried squid rings with salt and serve piping hot, garnished with lemon wedges for squeezing over. Accompany with a bowl of garlic mayonnaise for dipping.

blinis

ingredients

MAKES 8

4 oz/115 g/³/₄ cup
   buckwheat flour
4 oz/115 g/³/₄ cup
   white bread flour
¹/₆-oz/7-g sachet
   active dry yeast
1 tsp salt
13 fl oz/400 ml/scant
   1³/₄ cups tepid milk
2 eggs, 1 whole and
   1 separated
vegetable oil, for brushing
sour cream and smoked
   salmon, to serve

method

1 Sift both flours into a large, warmed bowl. Stir in the yeast and salt. Beat in the milk, whole egg, and egg yolk until smooth. Cover the bowl and let stand in a warm place for 1 hour.

2 Place the egg white in a spotlessly clean bowl and whisk until soft peaks form. Fold into the batter. Brush a heavy-bottom skillet with oil and set over medium-high heat. When the skillet is hot, pour enough of the batter onto the surface to make a blini about the size of a saucer.

3 When bubbles rise, turn the blini over with a spatula and cook the other side until light brown. Wrap in a clean dish towel to keep warm while cooking the remainder. Serve the warm blinis with sour cream and smoked salmon.

lunch & supper dishes

Fish is just made for lunch and supper dishes. It is light and easily digestible, so you won't find yourself needing to sleep off your lunch or be unable to sleep after supper. It works brilliantly in all sorts of dishes, from thick, delicious chowders to elegant tarts— for speed, try Smoked Salmon, Red Onion & Goat Cheese Tarts or Smoked Salmon, Feta & Dill Parcels, and if you have a little more time to spare, Smoked Fish & Gruyère Soufflé Tart melts in the mouth and tastes out of this world.

Fish marries well with eggs—try Scrambled Eggs with Smoked Salmon, the perfect brunch dish, a really satisfying Salmon Frittata, or Chinese fast food in the form of Shrimp Fu Yung. It is also a favorite ingredient in Mexican snacks such as Fish Tacos Ensenada-style and Fish Burritos.

Fish Cakes and Smoked Fish Pie are great for family meals, needing only a watercress salad or lightly cooked vegetables to accompany. For lunch or supper parties, Seafood in a Light Broth with Vegetables is a very attractive French dish, Potato, Herb & Smoked Salmon Gratin and Scallops in Saffron Sauce are definitely out of the ordinary, and soufflés never fail to draw a gasp of admiration from your guests. The Crab Soufflé will definitely do that!

scrambled eggs with smoked salmon

ingredients

SERVES 4

8 eggs

3 fl oz/90 ml/$\frac{1}{3}$ cup
   light cream

2 tbsp chopped fresh dill,
   plus extra for garnishing

salt and pepper

3$\frac{1}{2}$ oz/100 g smoked salmon,
   cut into small pieces

2 tbsp butter

slices rustic bread, toasted

method

1 Break the eggs into a large bowl and whisk together with the cream and dill. Season with salt and pepper. Add the smoked salmon and mix to combine.

2 Melt the butter in a large nonstick skillet and pour in the egg and smoked salmon mixture. Using a wooden spatula, gently scrape the egg away from the sides of the skillet as it starts to set and swirl the skillet slightly to allow the uncooked egg to fill the surface.

3 When the eggs are almost cooked but still creamy, remove from the heat and spoon on to the prepared toast. Serve at once, garnished with sprigs of dill.

salmon frittata

ingredients

SERVES 6

9 oz/250 g skinless, boneless
   salmon
3 fresh thyme sprigs
1 fresh parsley sprig plus
   2 tbsp chopped
   fresh parsley
5 black peppercorns
$^1/_2$ small onion, sliced
$^1/_2$ celery stalk, sliced
$^1/_2$ carrot, chopped
6 oz/175 g asparagus spears,
   chopped
3 oz/85 g baby carrots, halved
3$^1/_2$ tbsp butter
1 large onion, finely sliced
1 garlic clove, finely chopped
4 oz/115 g/1 cup fresh or
   frozen peas
8 eggs, lightly beaten
1 tbsp chopped fresh dill
salt and pepper
lemon wedges, to garnish
sour cream, salad, and crusty
   bread, to serve

method

1 Put the salmon in a pan with 1 thyme sprig, the parsley sprig, peppercorns, onion, celery, and carrot. Cover with cold water and bring slowly to a boil. Remove the pan from the heat and let stand for 5 minutes. Remove the fish with a slotted spoon, flake, and set aside. Discard the vegetables and cooking liquid.

2 Bring a large pan of salted water to a boil and blanch the asparagus for 2 minutes. Drain and refresh under cold running water. Blanch the baby carrots for 4 minutes. Drain and refresh under cold running water. Drain both again, pat dry and set aside.

3 Heat half the butter in a large skillet with an ovenproof handle over low-medium heat, add the onion, and cook, stirring, until softened. Add the garlic and remaining thyme and cook, stirring, for 1 minute. Add the asparagus, carrot, and peas and heat through.

4 Transfer to the eggs in a bowl with the chopped parsley, dill, and salmon. Season and stir briefly. Heat the remaining butter in the pan over low heat and return the mixture to the pan. Cover and cook for 10 minutes.

5 Cook under a preheated medium broiler for an additional 5 minutes until set and golden. Serve hot or cold in wedges, topped with a spoonful of sour cream, with salad and crusty bread. Garnish with lemon wedges.

fluffy shrimp omelet

ingredients

SERVES 2–4

4 oz/115 g cooked shelled
   shrimp, thawed if frozen

4 scallions, chopped

2 oz/55 g zucchini, grated

4 eggs, separated

few dashes of Tabasco sauce,
   to taste

3 tbsp milk

salt and pepper

1 tbsp corn or olive oil

1 oz/25 g sharp Cheddar
   cheese, grated

method

1 Pat the shrimp dry with paper towels, then mix with the scallions and zucchini in a bowl and set aside.

2 Using a fork, beat the egg yolks with the Tabasco, milk, salt, and pepper in a separate bowl.

3 Whisk the egg whites in a large bowl until stiff, then gently stir the egg yolk mixture into the egg whites, taking care not to overmix.

4 Heat the oil in a large, nonstick skillet and when hot pour in the egg mixture. Cook over low heat for 4–6 minutes, or until lightly set. Preheat the broiler.

5 Spoon the shrimp mixture on top of the eggs and sprinkle with the cheese. Cook under the preheated broiler for 2–3 minutes, or until set and the top is golden brown. Cut into wedges and serve at once.

shrimp fu yung

ingredients

SERVES 4–6

1 tbsp vegetable or peanut oil

4 oz/115 g raw shrimp,
    shelled and deveined

4 eggs, lightly beaten

1 tsp salt

pinch of white pepper

2 tbsp finely chopped
    Chinese chives

method

1 In a preheated wok or skillet, heat the vegetable or peanut oil and stir-fry the shrimp until they begin to turn pink.

2 Season the beaten eggs with the salt and pepper and pour over the shrimp. Stir-fry for 1 minute, then add the chives.

3 Cook for an additional 4 minutes, stirring all the time, until the eggs are cooked through but still soft in texture, and serve immediately.

crab soufflé

ingredients

SERVES 4–6

1 oz/25 g/¼ cup dried bread
　　crumbs

3 tbsp butter, plus extra
　　for greasing

1 small onion, finely chopped

1 garlic clove, crushed

2 tsp mustard powder

1 oz/25 g/scant ½ cup
　　all-purpose flour

8 fl oz/225 ml/1 cup milk

1¾ oz/50 g Gruyère cheese,
　　grated

3 eggs, separated

8 oz/225 g fresh crabmeat,
　　thawed if frozen

2 tbsp snipped fresh chives

pinch of cayenne pepper

salt and pepper

method

1 Generously grease a 48-fl oz/1.5-liter/ 6-cup soufflé dish. Add the bread crumbs and shake around the dish to coat completely, shaking out any excess. Set aside on a cookie sheet.

2 Melt the butter in a large pan over low heat, add the onion, and cook, stirring occasionally, for 8 minutes, until softened but not browned. Add the garlic and cook, stirring, for 1 minute. Then add the mustard powder and flour and continue stirring for another minute. Gradually add the milk, stirring constantly, until smooth. Increase the heat slightly and bring slowly to a boil, stirring constantly. Let simmer gently for 2 minutes. Remove from the heat and stir in the cheese. Let cool slightly.

3 Lightly beat in the egg yolks, then fold in the crabmeat, chives, cayenne, salt, and pepper.

4 Whisk the egg whites in a large, clean, greasefree bowl until they hold stiff peaks. Add a large spoonful of the egg whites to the crab mixture and fold together to slacken. Add the remaining egg whites and fold together carefully but thoroughly. Spoon into the prepared dish.

5 Cook in a preheated oven, 400°F/200°C, for 25 minutes until well risen and golden. Serve at once.

seafood in a light broth with vegetables

ingredients

SERVES 4

small pinch of saffron threads

2 oz/55 g unsalted butter

2 carrots, peeled and cut into julienne strips

2 celery stalks, cut into julienne strips

1 zucchini, cut into julienne strips

1 shallot, very finely chopped

2 garlic cloves, very finely chopped

1 bouquet garni

salt and pepper

7 fl oz/200 ml/generous $^3/_4$ cup dry white wine

7 fl oz/200 ml/generous $^3/_4$ cup water

8 pieces of mixed fresh fish, such as salmon fillets and monkfish medallions, or only 1 type of fish, all skin and bones removed, each piece about $4^1/_2$ oz/125 g

9 fl oz/250 ml/generous 1 cup sour cream

fresh chervil sprigs, to garnish

method

1 Put the saffron threads in a small dry skillet over high heat and toast, stirring constantly, for 1 minute, or until you can smell the aroma. Immediately tip out of the pan and set aside.

2 Melt the butter over medium heat in a large skillet with a tight-fitting lid. Add the carrots, celery, zucchini, shallot, garlic, bouquet garni, salt, and pepper. Sauté for 3 minutes, without letting the vegetables color.

3 Meanwhile, bring the wine and water to a boil in a pan over high heat, then boil for 2 minutes. Pour the boiling liquid over the vegetables, then reduce the heat to low and simmer for 5 minutes. Remove from the heat and discard the bouquet garni.

4 Place the fish over the vegetables in a single layer, then cover and simmer for 5 minutes, or until the fish is cooked through and flakes easily. Transfer the fish and vegetables to a warmed bowl and spoon over a little of the poaching liquid. Cover with foil and set aside.

5 Stir the sour cream and saffron threads into the poaching liquid and bring to a boil, stirring. Boil for 3–5 minutes to reduce. Place a mound of vegetables in the center of 4 soup plates and top with the fish. Spoon over the reduced liquid and garnish with the chervil.

smoked fish chowder

ingredients

SERVES 4

2 tbsp butter

1 onion, finely chopped

1 small celery stalk, finely diced

9 oz/250 g potatoes, diced

2 oz/55 g carrots, diced

10 fl oz/300 ml/1¼ cups
boiling water

salt and pepper

12 oz/350 g smoked cod
fillets, skinned and cut
into bite-size pieces

10 fl oz/300 ml/1¼ cups milk

method

1 Melt the butter in a large pan over low heat, add the onion and celery, and cook, stirring frequently, for 5 minutes, or until softened but not browned.

2 Add the potatoes, carrots, water, salt, and pepper. Bring to a boil, then reduce the heat and let simmer for 10 minutes, or until the vegetables are tender. Add the fish to the chowder and cook for an additional 10 minutes.

3 Pour in the milk and heat gently. Taste and adjust the seasoning, if necessary. Serve hot.

caribbean fish chowder

ingredients

SERVES 4

3 tbsp vegetable oil

1 tsp cumin seeds, crushed

1 tsp dried thyme or oregano

1 onion, diced

$1/2$ green bell pepper, seeded and diced

1 sweet potato, diced

2–3 fresh green chiles, seeded and very finely chopped

1 garlic clove, very finely chopped

32 fl oz/1 liter/4 cups chicken stock

salt and pepper

14 oz/400 g red snapper fillets, skinned and cut into chunks

1 oz/25 g/$1/4$ cup frozen peas

1 oz/25 g/$1/4$ cup frozen corn kernels

4 fl oz/125 ml/$1/2$ cup light cream

3 tbsp chopped fresh cilantro, to garnish

method

1 Heat the oil with the cumin seeds and thyme in a large pan over medium heat. Add the onion, bell pepper, sweet potato, chiles, and garlic and cook, stirring constantly, for 1 minute.

2 Reduce the heat to medium-low, cover, and cook for 10 minutes, or until beginning to soften.

3 Pour in the stock and season generously with salt and pepper. Bring to a boil, then reduce the heat to low-medium, cover, and let simmer for 20 minutes.

4 Add the snapper, peas, corn kernels, and cream. Cook over low heat, uncovered and without boiling, for 7–10 minutes until the fish is just cooked. Serve at once, garnished with chopped cilantro.

potato, herb & smoked salmon gratin

ingredients

SERVES 6

14 fl oz/425 ml/1³/₄ cups milk

3 whole cloves

2 bay leaves

1³/₄ oz/50 g onion, sliced

3 oz/85 g leek, chopped

3¹/₂ oz/100 g lightly cured smoked salmon, finely sliced into strips

12 oz/350 g potatoes, cut into ¹/₁₆-inch/2-mm slices

2 tbsp finely chopped fresh chives

2 tbsp finely chopped fresh dill

1 tbsp finely chopped fresh tarragon

2 tsp wholegrain mustard

pepper

1¹/₄ oz/35 g watercress

method

1 Pour the milk into a large, heavy-bottom pan, add the cloves, bay leaves, onion, leek, and smoked salmon and heat over a low heat. When the milk is just about to reach simmering point, carefully remove the smoked salmon with a slotted spoon and let cool on a plate.

2 Add the potatoes to the milk and stir with a wooden spoon. Return to a simmer and cook, stirring occasionally to prevent the potatoes from sticking, for 12 minutes, or until the potatoes are just beginning to soften and the milk has thickened slightly from the potato starch. Remove the cloves and bay leaves.

3 Add the herbs, mustard, and pepper and stir well. Pour the mixture into a greased and base-lined 7¹/₂-inch/19-cm shallow cake pan. Cover with a layer of greaseproof paper and then foil and bake in a preheated oven, 400°F/200°C, for 30 minutes.

4 Remove from the oven and place a pan on top. Leave to cool for 20 minutes before turning out onto a cookie sheet. Put under a preheated hot broiler to brown the top.

5 Cut the gratin into 6 wedges and serve with the smoked salmon, tossed with watercress.

broiled tuna & vegetable kabobs

ingredients

SERVES 4

4 tuna steaks, about 5 oz/
   140 g each

2 red onions

12 cherry tomatoes

1 red bell pepper, seeded and
   diced into 1-inch/2.5-cm
   pieces

1 yellow bell pepper, seeded
   and diced into 1-inch/
   2.5-cm pieces

1 zucchini, sliced

1 tbsp chopped fresh oregano

4 tbsp olive oil

pepper

lime wedges, to garnish

selection of salads and
   cooked couscous, new
   potatoes, or bread,
   to serve

method

1 Cut the tuna into 1-inch/2.5-cm dice. Peel the onions, leaving the root intact, and cut each onion lengthwise into 6 wedges.

2 Divide the fish and vegetables evenly among 8 wooden skewers (presoaked to avoid burning) and arrange on the broiler pan.

3 Mix the oregano and oil together in a small bowl. Season with pepper. Lightly brush the kabobs with the oil and cook under a broiler preheated to high for 10–15 minutes or until evenly cooked, turning occasionally. If you cannot fit all the kabobs on the broiler pan at once, cook them in batches, keeping the cooked kabobs warm while cooking the remainder. Alternatively, these kabobs can be cooked on a barbecue.

4 Garnish with lime wedges and serve with a selection of salads, cooked couscous, new potatoes, or bread.

fresh sardines baked with lemon & oregano

ingredients

SERVES 4

2 lemons, plus extra lemon
  wedges, to garnish
12 large fresh sardines,
  cleaned
4 tbsp olive oil
4 tbsp chopped fresh oregano
salt and pepper

method

1 Slice 1 of the lemons, and grate the rind and squeeze the juice from the second lemon.

2 Cut the heads off the sardines. Put the fish in a shallow, ovenproof dish large enough to hold them in a single layer. Put the lemon slices between the fish. Drizzle the lemon juice and oil over the fish. Sprinkle over the lemon rind and oregano and season with salt and pepper.

3 Bake in a preheated oven, 375°F/190°C, for 20–30 minutes until the fish are tender. Serve garnished with lemon wedges.

shrimp & pineapple curry

ingredients

SERVES 4

16 fl oz/500 ml/2 cups
　　coconut cream
1/2 fresh pineapple, peeled
　　and chopped
2 tbsp Thai red curry paste
2 tbsp Thai fish sauce
2 tsp sugar
12 oz/350 g raw jumbo shrimp
2 tbsp chopped fresh cilantro
edible flower, to garnish
steamed jasmine rice, to serve

method

1 Place the coconut cream, pineapple, curry paste, fish sauce, and sugar in a large skillet. Heat gently over medium heat until almost boiling. Shell and devein the shrimp. Add the shrimp and chopped cilantro to the skillet and let simmer gently for 3 minutes, or until the shrimp are cooked.

2 Garnish with a fresh flower and serve with steamed jasmine rice.

garlic & herb shrimp

ingredients

SERVES 2

12 raw jumbo shrimp, in
   their shells
juice of $1/2$ lemon
2 garlic cloves, crushed
3 tbsp chopped fresh parsley
1 tbsp chopped fresh dill
3 tbsp softened butter
salt and pepper
lemon wedges, crusty bread,
   and salad, to serve

method

1 Rinse and peel the shrimp. Devein, using a sharp knife to slice along the back from the head end to the tail, and removing the thin black intestine.

2 Mix the lemon juice with the garlic, herbs, and butter to form a paste. Season well with salt and pepper. Spread the paste over the shrimp and let marinate for 30 minutes.

3 Cook the shrimp under a preheated medium broiler for 5–6 minutes. Alternatively, heat a skillet and fry the shrimp in the paste until cooked. Turn out onto hot plates and pour over the juices. Serve at once with lemon wedges, some crusty bread, and salad.

scallops in saffron sauce

ingredients

SERVES 8

5 fl oz/150 ml/²/₃ cup dry
    white wine
5 fl oz/150 ml/²/₃ cup
    fish stock
large pinch of saffron threads
2 lb/900 g shucked scallops,
    preferably large ones,
    with corals
salt and pepper
3 tbsp olive oil
1 small onion, finely chopped
2 garlic cloves, finely chopped
5 fl oz/150 ml/²/₃ cup heavy
    cream
squeeze of lemon juice
chopped fresh flat-leaf
    parsley, to garnish
crusty bread, to serve

method

1 Put the wine, fish stock, and saffron in a pan and bring to a boil. Lower the heat, cover, and let simmer gently for 15 minutes.

2 Meanwhile, remove and discard from each scallop the tough, white muscle that is found opposite the coral, and separate the coral from the scallop. Slice the scallops and corals vertically into thick slices. Dry well on paper towels, then season with salt and pepper.

3 Heat the olive oil in a large, heavy-bottom skillet. Add the onion and garlic and cook until softened and lightly browned. Add the sliced scallops to the skillet and cook gently for 5 minutes, stirring occasionally, or until they turn just opaque. Overcooking the scallops will make them tough and rubbery.

4 Using a slotted spoon, remove the scallops from the skillet and transfer to a warmed plate. Add the saffron liquid to the skillet, bring to a boil, and boil rapidly until reduced to about half. Lower the heat and gradually stir in the cream, just a little at a time. Let simmer gently until the sauce thickens.

5 Return the scallops to the skillet and let simmer for 1–2 minutes just to heat through. Add a squeeze of lemon juice and season with salt and pepper. Serve the scallops hot, garnished with the parsley, with slices or chunks of crusty bread.

fish cakes

ingredients

SERVES 4

1 lb/450 g mealy potatoes,
   such as Russet Burbank,
   Russet Arcadia, or Butte,
   peeled and cut into chunks
1 lb/450 g mixed fish fillets,
   such as cod and salmon,
   skinned
2 tbsp chopped fresh tarragon
grated rind of 1 lemon
2 tbsp heavy cream
salt and pepper
1 tbsp all-purpose flour
1 egg, beaten
4 oz/115 g/1 cup bread
   crumbs, made from day-
   old white or whole wheat
   bread
4 tbsp vegetable oil
lemon wedges, to garnish
watercress salad, to serve

method

1 Bring a large pan of salted water to a boil, add the potatoes, and cook for 15–20 minutes. Drain well, then mash with a potato masher or fork until smooth.

2 Put the fish in a skillet and just cover with water. Bring to a boil over medium heat, then reduce the heat to low, cover, and let simmer gently for 5 minutes until cooked. Remove with a slotted spoon and drain on a plate. When cool enough to handle, flake the fish coarsely into good-size pieces, removing and discarding any bones.

3 Mix the mashed potatoes with the fish, tarragon, lemon rind, and cream in a bowl. Season well with salt and pepper and shape into 4 round cakes or 8 smaller ones.

4 Put the flour, egg, and bread crumbs in separate bowls. Dust the fish cakes with flour, dip into the beaten egg, then coat thoroughly in the bread crumbs. Put on a cookie sheet, cover, and let chill in the refrigerator for at least 30 minutes.

5 Heat the oil in the skillet over medium heat, add the fish cakes, and cook for 5 minutes on each side, turning them with a spatula. Serve hot, garnished with lemon wedges, with a watercress salad to accompany.

fish tacos ensenada-style

ingredients

SERVES 4

1 lb/450 g firm-fleshed white
　fish, such as red snapper
　or cod

$1/4$ tsp dried oregano

$1/4$ tsp ground cumin

1 tsp mild chili powder

2–3 garlic cloves, finely
　chopped

salt and pepper

3 tbsp all-purpose flour

vegetable oil, for frying

$1/4$ red cabbage, thinly sliced
　or shredded

juice of 2 limes

hot pepper sauce or salsa
　to taste

8 soft corn tortillas

1 tbsp chopped fresh cilantro

$1/2$ onion, chopped (optional)

salsa of your choice

method

1 Place the fish on a plate and sprinkle with half the oregano, cumin, chili powder, garlic, and salt and pepper, then dust with the flour.

2 Heat the oil in a skillet until it is smoking, then fry the fish in several batches until it is golden on the outside, and just tender in the middle. Remove from the pan and place on paper towels to drain.

3 Combine the cabbage with the remaining oregano, cumin, chili, and garlic, then stir in the lime juice, and season with salt and hot pepper sauce. Set aside.

4 Heat the tortillas in an ungreased nonstick skillet, sprinkling with a few drops of water as they heat; wrap the tortillas in a clean dish towel as you work to keep them warm. Alternatively, heat through in a stack in the pan, alternating the top and bottom tortillas so that they warm evenly.

5 Place some of the warm fried fish in each tortilla, along with a big spoonful of the cabbage salad. Sprinkle with fresh cilantro and onion, if using. Add salsa to taste and serve at once.

fish burritos

ingredients

SERVES 4–6

about 1 lb/450 g firm-fleshed
    white fish fillets, such as
    red snapper or cod, skinned
salt and pepper
$^1/_4$ tsp ground cumin
pinch of dried oregano
4 garlic cloves, finely chopped
4 fl oz/125 ml/$^1/_2$ cup fish
    stock
juice of $^1/_2$ lemon or lime
8 flour tortillas
2–3 romaine lettuce leaves,
    shredded
2 ripe tomatoes, diced
salsa of your choice
lemon wedges, to garnish

method

1 Season the fish with salt and pepper, then put in a pan with the cumin, oregano, garlic, and enough stock to cover.

2 Bring to a boil and boil for 1 minute. Remove the pan from the heat and let the fish cool in the cooking liquid for about 30 minutes.

3 Remove the fish with a slotted spoon. Flake the fish into bite-size pieces and put in a nonmetallic bowl. Sprinkle with the lemon juice and set aside.

4 Heat the tortillas in a dry nonstick skillet over medium heat, sprinkling with a few drops of water as they heat; wrap in a clean dish towel as you work to keep them warm. Alternatively, heat through in a stack in the pan, alternating the tortillas from the top to the bottom to warm evenly.

5 Arrange some lettuce in the center of 1 tortilla, spoon on a few fish chunks, then sprinkle with a little tomato. Top with some salsa. Repeat with the other tortillas and serve at once, garnished with lemon wedges.

smoked fish pie

ingredients

SERVES 6

1 lb 8 oz/675 g potatoes,
   unpeeled
2 tbsp olive oil
1 onion, finely chopped
1 leek, thinly sliced
1 carrot, diced
1 celery stalk, diced
4 oz/115 g mushrooms, halved
grated rind 1 lemon
12 oz/350 g skinless,
   boneless smoked cod or
   haddock fillet, cubed
12 oz/350 g skinless,
   boneless white fish, cubed
8 oz/225 g cooked
   shelled shrimp
2 tbsp chopped fresh parsley
1 tbsp chopped fresh dill,
   plus sprigs to garnish
salt and pepper
4 tbsp butter, melted
1 oz/25 g Gruyère
   cheese, grated
cooked vegetables, to serve

sauce

4 tbsp butter
4 tbsp all-purpose flour
1 tsp mustard powder
20 fl oz/625 ml/2$^{1}/_{2}$ cups milk
3 oz/85 g Gruyère
   cheese, grated

method

1 For the sauce, melt the butter in a large pan, add the flour and mustard powder, and stir until smooth. Cook over very low heat for 2 minutes. Slowly beat in the milk, while heating, until smooth. Let simmer gently for 2 minutes then stir in the cheese until smooth. Remove from the heat and cover the surface of the sauce with plastic wrap. Set aside.

2 Meanwhile, boil the whole potatoes in plenty of salted water for 15 minutes. Drain well and set aside until cool enough to handle.

3 Heat the oil in a clean pan. Add the onion and cook for 5 minutes until softened. Add the leek, carrot, celery, and mushrooms and cook for an additional 10 minutes, or until the vegetables have softened. Stir in the lemon rind and cook briefly. Add the vegetables with the fish, shrimp, parsley, and dill to the sauce. Season and transfer to a greased 56-fl oz/1.75-liter/7-cup casserole dish.

4 Peel the cooled potatoes and grate them coarsely. Mix with the melted butter. Cover the filling with the grated potato and sprinkle with grated Gruyère cheese. Cover loosely with foil and bake in a preheated oven, 400°F/200°C, for 30 minutes. Remove the foil and bake for an additional 30 minutes, or until the topping is golden and the filling is bubbling. Garnish with dill sprigs and serve with vegetables.

smoked fish & gruyère soufflé tart

ingredients

SERVES 6

pie dough

4 1/2 oz/125 g/scant 1 cup all-purpose flour, plus extra for dusting

pinch of salt

1/2 tsp English mustard powder

4 tbsp cold butter, diced, plus extra for greasing

1 egg yolk, mixed with a little cold water

filling

10 fl oz/300 ml/1 1/4 cups milk

1 bay leaf

9 oz/250 g skinless, boneless, undyed smoked fish

2 tbsp butter

1 oz/25 g/scant 1/4 cup all-purpose flour

1/2 tsp ground nutmeg

white pepper

4 1/2 oz/125 g Gruyère cheese, grated

2 eggs, separated

method

1 Sift the flour, salt, and mustard into a food processor, add the butter, and process to resemble bread crumbs. Add the egg yolk and pulse to bring the dough together. Roll out the dough on a lightly floured counter and use to line a greased 9-inch/23-cm loose-bottom fluted tart pan. Trim the edge, line the tart shell with parchment paper, and fill with dried beans. Let chill for 30 minutes, then bake in a preheated oven, 375°F/190°C, for 10 minutes. Remove the paper and beans, bake for 5 minutes more, then remove from the oven. Increase the temperature to 400°F/200°C.

2 Bring the milk and bay leaf to a simmer in a skillet, add the fish and cook for 3–5 minutes until just cooked. Remove the fish with a slotted spoon, reserving the milk but discarding the bay leaf. Cool then flake the fish.

3 Melt the butter in a pan, stir in the flour, and cook, stirring, for 2–3 minutes. Slowly add the reserved milk and cook, stirring, until thickened. Stir in nutmeg and pepper, then the cheese. Remove from the heat, stir in the egg yolks and fish, and let cool slightly. Whisk the egg whites in a clean bowl until stiff, then fold quickly into the fish mixture. Pour into the tart shell and bake for 15 minutes until risen and browned. Let rest for 10 minutes, then serve.

smoked cod & shrimp tart

ingredients

SERVES 4–6

14 oz/400 g undyed smoked
   cod fillet, rinsed and dried
10 fl oz/300 ml/1$\frac{1}{4}$ cups milk
5$\frac{1}{2}$ oz/150 g cooked shelled
   shrimp
7 oz/200 g/scant 1 cup cream
   cheese
3 eggs, beaten
3 tbsp snipped fresh chives
pepper

pie dough

7 oz/200 g/scant 1$\frac{1}{2}$ cups
   all-purpose flour
large pinch of salt
3$\frac{1}{2}$ oz/100 g margarine,
   diced, plus extra for
   greasing
1 egg yolk
3 tbsp ice-cold water

method

1 To make the pie dough, sift the flour and salt into a mixing bowl, then rub in the margarine until the mixture resembles coarse bread crumbs. Stir in the egg yolk, followed by the water, then bring the mixture together into a ball. Turn out on to a lightly floured counter and knead until smooth. Wrap in plastic wrap and let chill in the refrigerator for 30 minutes.

2 Meanwhile, put the fish into a shallow pan with the milk. Heat gently until simmering and let simmer for 10 minutes, or until just cooked and opaque. Remove the fish with a slotted spoon, let cool a little, then peel away the skin and discard any bones. Flake the fish into large chunks and set aside. Set aside 4 fl oz/ 125 ml/$\frac{1}{2}$ cup of the cooking liquid.

3 Roll out the dough and use to line a lightly greased 10$\frac{1}{2}$-inch/26-cm tart pan. Line the tart shell with parchment paper and dried beans and bake in a preheated oven, 400°F/ 200°C, for 8 minutes. Remove the paper and beans and bake for 5 minutes more.

4 Arrange the fish and shrimp in the tart shell. Beat the cream cheese, reserved cooking liquid, eggs, chives, and pepper in a bowl, then pour over the seafood. Bake for 30 minutes, or until set and golden brown.

smoked salmon, red onion & goat cheese tarts

ingredients

SERVES 4

9 oz/250 g good quality puff
    pastry
all-purpose flour, for rolling
1 egg, lightly beaten with
    1 tbsp milk
1 small red onion, sliced
3^1/$_2$ oz/100 g goat cheese,
    crumbled
4 slices smoked salmon
pepper

method

1 Roll the puff pastry out to ^{1}/$_4$ inch/5 mm thick on a lightly floured counter and cut into 4 even-size squares. Place on an ungreased cookie sheet and brush each square lightly with the egg mixture. Divide the sliced onion evenly among the tarts and top with goat cheese.

2 Bake in a preheated oven, 400°F/200°C, for 20–25 minutes, or until the pastry has risen and is golden brown. Let cool slightly, then top with the slices of smoked salmon and season with pepper. Serve at once.

smoked salmon, feta & dill filo packages

ingredients

MAKES 6 PACKAGES

5¹/₂ oz/150 g feta cheese, crumbled

9 oz/250 g/generous 1 cup ricotta cheese

5¹/₂ oz/150 g smoked salmon, diced

2 tbsp chopped fresh dill

2 tbsp snipped fresh chives

pepper

12 sheets filo pastry

3¹/₂ oz/100 g butter, melted, plus extra for greasing

4 tbsp dried bread crumbs

6 tsp fennel seeds

method

1 In a large bowl, combine the feta, ricotta, smoked salmon, dill, and chives. Season with pepper.

2 Lay out a sheet of pastry on the counter and brush well with melted butter. Sprinkle over 2 teaspoons of the bread crumbs and cover with a second sheet of pastry. Brush with butter and spread a large tablespoon of the salmon mixture on one end of the pastry. Roll the pastry up, folding in the sides, to enclose the salmon completely and create a neat package. Place on a lightly greased cookie sheet, brush the top of the package with butter and sprinkle over 1 teaspoon of the fennel seeds. Repeat with the remaining ingredients to make 6 packages.

3 Bake the packages in a preheated oven, 350°F/180°C, for 25–30 minutes, or until the pastry is golden brown. Serve warm.

crab & watercress tart

ingredients

SERVES 6

pie dough

$4^1/2$ oz/125 g/scant 1 cup all-purpose flour, plus extra for dusting

pinch of salt

4 tbsp cold butter, diced, plus extra for greasing

ice-cold water

filling

$10^1/2$ oz/300 g fresh white and brown crabmeat, thawed if frozen

1 bunch of watercress, leaves picked from the stems

2 fl oz/50 ml/$^1/4$ cup milk

2 large eggs plus 3 egg yolks

7 fl oz/200 ml/scant 1 cup heavy cream

salt and pepper

$^1/2$ tsp ground nutmeg

$^1/2$ bunch of fresh chives, snipped

2 tbsp freshly grated Parmesan cheese

method

1 Lightly grease a 9-inch/23-cm loose-bottom fluted tart pan. Sift the flour with the salt into a food processor, add the butter, and process until the mixture resembles fine bread crumbs. Tip the mixture into a large bowl and add a little cold water, just enough to bring the dough together. Turn out on to a lightly floured counter. Roll out to $3^1/4$ inches/8 cm larger than the pan. Line the pan with the dough and trim the edge. Line the tart shell with parchment paper and fill with dried beans. Let chill in the refrigerator for 30 minutes.

2 Remove the tart shell from the refrigerator and bake in a preheated oven, 375°F/190°C, for 10 minutes. Remove the paper and beans and bake the tart shell for 5 minutes more. Remove from the oven and reduce the oven temperature to 325°F/160°C.

3 Arrange the crabmeat and watercress in the tart shell, reserving a few watercress leaves for garnishing. Whisk the milk, eggs, and egg yolks together in a bowl. Bring the cream to simmering point in a pan and pour over the egg mixture, whisking all the time. Season with salt and pepper and stir in the nutmeg and chives. Carefully pour over the crab and watercress and sprinkle over the cheese. Bake for 35–40 minutes until golden and set. Let the tart rest for 10 minutes before serving, garnished with the reserved watercress.

main meals

One of the most rewarding aspects of making fish the centerpiece of your main meal is that it requires so little in the way of cooking, yet looks as if you've put in a huge amount of effort! Add a simple sauce and you have a taste sensation. Monkfish with Lime & Chile Sauce is a delectable example that takes little more than five minutes to prepare and cook—in fact, cooking the rice to accompany it will take longer!

Roasting is a delicious and trouble-free way to cook fish. Try Roast Monkfish with Romesco Sauce, Italian Fish, Garlic-crusted Roast Fish, Roast Red Snapper with Fennel, Roast Salmon with Lemon & Herbs, or Roast Tuna with Orange & Anchovies. It is also wonderful in stews such as Spanish Swordfish Stew or Moroccan Fish Tagine, which is served with couscous.

Fish goes beautifully with butter, although this somewhat cancels out its virtue of being low in fat! For the occasional treat, however, serve Sole à la Meunière or Skate in Black Butter Sauce, and schedule in a brisk walk to follow!

For something a little different, try Fish with Yucatan Flavors—swordfish steaks marinated in a spicy, herby, fruity dressing, then steamed in banana leaves. Very tasty, and a great talking point when you serve each portion of fish in its leaf!

monkfish with lime & chile sauce

ingredients

SERVES 4

4 x 4-oz/115-g
   monkfish fillets
1 oz/25 g/$^1/_4$ cup rice flour
   or cornstarch
6 tbsp vegetable or peanut oil
4 garlic cloves, crushed
2 large fresh red chiles,
   seeded and sliced
2 tsp jaggery or soft light
   brown sugar
juice of 2 limes
grated rind of 1 lime
boiled rice, to serve

method

1 Toss the fish in the flour, shaking off any excess. Heat the oil in a wok and cook the fish on all sides until browned and cooked through, taking care when turning not to break it up.

2 Lift the fish out of the wok and keep warm. Add the garlic and chiles and stir-fry for 1–2 minutes, until they have softened.

3 Add the sugar, the lime juice and rind, and 2–3 tablespoons of water and bring to a boil. Let simmer gently for 1–2 minutes, then spoon the mixture over the fish. Serve immediately with rice.

roast monkfish with romesco sauce

ingredients

SERVES 4

1 monkfish tail, about
    2 lb/900 g, membrane
    removed
2–3 slices serrano ham
olive oil, for brushing
salt and pepper

romesco sauce

1 red bell pepper, halved
    and seeded
4 garlic cloves, unpeeled
2 tomatoes, halved
4 fl oz/125 ml/$\frac{1}{2}$ cup olive oil
1 slice white bread, diced
4 tbsp blanched almonds
1 fresh red chile, seeded and
    chopped
2 shallots, chopped
1 tsp paprika
2 tbsp red wine vinegar
2 tsp sugar
1 tbsp water

method

1 Place the bell pepper, garlic, and tomatoes in a roasting pan and toss with 1 tablespoon of the oil. Roast in a preheated oven, 425°F/ 220°C, for 20–25 minutes, then cover with a dish towel, and set aside for 10 minutes. Peel off the skins and place the vegetables in a food processor.

2 Heat 1 tablespoon of the remaining oil in a skillet. Cook the bread cubes and almonds over low heat, stirring frequently, until golden. Remove with a slotted spoon and drain on paper towels. Add the chile, shallots, and paprika to the skillet and cook, stirring, for 5 minutes. Transfer both mixtures to the food processor, add the vinegar, sugar, and water, and process to a paste. With the motor running, add the remaining oil through the feeder tube.

3 Reduce the oven temperature to 400°F/ 200°C. Rinse the monkfish tail and pat it dry. Wrap the ham around the monkfish, brush lightly with oil, and season. Place the fish on a cookie sheet and roast for 20 minutes until the flesh is opaque and flakes easily.

4 Cut through the ham to remove the central bone and produce 2 thick fillets. Cut each fillet into 2 pieces and arrange on plates with a spoonful of romesco sauce. Serve at once.

spanish swordfish stew

ingredients

SERVES 4

4 tbsp olive oil

3 shallots, chopped

2 garlic cloves, chopped

8 oz/225 g canned chopped
   tomatoes

1 tbsp tomato paste

1 lb 7 oz/650 g potatoes, sliced

9 fl oz/250 ml/generous 1 cup
   vegetable stock

2 tbsp lemon juice

1 red bell pepper, seeded and
   chopped

1 orange bell pepper, seeded
   and chopped

20 black olives, pitted
   and halved

2 lb 4 oz/1 kg swordfish
   steak, skinned and cut
   into bite-size pieces

salt and pepper

parsley springs and lemon
   slices, to garnish

method

1 Heat the oil in a pan over low heat, add the
shallots, and cook, stirring frequently, for
4 minutes, or until softened. Add the garlic,
tomatoes, and tomato paste, cover, and let
simmer gently for 20 minutes.

2 Meanwhile, put the potatoes in an ovenproof
casserole with the stock and lemon juice.
Bring to a boil, then reduce the heat and add
the bell peppers. Cover and cook for 15 minutes.

3 Add the olives, swordfish, and the tomato
mixture to the potatoes. Season with salt and
pepper. Stir well, then cover and let simmer for
7–10 minutes, or until the swordfish is cooked
to your taste.

4 Remove from the heat and garnish with
parsley sprigs and lemon slices.

fish with yucatan flavors

ingredients

SERVES 8

4 tbsp annatto seeds, soaked
    in water overnight

3 garlic cloves, finely chopped

1 tbsp mild chili powder

1 tbsp paprika

1 tsp ground cumin

$1/2$ tsp dried oregano

2 tbsp beer or tequila

juice of 1 lime and I orange or
    3 tbsp pineapple juice

2 tbsp olive oil

2 tbsp chopped fresh cilantro

$1/4$ tsp ground cinnamon

$1/4$ tsp ground cloves

2 lb 4 oz/1 kg swordfish
    steaks

banana leaves, for wrapping
    (optional)

orange wedges, to serve

method

1 Drain the annatto, then crush them to a paste in a mortar with a pestle. Work in the garlic, chili powder, paprika, cumin, oregano, beer or tequila, fruit juice, olive oil, fresh cilantro, cinnamon, and cloves. Smear the paste on to the fish and let marinate in the refrigerator for at least 3 hours or overnight.

2 Wrap the fish steaks in banana leaves, tying with string to make packages. Bring water to a boil in a steamer, then add a batch of packages to the top part of the steamer and cook for about 15 minutes or until the fish is cooked through.

3 Alternatively, cook the fish without wrapping in the banana leaves. To cook on the grill, place in a hinged basket, or on a rack, and cook over the hot coals for 5-6 minutes on each side until cooked through; or cook the fish under a preheated broiler for 5-6 minutes on each side until cooked through.

4 Serve with orange wedges for squeezing over the fish.

italian fish

ingredients

SERVES 4

2 tbsp butter

1³/₄ oz/50 g/scant 1 cup
     fresh whole wheat
     bread crumbs

1 heaped tbsp
     chopped walnuts

grated rind and juice of
     2 lemons

2 fresh rosemary sprigs,
     stalks removed

2 tbsp chopped fresh parsley

4 cod fillets, about
     5¹/₂ oz/150 g each

1 garlic clove, crushed

1 small fresh red chile, diced

3 tbsp walnut oil

method

1 Melt the butter in a large pan over low heat, stirring constantly. Remove the pan from the heat and add the bread crumbs, walnuts, the rind and juice of 1 lemon, half the rosemary, and half the parsley, stirring until mixed.

2 Press the bread crumb mixture over the top of the cod fillets. Place the cod fillets in a shallow foil-lined roasting pan and roast in a preheated oven, 400°F/200°C, for 25–30 minutes.

3 Mix the garlic, the remaining lemon rind and juice, rosemary, and parsley, and the chile together in a bowl. Beat in the oil and mix to combine. Drizzle the dressing over the cod steaks as soon as they are cooked.

4 Transfer the fish to warmed serving plates and serve at once.

baked lemon cod with herb sauce

ingredients

SERVES 4

4 thick cod fillets
olive oil, for brushing
8 thin lemon slices
salt and pepper

herb sauce

4 tbsp olive oil
1 garlic clove, crushed
4 tbsp chopped fresh parsley
2 tbsp chopped fresh mint
juice of $1/2$ lemon

method

1 Rinse each cod fillet and pat dry with paper towels, then brush with oil. Place each fillet on a piece of parchment paper that is large enough to encase the fish in a package. Top each fillet with 2 lemon slices and season with salt and pepper. Fold over the parchment paper to encase the fish and bake in a preheated oven, 400°F/200°C, for 20 minutes, or until just cooked and opaque.

2 Meanwhile, to make the herb sauce, put all the ingredients into a food processor and process until finely chopped. Season with salt and pepper.

3 Carefully unfold each package and place it on a serving plate. Pour a spoonful of herb sauce over each piece of fish before serving.

cod with catalan spinach

ingredients

SERVES 4

2 oz/55 g/$^1/_2$ cup raisins

2 oz/55 g/$^1/_2$ cup pine nuts

4 tbsp extra-virgin olive oil

3 garlic cloves, crushed

1 lb 2 oz/500 g baby spinach
leaves, rinsed and
shaken dry

4 cod fillets, each about
6 oz/175 g

olive oil

salt and pepper

tomato halves and lemon
wedges, to serve

method

1 Put the raisins in a small bowl, cover with hot water, and set aside to soak for 15 minutes; drain well.

2 Meanwhile, put the pine nuts in a dry skillet over medium-high heat and dry-fry for 1–2 minutes, shaking frequently, until toasted and golden brown: watch closely because they burn quickly.

3 Heat the oil in a large, lidded skillet over medium-high heat. Add the garlic and cook for 2 minutes, or until golden, but not brown. Remove with a slotted spoon and discard.

4 Add the spinach to the oil with only the rinsing water clinging to its leaves. Cover and cook for 4–5 minutes until wilted. Uncover, stir in the drained raisins and pine nuts and continue cooking until all the liquid evaporates. Season with salt and pepper and keep warm.

5 To cook the cod, brush the fillets lightly with oil and sprinkle with salt and pepper. Place under a preheated hot broiler about 4 inches/ 10 cm from the heat and broil for 8–10 minutes until the flesh is opaque and flakes easily.

6 Divide the spinach among 4 plates and place the cod fillets on top. Serve with the tomato halves and lemon wedges.

hake in white wine

ingredients

SERVES 4

about 2 tbsp all-purpose flour

salt and pepper

4 hake fillets, about
5 oz/140 g each

4 tbsp extra-virgin olive oil

4 fl oz/125 ml/$1/2$ cup dry
white wine, such
as a white Rioja

2 large garlic cloves,
very finely chopped

6 scallions, finely sliced

1 oz/25 g fresh parsley,
very finely chopped

method

1 Spread the flour out on a large, flat plate and season well with salt and pepper. Dredge the skin side of the hake fillets in the seasoned flour, then shake off any excess. Set aside.

2 Heat a shallow, ovenproof casserole over high heat until you can feel the heat rising. Add the oil and heat until a cube of bread sizzles in 30 seconds. Add the hake fillets, skin-side down, and cook for 3 minutes until the skin is golden brown.

3 Turn the fish over and season with salt and pepper. Pour in the wine and add the garlic, scallions, and parsley. Transfer the casserole to a preheated oven, 450°F/230°C, and bake, uncovered, for 5 minutes, or until the flesh flakes easily. Serve the fish straight from the casserole.

nut-crusted halibut

ingredients

SERVES 4

3 tbsp butter, melted

1 lb 10 oz/750 g hallibut fillet

2 oz/55 g/generous $1/3$ cup
   pistachios, shelled and
   very finely chopped

method

1 Brush the melted butter over the halibut fillet. Spread the nuts out on a large, flat plate. Roll the fish in the nuts, pressing down gently.

2 Preheat a ridged stovetop grill pan over medium heat. Cook the halibut, turning once, for 10 minutes, or until firm but tender—the exact cooking time will depend on the thickness of the fillet.

3 Remove the fish and any loose pistachio pieces from the heat and transfer to a large, warmed serving platter. Serve at once.

garlic-crusted roast fish

ingredients

SERVES 4

2 lb/900 g mealy potatoes

4 fl oz/125 ml/^{1}/$_2$ cup milk

2 oz/55 g butter

salt and pepper

4 haddock fillets, about
    8 oz/225 g each

1 tbsp corn oil

4 garlic cloves, finely chopped

2 tbsp chopped fresh parsley,
    to garnish

method

1 Cut the potatoes into chunks and cook in a pan of lightly salted water for 15 minutes, or until tender. Drain well. Mash in the pan until smooth. Set over low heat and beat in the milk, butter, and salt and pepper.

2 Place the haddock fillets in a roasting pan and brush the fish with the oil. Sprinkle the garlic on top, add salt and pepper, then spread with the mashed potatoes. Roast in a preheated oven, 450°F/230°C, for 8–10 minutes, or until the fish is just tender.

3 Meanwhile, preheat the broiler. Transfer the fish to the broiler and cook for about 2 minutes, or until golden brown. Sprinkle with the chopped parsley and serve at once.

fish parcels with fresh herbs

ingredients

SERVES 4

vegetable oil spray

4 flounder fillets, skinned

6 tbsp chopped fresh herbs,
    such as dill, parsley, chives,
    thyme, or marjoram

finely grated rind and
    juice of 2 lemons

1 small onion, sliced thinly

1 tbsp capers, rinsed
    (optional)

salt and pepper

method

1 Cut 4 large squares of aluminum foil, each large enough to hold a fish and form a packet, and spray with oil.

2 Place each fish fillet on a foil sheet and sprinkle with the herbs, lemon rind and juice, onion, capers (if using), salt, and pepper. Fold the foil to make a secure packet and place on a cookie sheet.

3 Bake the packets in a preheated oven, 375°F/190°C, for 15 minutes, or until tender. Serve the fish piping hot, in their loosely opened packets.

sole à la meunière

ingredients

SERVES 4

4 tbsp all-purpose flour

1 tsp salt

4 x 14-oz/400-g Dover sole,
    cleaned and skinned

5^1/$_2$ oz/150 g butter

3 tbsp lemon juice

1 tbsp chopped fresh parsley

^{1}/$_4$ of a preserved lemon,
    finely chopped (optional)

fresh parsley sprigs, to garnish

lemon wedges, to serve

method

1 Mix the flour with the salt and place on a large plate. Drop the fish into the flour, one at a time, and shake well to remove any excess. Melt 3 tablespoons of the butter in a small pan and use to brush the fish liberally all over. Place the fish under a broiler preheated to medium and cook for 5 minutes on each side.

2 Meanwhile, melt the remaining butter in a pan. Pour cold water into a bowl that is large enough to take the bottom of the pan and keep near by.

3 Heat the butter until it turns a golden brown and begins to smell nutty. Remove at once from the heat and immerse the bottom of the pan in the cold water, to stop the cooking.

4 Place the fillets on individual plates, drizzle with the lemon juice, and sprinkle with the parsley and preserved lemon, if using. Pour over the browned butter, garnish with parsley sprigs, and serve immediately with lemon wedges for squeezing over.

sole florentine

ingredients

SERVES 4

20 fl oz/625 ml/2^1/$_2$ cups milk

2 strips of lemon rind

2 fresh tarragon sprigs

1 fresh bay leaf

^{1}/$_2$ onion, sliced

3^1/$_2$ tbsp butter, plus extra
for greasing

1^3/$_4$ oz/50 g/generous ^{1}/$_3$ cup
all-purpose flour

2 tsp mustard powder

1 oz/25 g/^{1}/$_4$ cup freshly
grated Parmesan cheese

10 fl oz/300 ml/1^1/$_4$ cups
heavy cream

pinch of freshly grated nutmeg

salt and pepper

1 lb/450 g spinach leaves

4 Dover sole or sole quarter-cut
fillets (two from each side
of the fish), about
1 lb 10 oz/750 g in total

crisp green salad, to serve

method

1 Put the milk, lemon rind, tarragon, bay leaf, and onion in a pan over medium heat and bring slowly to a boil. Remove from the heat and let infuse for 30 minutes.

2 Melt the butter in a separate pan over medium heat and stir in the flour and mustard powder until smooth. Strain the infused milk, discarding the lemon, herbs, and onion. Gradually beat the milk into the butter and flour until smooth. Bring slowly to a boil, stirring constantly, until thickened. Let simmer gently for 2 minutes. Remove from the heat and stir in the cheese, cream, nutmeg, salt, and pepper. Cover the surface of the sauce with parchment paper or plastic wrap. Set aside.

3 Lightly grease a large baking dish. Bring a large pan of salted water to a boil, add the spinach, and blanch for 30 seconds. Drain and refresh under cold running water. Drain again and pat dry with paper towels. Put the spinach in a layer in the base of the dish.

4 Wash and dry the fish fillets. Season with salt and pepper and roll up. Arrange on top of the spinach and pour over the cheese sauce. Bake in a preheated oven, 400°F/200°C, for 35 minutes until bubbling and golden. Serve at once with a green salad.

porgy en papillote

ingredients

SERVES 4

2 porgy, filleted

4 oz/115 g/²/₃ cup pitted
    black olives

12 cherry tomatoes, halved

4 oz/115 g green beans

handful of fresh basil leaves,
    plus extra to garnish

4 lemon slices

4 tsp olive oil

salt and pepper

boiled new potatoes, to serve

method

1 Wash and dry the fish fillets and set aside. Cut 4 large rectangles of parchment paper, each measuring about 18 x 12 inches/ 46 x 30 cm. Fold in half to make a 9 x 12-inch/ 23 x 30-cm rectangle. Cut this into a large heart shape and open out.

2 Lay a porgy fillet on one half of the paper heart. Top with a quarter of the olives, tomatoes, beans, basil, and 1 lemon slice. Drizzle over 1 teaspoon of the oil and season well with salt and pepper.

3 Fold over the other half of the paper and bring the edges of the paper together to enclose. Repeat to make 4 packages. Put the packages on a cookie sheet and cook in a preheated oven, 400°F/200°C, for 15 minutes, or until the fish is tender.

4 Transfer each package to a serving plate, unopened. Garnish with basil leaves and serve with new potatoes.

skate in black butter sauce

ingredients

SERVES 4

4 skate wings, about
6 oz/175 g each
20 fl oz/625 ml/2^1/$_2$ cups
fish stock
8 fl oz/225 ml/1 cup
dry white wine
salt and pepper
4 tbsp butter
2 tbsp lemon juice
2 tsp capers in brine, rinsed
2 tbsp chopped fresh parsley

method

1 Put the fish in a large, heavy-bottom skillet or ovenproof casserole, pour in the stock and wine, and season with salt and pepper. Bring to a boil, then reduce the heat and let simmer for 10–15 minutes until the fish is tender.

2 Meanwhile, melt the butter in a large, heavy-bottom skillet over very low heat and cook until it turns brown but not black. Stir in the lemon juice, capers, and parsley and heat for an additional 1–2 minutes.

3 Transfer the skate wings to warmed serving plates with a spatula, pour the black butter sauce over, and serve at once.

moroccan fish tagine

ingredients

SERVES 4

2 tbsp olive oil

1 large onion, finely chopped

large pinch of saffron threads

$^1/_2$ tsp ground cinnamon

1 tsp ground coriander

$^1/_2$ tsp ground cumin

$^1/_2$ tsp ground turmeric

7 oz/200 g canned chopped
   tomatoes

10 fl oz/300 ml/1$^1/_4$ cups
   fish stock

4 small red snapper, cleaned,
   boned, and heads and
   tails removed

1$^3/_4$ oz/50 g/$^1/_3$ cup pitted
   green olives

1 tbsp chopped preserved
   lemon

3 tbsp chopped fresh cilantro

salt and pepper

freshly prepared couscous,
   to serve

method

1 Heat the oil in a large pan or ovenproof casserole over low heat, add the onion, and cook, stirring occasionally, for 10 minutes until softened, but not browned. Add the saffron, cinnamon, coriander, cumin, and turmeric and cook, stirring constantly, for an additional 30 seconds.

2 Add the tomatoes and stock and stir well. Bring to a boil, then reduce the heat, cover, and let simmer for 15 minutes. Uncover and let simmer for an additional 20–35 minutes, until thickened.

3 Cut each snapper in half, then add the pieces to the pan, pushing them into the sauce. Let simmer gently for an additional 5–6 minutes until the fish is just cooked.

4 Carefully stir in the olives, preserved lemon, and cilantro. Season with salt and pepper and serve with couscous.

blackened snapper with corn papaya relish

ingredients

SERVES 4

4 x 3-oz/85-g snapper fillets

vegetable oil spray

2 lemons, halved, to serve

relish

2 tbsp finely chopped onion

1 tsp sugar

2 tbsp white wine vinegar

2 tbsp cooked or canned corn kernels

$1/4$ tsp finely chopped habanero chile or other type of chile

$3^1/2$ fl oz/100 ml/$1/3$ cup water

$1/4$ tsp yellow mustard seeds

pinch of ground turmeric

1 tsp cornstarch, blended with a little cold water

$1^3/4$ oz/50 g papaya, cut into $1/4$-inch/5-mm cubes

seasoning mix

$1/4$ tsp paprika

$1/2$ tsp onion powder

$1/4$ tsp dried thyme

$1/4$ tsp dried oregano

$1/4$ tsp cayenne pepper

$1/4$ tsp pepper

$1/2$ tsp cornstarch

method

1 To make the relish, place the onion, sugar, vinegar, corn, chile, water, mustard seeds, and turmeric into a small pan over medium heat and bring to a boil. Let simmer for 10 minutes, then add the cornstarch mixture, stirring constantly, and cook until it is the required consistency (it will thicken slightly when cooled). Stir in the papaya and let cool.

2 To make the seasoning mix, put all the ingredients into a bowl and mix thoroughly.

3 Sprinkle the seasoning mix over the snapper fillets on both sides and pat into the flesh, then shake off any excess. Lay the fillets on a board.

4 Heat a nonstick skillet over high heat until smoking. Lightly spray both sides of the fillets with oil, then put into the hot skillet and cook for 2 minutes. Turn the fillets and cook all the way through. (If the fillets are thick, finish the cooking under a preheated broiler as the less intense heat will prevent the seasoning mix from burning.) Remove the fish from the skillet.

5 Add the lemon halves, cut-side down, and cook over high heat for 2–5 minutes, until browned. Serve the fillets, topped with relish, on warmed plates, with the lemon halves.

roast red snapper with fennel

ingredients

SERVES 4

9 oz/250 g/2¹/₄ cups dried, white bread crumbs

2 tbsp milk

1 fennel bulb, sliced thinly, fronds reserved for garnish

1 tbsp lemon juice

2 tbsp sambuca

1 tbsp chopped fresh thyme

1 bay leaf, crumbled

3 lb 5 oz/1.5 kg whole red snapper, cleaned, scaled, and boned

salt and pepper

3 tbsp olive oil, plus extra for brushing

1 red onion, chopped

10 fl oz/300 ml/1¹/₄ cups dry white wine

method

1 Place the bread crumbs in a bowl, add the milk, and set aside for 5 minutes to soak. Place the fennel in another bowl and add the lemon juice, sambuca, thyme, and bay leaf. Squeeze the bread crumbs and add them to the mixture, stirring well.

2 Rinse the fish inside and out under cold running water and pat dry with paper towels. Season with salt and pepper. Spoon the fennel mixture into the cavity, then bind the fish with trussing thread or kitchen string.

3 Brush a large ovenproof dish with olive oil and sprinkle the onion over the bottom. Lay the fish on top and pour in the wine—it should reach about one third of the way up the fish. Drizzle the red snapper with the olive oil and cook in preheated oven, 375°F/190°C, for 25–30 minutes. Baste the fish occasionally with the cooking juices and if it starts to brown, cover with a piece of foil to protect it.

4 Carefully lift out the fish, remove the string, and place on a warmed serving platter. Garnish with the reserved fennel fronds and serve at once.

grilled sea bass with stewed artichokes

ingredients

SERVES 4

4 lb/1.8 kg baby globe
   artichokes
2¹/₂ tbsp fresh lemon juice,
   plus the cut halves of
   the lemon
5 fl oz/150 ml/²/₃ cup olive oil
10 garlic cloves, finely sliced
1 tbsp chopped fresh thyme,
   plus extra to garnish
salt and pepper
6 x 4-oz/115-g sea bass fillets
1 tbsp olive oil, for brushing
crusty bread, to serve

method

1 Peel away the tough outer leaves of each artichoke until the yellow-green heart is revealed. Slice off the pointed top at about halfway between the point and the top of the stem. Cut off the stem and pare off what is left of the dark green leaves around the bottom of the artichoke.

2 Submerge the prepared artichokes in water containing the cut halves of the lemon to prevent discoloration. When all the artichokes have been prepared, turn them choke side down and slice thickly.

3 Heat the olive oil in a large pan. Add the artichoke pieces, garlic, thyme, lemon juice, salt, and pepper, cover, and cook the artichokes over low heat for 20–30 minutes, without coloring, until tender.

4 Meanwhile, preheat a ridged stovetop grill pan or light a barbecue. Brush the sea bass fillets with the 1 tablespoon of olive oil and season well. Cook on the grill pan or over hot coals for 3–4 minutes on each side until just tender.

5 Divide the stewed artichokes among individual plates and top each with a fish fillet. Garnish with chopped thyme and serve with crusty bread.

sweet-&-sour sea bass

ingredients

SERVES 2

$2^{1}/_{4}$ oz/60 g bok choy, shredded

$1^{1}/_{2}$ oz/40 g bean sprouts

$1^{1}/_{2}$ oz/40 g shiitake mushrooms, sliced

$1^{1}/_{2}$ oz/40 g oyster mushrooms, torn

$^{3}/_{4}$ oz/20 g scallion, finely sliced

1 tsp finely grated gingerroot

1 tbsp finely sliced lemongrass

2 x $3^{1}/_{4}$-oz/90-g sea bass fillets, skinned and boned

$^{1}/_{4}$ oz/10 g sesame seeds, toasted

sweet-&-sour sauce

3 fl oz/90 ml/scant $^{1}/_{2}$ cup unsweetened pineapple juice

1 tbsp sugar

1 tbsp red wine vinegar

2 star anise, crushed

3 fl oz/90 ml tomato juice

1 tbsp cornstarch, blended with a little cold water

method

1 Cut 2 x 15-inch/38-cm squares of parchment paper and 2 x 15-inch/38-cm squares of aluminum foil.

2 To make the sauce, heat the pineapple juice, sugar, red wine vinegar, star anise, and tomato juice. Let simmer for 1–2 minutes, then thicken with the cornstarch and water mixture, whisking continuously. Pass through a fine strainer into a small bowl to cool.

3 In a separate large bowl mix together the bok choy, bean sprouts, mushrooms, and scallions, then add the gingerroot and lemongrass. Toss all the ingredients together.

4 Put a square of greaseproof paper on top of a square of foil and fold into a triangle. Open up and place half the vegetable mix in the center, pour half the sweet and sour sauce over the vegetables, and place the sea bass on top. Sprinkle with a few sesame seeds. Close the triangle over the mixture and, starting at the top, fold the right corner and crumple the edges together to form an airtight triangular bag. Repeat to make another bag.

5 Place on a cookie sheet and cook in a preheated oven, 400°F/200°C, for 10 minutes, until the foil bags puff with steam. To serve, place on individual plates and snip open at the table.

seared salmon with quick hollandaise sauce

ingredients

SERVES 4

1 tbsp dried thyme

1 tbsp dried rosemary

1 tbsp dried oregano

1 tbsp mild paprika

1 tsp garlic powder

2 tsp cumin seeds

1 tbsp sea salt

4 salmon fillets, skin removed

1 tbsp vegetable oil

5$\frac{1}{2}$ oz/150 g baby spinach

quick hollandaise sauce

3 egg yolks

7 oz/200 g butter

1 tbsp lemon juice

pepper

method

1 Combine the dried herbs, paprika, garlic powder, cumin seeds, and sea salt in a small grinder and process until smooth. Alternatively, grind by hand using a pestle in a mortar. Rub 1 tablespoon of the mixture into the top of each of the salmon fillets.

2 Heat the oil in a large skillet and cook the salmon, spice-side down, for 2–3 minutes, or until golden brown. Turn over and continue cooking until the salmon is cooked to your liking. Do not overcook or the salmon will be dry.

3 To make the hollandaise sauce, place the egg yolks in a blender or food processor. Melt the butter in a small pan until bubbling. With the motor running, gradually add the hot butter in a steady stream until the sauce is thick and creamy. Add the lemon juice, and a little warm water if the sauce is too thick, then season with pepper. Remove from the blender or food processor and keep warm.

4 Divide the baby spinach equally among 4 plates, place the cooked salmon on top, and spoon over the sauce. Serve at once.

roast salmon with lemon & herbs

ingredients

SERVES 4

6 tbsp extra-virgin olive oil

1 onion, sliced

1 leek, sliced

juice of $\frac{1}{2}$ lemon

2 tbsp chopped fresh parsley

2 tbsp chopped fresh dill

salt and pepper

1 lb 2 oz/500 g salmon fillets

freshly cooked baby spinach
    leaves, to serve

lemon slices, to garnish

method

1 Heat 1 tablespoon of the oil in a skillet over medium heat. Add the onion and leek and cook, stirring occasionally, for 4 minutes, or until slightly softened.

2 Meanwhile, place the remaining oil in a small bowl with the lemon juice and herbs and season with salt and pepper. Stir together well. Rinse the fish under cold running water, then pat dry with paper towels. Arrange the fish in a shallow ovenproof dish.

3 Remove the skillet from the heat and spread the onion and leek over the fish. Pour the oil mixture over the top, making sure that everything is well coated. Roast in the center of a preheated oven, 400°F/200°C, for 10 minutes, or until the fish is cooked through.

4 Arrange the cooked spinach on serving plates. Remove the fish and vegetables and serve next to the spinach with the vegetables arranged on top of the fish. Garnish with lemon slices and serve at once.

ginger-marinated salmon & scallops

ingredients

SERVES 4

7 oz/200 g/1 cup brown basmati rice

1/2 cucumber, diced

4 scallions, sliced

1/2 bunch fresh cilantro, chopped

1 red bell pepper, seeded and diced

1 fresh green chile, seeded and thinly sliced

juice of 1 lime

2 tbsp toasted sesame oil

1 lb 2 oz/500 g salmon fillet, skinned and cut into chunks

8 scallops, without corals, cleaned

1³/₄ oz/50 g fresh gingerroot

juice of 1 lemon

1 tbsp olive oil

green salad, to serve

method

1 Bring a large pan of water to a boil, add the rice, and cook for 25 minutes, or until tender. Drain and let cool. Mix the cooled rice with the cucumber, scallions, cilantro, red bell pepper, chile, lime juice, and sesame oil in a bowl. Cover and set aside for the flavors to develop.

2 Meanwhile, put the salmon chunks into a shallow, nonmetallic bowl. Cut each scallop in half and add to the bowl. Using a garlic press or the back of a knife, crush the gingerroot to extract the juice. Mix the ginger juice with the lemon juice and olive oil in a small bowl or pitcher and pour over the seafood. Turn the seafood to coat in the marinade. Cover and let marinate in the refrigerator for 30 minutes. Soak 8 wooden skewers in cold water for 30 minutes, then drain.

3 Thread an equal quantity of the salmon and scallops onto the skewers. Cook under a broiler preheated to high for 3–4 minutes on each side, or until cooked through. Serve the hot seafood skewers with the rice salad and a green salad.

mexican-style salmon

ingredients

SERVES 4

4 salmon steaks, about
    6–8 oz/175–225 g each
tomato wedges, 3 finely
    chopped scallions, and
    shredded lettuce, to serve
lime slices, to garnish

marinade

4 garlic cloves, finely chopped
2 tbsp extra-virgin olive oil
pinch of ground allspice
pinch of ground cinnamon
juice of 2 limes
1–2 tsp marinade from
    canned chipotle chiles or
    bottled chipotle chile salsa
$1/4$ tsp ground cumin
pinch of sugar
salt and pepper

method

1 To make the marinade, finely chop the garlic and place in a bowl with the olive oil, allspice, cinnamon, lime juice, chipotle marinade, cumin, and sugar. Add salt and pepper and stir to combine.

2 Coat the salmon with the garlic mixture, then place in a nonmetallic dish. Leave to marinate for at least 1 hour or overnight in the refrigerator.

3 Transfer to a broiler pan and cook under a preheated broiler for 3–4 minutes on each side. Alternatively, cook the salmon over hot coals on a grill until cooked through.

4 To serve, mix the tomato wedges with the scallions. Place the salmon on individual plates and arrange the tomato salad and shredded lettuce alongside. Garnish with lime slices and serve.

roast tuna
with orange & anchovies

ingredients

SERVES 4–6

scant 1 cup freshly squeezed
orange juice

3 tbsp extra-virgin olive oil

2 oz/55 g anchovy fillets in oil,
coarsely chopped, with the
oil reserved

small pinch of dried red
pepper flakes, or to taste

1 tuna fillet, about
1 lb 5 oz/600 g

pepper

method

1 Combine the orange juice, 2 tablespoons of the olive oil, the anchovies and their oil, and red pepper flakes in a nonmetallic bowl large enough to hold the tuna and season with pepper. Add the tuna and spoon the marinade over it. Cover with plastic wrap and let marinate in the refrigerator for 2 hours, turning the tuna occasionally. Remove the bowl from the refrigerator about 20 minutes before cooking to return the fish to room temperature.

2 Remove the tuna from the marinade, reserving the marinade, and wipe dry. Heat the remaining oil in a large skillet over high heat. Add the tuna and sear for 1 minute on each side until lightly browned and crisp. Place in a roasting pan. Cover the pan tightly with foil.

3 Roast in a preheated oven, 425°F/220°C, for 8 minutes for medium-rare and 10 minutes for medium-well done. Remove from the oven and set aside to rest for 2 minutes before slicing.

4 Meanwhile, place the marinade in a small pan over high heat and bring to a rolling boil. Boil for 2 minutes.

5 Transfer the tuna to a serving platter and carve into thick slices, which will probably break into chunks as you cut them. Serve the sauce separately for spooning over.

charbroiled tuna with chile salsa

ingredients

SERVES 4

4 tuna steaks, about
  6 oz/175 g each
grated rind and juice of 1 lime
2 tbsp olive oil
salt and pepper
green salad, to serve

chile salsa
2 orange bell peppers
1 tbsp olive oil
juice of 1 lime
juice of 1 orange
2–3 fresh red chiles, seeded
  and chopped
pinch of cayenne pepper

method

1 Rinse the tuna thoroughly under cold running water and pat dry with paper towels, then place in a large shallow nonmetallic dish. Sprinkle the lime rind and juice and the oil over the fish. Season with salt and pepper, cover with plastic wrap, and let marinate in the refrigerator for up to 1 hour.

2 Preheat the grill. To make the salsa, brush the bell peppers with the olive oil and cook over hot coals, turning frequently, for 10 minutes, or until the skin is blackened and charred. Remove from the grill and let cool slightly, then peel off the skins and discard the seeds. Place the bell peppers in a food processor with the remaining salsa ingredients and process to a purée. Transfer to a bowl and season with salt and pepper.

3 Cook the tuna over hot coals for 4–5 minutes on each side until golden. Transfer to plates, and serve immediately with the green salad and the salsa.

rice, pasta & noodles

Italy and Spain are bordered by miles of Mediterranean coastline, so it is not surprising that fish features prominently in the culinary tradition of these two countries. In Spain, fish and seafood go into what has almost become the national dish—paella. It is often mixed with meat, usually chicken, but Paella with Mussels & White Wine and Seafood Paella with Lemon & Herbs make the most of the daily catch from the sea. The classic Italian rice dish, risotto—a gloriously creamy, rich delight—also works wonderfully well with fish and seafood. Shrimp & Asparagus Risotto and Saffron & Lemon Risotto are both simple yet sophisticated, and if you really love things in shells, Venetian Seafood Risotto is packed with shrimp, mussels, and clams.

Pasta, another Italian favorite, is also a great partner for fish. Smoked salmon goes especially well—try Fettucine with Smoked Salmon or Linguine with Smoked Salmon & Arugula, both light, delicious recipes. Noodles, the Asian version of pasta, are particularly useful if you have a gluten intolerance—you can choose recipes such as Fish Curry with Rice Noodles, Thai Fisherman's Catch, Malaysian-style Coconut Noodles with Shrimp, and Shrimp Laksa, which have all the satisfying texture of noodles but not a hint of wheat!

paella with mussels & white wine

ingredients

SERVES 4–6

5^1/$_2$ oz/150 g cod fillet, skinned
  and rinsed in cold water

44 fl oz/1.35 liters/5^1/$_2$ cups
  simmering fish stock

7 oz/200 g live mussels,
  prepared (see page 38)

3 tbsp olive oil

1 large red onion, chopped

2 garlic cloves, crushed

^{1}/$_2$ tsp cayenne pepper

^{1}/$_2$ tsp saffron threads infused
  in 2 tbsp hot water

8 oz/225 g tomatoes, peeled
  and cut into wedges

1 red bell pepper, seeded
  and sliced

1 green bell pepper, seeded
  and sliced

13 oz/375 g/generous
  1^1/$_2$ cups medium-grain
  paella rice

3^1/$_2$ fl oz/100 ml/generous
  ^{1}/$_3$ cup white wine

5^1/$_2$ oz/150 g/generous 1 cup
  shelled peas

1 tbsp chopped fresh dill,
  plus extra to garnish

salt and pepper

lemon wedges, to serve

method

1 Cook the cod in the pan of simmering stock for 5 minutes. Transfer to a colander, rinse under cold running water, and drain. Cut into chunks, then transfer to a bowl and set aside. Cook the mussels in the stock for 5 minutes, or until opened, then transfer to the bowl with the cod, discarding any that remain closed.

2 Heat the oil in a paella pan and stir the onion over medium heat until softened. Add the garlic, cayenne pepper, and saffron and its soaking liquid and cook, stirring constantly, for 1 minute. Add the tomatoes and bell peppers and cook, stirring, for 2 minutes.

3 Add the rice and cook, stirring, for 1 minute. Add the wine and most of the stock and bring to a boil, then let simmer for 10 minutes. Do not stir during cooking, but shake the pan once or twice and when adding ingredients. Add the peas, dill, salt, and pepper. Cook for 10 minutes, or until the rice is almost cooked, adding more stock if necessary. Add the cod and mussels and cook for 3 minutes.

4 When all the liquid has been absorbed and you detect a faint toasty aroma coming from the rice, remove from the heat immediately. Cover with foil and let stand for 5 minutes. Garnish with dill and serve with lemon wedges.

seafood paella with lemon & herbs

ingredients

SERVES 4–6

$^1/_2$ tsp saffron threads

2 tbsp hot water

5$^1/_2$ oz/150 g cod fillet, skinned and rinsed under cold running water

42 fl oz/1.25 liters/5$^1/_2$ cups simmering fish stock

12 large raw shrimp, shelled and deveined

1 lb/450 g raw squid, cleaned and cut into rings or bite-size pieces (or use the same quantity of shucked scallops)

3 tbsp olive oil

1 large red onion, chopped

2 garlic cloves, crushed

1 small fresh red chile, seeded and minced

8 oz/225 g tomatoes, peeled and cut into wedges

13 oz/375 g/generous 1$^1/_2$ cups medium-grain paella rice

1 tbsp chopped fresh parsley

2 tsp chopped fresh dill

salt and pepper

1 lemon, cut into halves, to serve

method

1 Put the saffron threads and water in a small bowl and let infuse for a few minutes.

2 Add the cod to the pan of simmering stock and cook for 5 minutes, then transfer to a colander, rinse under cold running water and drain. Add the shrimp and squid to the stock and cook for 2 minutes. Cut the cod into chunks, then transfer with the other seafood to a bowl and set aside. Let the stock simmer.

3 Heat the oil in a paella pan and stir the onion over medium heat until softened. Add the garlic, chile, and saffron and its soaking liquid and cook, stirring, for 1 minute. Add the tomato wedges and cook, stirring, for 2 minutes. Add the rice and herbs and cook, stirring, for 1 minute. Add most of the stock and bring to a boil. Let simmer, uncovered, for 10 minutes. Do not stir during cooking, but shake the pan once or twice and when adding ingredients. Season and cook for 10 minutes, until the rice is almost cooked. Add more stock if necessary. Add the seafood and cook for 2 minutes.

4 When all the liquid has been absorbed and you detect a faint toasty aroma coming from the rice, remove from the heat immediately. Cover with foil and let stand for 5 minutes. Serve with the lemon halves.

risotto with tuna & pine nuts

ingredients

SERVES 4

3 tbsp butter

4 tbsp olive oil

1 small onion, finely chopped

10 oz/280 g/1$^1/_2$ cups
  Arborio rice

40 fl oz/1.25 liters/5 cups
  simmering fish or chicken
  stock

salt and pepper

8 oz/225 g tuna, canned
  and drained, or broiled
  fresh steaks

8–10 black olives, pitted
  and sliced

1 small pimiento, thinly sliced

1 tsp finely chopped
  fresh parsley

1 tsp finely chopped
  fresh marjoram

2 tbsp white wine vinegar

2 oz/55 g/$^3/_8$ cup pine nuts

1 garlic clove, chopped

8 oz/225 g fresh tomatoes,
  peeled, seeded, and diced

3 oz/85 g/$^3/_4$ cup Parmesan
  or Grana Padano cheese

method

1 Melt 2 tablespoons of the butter with 1 tablespoon of the oil in a deep pan over medium heat. Add the onion and cook, stirring occasionally, until soft and starting to turn golden. Reduce the heat, add the rice, and mix to coat in oil and butter. Cook, stirring constantly, until the grains are translucent. Add the hot stock, a ladleful at a time, stirring constantly, until all the liquid is absorbed and the rice is creamy. Season to taste.

2 While the risotto is cooking, flake the tuna into a bowl and mix in the olives, pimiento, parsley, marjoram, and vinegar. Season with salt and pepper.

3 Heat the remaining oil in a small skillet over high heat. Add the pine nuts and garlic. Cook, stirring constantly, for 2 minutes, or until they just start to brown. Add the tomatoes and mix well. Continue cooking over medium heat for 3–4 minutes or until they are thoroughly warm. Pour the tomato mixture over the tuna mixture and mix. Fold into the risotto 5 minutes before the end of the cooking time.

4 Remove the risotto from the heat when all the liquid has been absorbed and add the remaining butter. Mix well, then stir in the Parmesan until it melts. Serve at once.

risotto with sole & tomatoes

ingredients

SERVES 4

3 tbsp butter

3 tbsp olive oil

1 small onion, finely chopped

10 oz/280 g/1½ cups
  Arborio rice

40 fl oz/1.25 liters/5 cups
  simmering fish or chicken
  stock

salt and pepper

1 lb/450 g tomatoes, peeled,
  seeded, and cut into strips

6 sun-dried tomatoes in olive
  oil, drained and thinly sliced

3 tbsp tomato paste

2 fl oz/50 ml/¼ cup red wine

1 lb/450 g sole or flounder
  fillets, skinned

4 oz/115 g/1 cup freshly
  grated Parmesan or Grana
  Padano cheese

2 tbsp finely chopped fresh
  cilantro, to garnish

method

1 Melt 2 tablespoons of the butter with 1 tablespoon of the oil in a deep pan over medium heat. Stir in the onion and cook, stirring occasionally, for 5 minutes, or until soft and starting to turn golden. Reduce the heat, add the rice, and mix to coat in oil and butter. Cook, stirring constantly, for 2–3 minutes, or until the grains are translucent. Add the hot stock, a ladleful at a time, stirring constantly, until all the liquid is absorbed and the rice is creamy. Season with salt and pepper.

2 Meanwhile, heat the remaining oil in a large, heavy-bottom skillet. Add the fresh and dried tomatoes. Stir well and cook over medium heat for 10–15 minutes, or until soft and slushy. Stir in the tomato paste and wine. Bring to a boil, then reduce the heat until it is just simmering. Cut the fish into strips and gently stir into the sauce. Cook for 5 minutes, or until the fish flakes when checked with a fork. Most of the liquid should be absorbed but, if it isn't, remove the fish and then increase the heat to reduce the sauce.

3 Remove the risotto from the heat when all the liquid has been absorbed and add the remaining butter. Mix well, then stir in the Parmesan until it melts. Place the risotto on serving plates and arrange the fish and sauce on top. Garnish with chopped fresh cilantro and serve at once.

venetian seafood risotto

ingredients

SERVES 4

8 oz/225 g prepared raw
   shrimp, heads and
   shells reserved

2 garlic cloves, halved

1 lemon, sliced

8 oz/225 g live mussels*,
   scrubbed and debearded

8 oz/225 g live clams*,
   scrubbed

20 fl oz/625 ml/2^1/$_2$ cups
   water

4 oz/115 g butter

1 tbsp olive oil

1 onion, finely chopped

2 tbsp chopped fresh
   flat-leaf parsley

12 oz/350 g/1^3/$_4$ cups
   Arborio rice

4 fl oz/125 ml/^{1}/$_2$ cup
   dry white wine

8 oz/225 g cleaned raw
   squid, cut into small
   pieces, or squid rings

4 tbsp Marsala

salt and pepper

* discard any mussels or
clams that remain closed
after cooking

method

1 Wrap the shrimp heads and shells in a square of cheesecloth and pound with a pestle. Put the wrapped shells and their liquid in a pan with the garlic, lemon, mussels, and clams. Add the measured water, cover, and bring to a boil over high heat. Cook, shaking the pan frequently, for 5 minutes until the shellfish have opened. Let cool, shell and set aside. Strain the cooking liquid through a strainer lined with cheesecloth and add water to make 40 fl oz/1.25 liters/5 cups. Bring to a boil in a pan, then simmer gently over low heat.

2 Melt 2 tablespoons of butter with the olive oil in a pan. Cook the onion and half the parsley over medium heat, stirring occasionally, until softened. Reduce the heat, stir in the rice, and cook, stirring, until the grains are translucent. Add the wine and cook, stirring, for 1 minute until reduced. Add the hot cooking liquid a ladleful at a time, stirring constantly, until all the liquid is absorbed and the rice is creamy.

3 Melt 2 oz/55 g of the remaining butter in a pan. Cook the squid, stirring frequently, for 3 minutes. Add the shrimp and cook for 2–3 minutes, until the squid is opaque and the shrimp have changed color. Add the Marsala, bring to a boil, and cook until the liquid has evaporated. Stir all the seafood into the rice, add the remaining butter and parsley, and season. Heat gently and serve at once.

lobster risotto

ingredients

SERVES 2

1 cooked lobster, about
 14 oz–1 lb/400–450 g

1 tbsp olive oil

2 oz/55 g butter

1/2 onion, finely chopped

1 garlic clove, finely chopped

1 tsp chopped fresh thyme
 leaves

6 oz/175 g/generous 3/4 cup
 Arborio rice

5 fl oz/150 ml/2/3 cup
 sparkling white wine

20 fl oz/625 ml/2 1/2 cups
 simmering fish stock

1 tsp green or pink
 peppercorns in brine,
 drained and coarsely
 chopped

1 tbsp chopped fresh parsley

method

1 To prepare the lobster, remove the claws by twisting them. Crack the claws using the back of a large knife and set aside. Split the body lengthwise. Remove and discard the intestinal vein, the stomach sac, and the spongy gills. Remove the meat from the tail and coarsely chop. Set aside with the claws.

2 Heat the oil with half the butter in a large pan over medium heat. Add the onion and cook, stirring occasionally, for 5 minutes until softened. Add the garlic and cook for an additional 30 seconds. Stir in the thyme. Reduce the heat, add the rice, and mix to coat in butter and oil. Cook, stirring constantly, for 2–3 minutes, or until the grains are translucent.

3 Stir in the wine and cook, stirring constantly, for 1 minute until reduced. Gradually add the hot stock, a ladleful at a time. Stir constantly and add more liquid as the rice absorbs each addition. Increase the heat to medium so that the liquid bubbles. Cook for 20 minutes, or until all the liquid is absorbed and the rice is creamy. Five minutes before the end of cooking time, add the lobster meat and claws.

4 Remove the pan from the heat and stir in the peppercorns, remaining butter, and the parsley. Spoon on to warmed plates and serve at once.

shrimp & asparagus risotto

ingredients

SERVES 4

40 fl oz/1.25 liters/5 cups
vegetable stock

12 oz/375 g fresh asparagus
spears, cut into 2-inch/
5-cm lengths

2 tbsp olive oil

1 onion, finely chopped

1 garlic clove, finely chopped

12 oz/350 g/1$3/4$ cups
Arborio rice

1 lb/450 g raw jumbo shrimp,
shelled and deveined

2 tbsp olive paste or tapenade

2 tbsp chopped fresh basil

salt and pepper

fresh Parmesan cheese and
fresh basil sprigs,
to garnish

method

1 Bring the stock to a boil in a large pan. Add the asparagus and cook for 3 minutes until just tender. Strain, reserving the stock, and refresh the asparagus under cold running water. Drain and set aside. Return the stock to the pan and keep simmering gently over low heat while you are cooking the risotto.

2 Heat the olive oil in a large, heavy-bottom pan. Add the onion and cook over medium heat, stirring occasionally, for 5 minutes until softened. Add the garlic and cook for an additional 30 seconds. Reduce the heat, add the rice, and mix to coat in oil. Cook, stirring constantly, for 2–3 minutes, or until the grains are translucent.

3 Gradually add the hot stock, a ladleful at a time. Stir constantly and add more liquid as the rice absorbs each addition. Increase the heat to medium so that the liquid bubbles. Cook for 20 minutes, until all the liquid is absorbed and the rice is creamy. Add the shrimp and asparagus when you add the last ladleful of stock.

4 Remove the pan from the heat, stir in the olive paste and basil, and season with salt and pepper. Spoon the risotto onto warmed plates and serve at once, garnished with Parmesan cheese and basil sprigs.

saffron & lemon risotto with scallops

ingredients

SERVES 4

16 live scallops, shucked

juice of 1 lemon, plus extra
for seasoning

3 tbsp butter

1 tbsp olive oil, plus extra for
brushing

1 small onion, finely chopped

10 oz/280 g/1 1/2 cups
Arborio rice

1 tsp crumbled saffron
threads

40 fl oz/1.25 liters/5 cups
simmering fish or
vegetable stock

salt and pepper

2 tbsp vegetable oil

4 oz/115 g/1 cup freshly
grated Parmesan or Grana
Padano cheese

1 lemon, cut into wedges and
2 tsp lemon zest, to
garnish

method

1 Place the scallops in a nonmetallic bowl and mix with the lemon juice. Cover the bowl with plastic wrap and let chill for 15 minutes.

2 Melt 2 tablespoons of the butter with the oil in a deep pan over medium heat. Add the onion and cook, stirring occasionally, until soft and starting to turn golden. Add the rice and mix to coat in oil and butter. Cook, stirring, until the grains are translucent. Dissolve the saffron in 4 tablespoons of hot stock and add to the rice. Gradually add the remaining stock a ladleful at a time, stirring constantly, until all the liquid is absorbed and the rice is creamy. Season with salt and pepper.

3 When the risotto is nearly cooked, preheat a grill pan over high heat. Brush the scallops with oil and sear on the grill pan for 3–4 minutes on each side, depending on their thickness. Take care not to overcook or they will be rubbery.

4 Remove the risotto from the heat and add the remaining butter. Mix well, then stir in the Parmesan until it melts. Season with lemon juice, adding just 1 teaspoon at a time and tasting as you go. Serve the risotto at once with the scallops and lemon wedges arranged on top, sprinkled with lemon zest.

risotto with squid & garlic butter

ingredients

SERVES 4

8–12 raw baby squid,
    cleaned, rinsed, and
    patted dry
5^1/$_2$ oz/150 g butter
1 tbsp olive oil
1 small onion, finely chopped
10 oz/280 g/scant 1^1/$_2$ cups
    Arborio rice
40 fl oz/1.25 liters/5 cups
    simmering fish
    or chicken stock
salt and pepper
3 garlic cloves, crushed
3 oz/85 g/^{3}/$_4$ cup freshly
    grated Parmesan or Grana
    Padano cheese
2 tbsp finely chopped fresh
    parsley, to garnish

method

1 Cut the squid in half lengthwise, then score with a sharp knife, making horizontal and vertical cuts. Dice the larger tentacles.

2 Melt 2 tablespoons of the butter with the oil in a deep pan over medium heat. Cook the onion, stirring, until soft and starting to turn golden. Stir in the rice and cook, stirring, until the grains are translucent. Gradually add the hot stock, a ladleful at a time. Stir constantly and add more liquid as the rice absorbs each addition. Cook for 20 minutes, or until all the liquid is absorbed and the rice is creamy. Season with salt and pepper.

3 When the risotto is nearly cooked, melt 4 oz/115 g of the remaining butter in a heavy-bottom skillet. Add the garlic and cook over low heat until soft. Increase the heat to high, add the squid, and toss to cook for no more than 2–3 minutes or the squid will become tough. Remove the squid from the skillet, draining carefully and reserving the garlic butter.

4 Remove the risotto from the heat and stir in the remaining butter, then stir in the Parmesan until it melts. Spoon onto warmed serving plates and arrange the squid on top. Spoon some of the garlic butter over each portion. Serve at once, sprinkled with chopped parsley.

shrimp with coconut rice

ingredients

SERVES 4

4 oz/115 g/1 cup dried
   Chinese mushrooms
2 tbsp vegetable or
   peanut oil
6 scallions, chopped
2 oz/55 g/scant $^1/_2$ cup dry
   unsweetened coconut
1 fresh green chile, seeded
   and chopped
8 oz/225 g/generous 1 cup
   jasmine rice
5 fl oz/150 ml/$^2/_3$ cup
   fish stock
14 fl oz/425 ml/1$^3/_4$ cups
   coconut milk
12 oz/350 g cooked shelled
   shrimp
6 sprigs fresh Thai basil

method

1 Place the mushrooms in a small bowl, cover with hot water, and set aside to soak for 30 minutes. Drain, then cut off and discard the stalks and slice the caps.

2 Heat 1 tablespoon of the oil in a wok and stir-fry the scallions, coconut, and chile for 2–3 minutes, until lightly browned. Add the mushrooms and stir-fry for 3–4 minutes.

3 Add the rice and stir-fry for 2–3 minutes, then add the stock and bring to a boil. Reduce the heat and add the coconut milk. Let simmer for 10–15 minutes, until the rice is tender. Stir in the shrimp and basil, heat through, and serve.

smoked fish with tagliatelle verde

ingredients

SERVES 4

1 lb/450 g smoked haddock
　fillets, skinned

10 oz/280 g dried tagliatelle
　verde

20 fl oz/625 ml/2^1/2 cups
　skim or lowfat milk

4 tbsp cornstarch

2 shallots, finely chopped

2 tbsp snipped fresh chives

pepper

method

1 Cut the fish into chunks, removing any remaining bones.

2 Bring a large pan of water to a boil, add the tagliatelle, and return to a boil. Cook for 8–10 minutes, or until just tender.

3 Meanwhile, blend 4 fl oz/125 ml/^{1}/2 cup of the milk with the cornstarch in a heatproof 28-fl oz/875-ml/3^1/2-cup bowl. Place the remaining milk in a pan with the shallots and bring to a boil. Pour the boiling milk over the cornstarch mixture, stirring constantly. Return the milk to the pan and return to a boil, stirring constantly, until the sauce thickens.

4 Stir the fish into the sauce, reduce the heat to low, and let simmer gently for 5 minutes, or until the fish is cooked. Stir in half of the chives.

5 Drain the tagliatelle and return to the pan, stir in the haddock sauce, and season with pepper. Serve at once, garnished with the remaining chives.

fettuccine with smoked salmon

ingredients

SERVES 4

8 oz/225 g dried fettuccine

1 tsp olive oil

1 garlic clove, finely chopped

2 oz/55 g smoked salmon,
     cut into thin strips

2 oz/55 g watercress leaves,
     plus extra to garnish

salt and pepper

method

1 Bring a large pan of lightly salted water to a boil over medium heat. Add the pasta, return to a boil and cook for 8–10 minutes, or until tender but still firm to the bite.

2 Meanwhile, heat the olive oil in a large nonstick skillet. Add the garlic and cook over low heat, stirring constantly, for 30 seconds. Add the salmon and watercress, season with pepper, and cook for an additional 30 seconds, or until the watercress has wilted.

3 Drain the cooked pasta and return to the pan. Mix the salmon and watercress with the pasta. Toss the mixture thoroughly using 2 large forks. Divide among 4 large serving plates and garnish with extra watercress leaves. Serve immediately.

linguine with smoked salmon & arugula

ingredients

SERVES 4

12 oz/350 g dried linguine

2 tbsp olive oil

1 garlic clove, finely chopped

4 oz/115 g smoked salmon,
     cut into thin strips

2 oz/55 g arugula

salt and pepper

lemon halves, to garnish

method

1 Bring a large, heavy-bottom pan of lightly salted water to a boil. Add the pasta, return to a boil, and cook for 8–10 minutes, or until tender but still firm to the bite.

2 Just before the end of the cooking time, heat the olive oil in a heavy-bottom skillet. Add the garlic and cook over low heat, stirring constantly, for 1 minute. Do not allow the garlic to brown or it will taste bitter. Add the salmon and arugula. Season with salt and pepper and cook, stirring constantly, for 1 minute. Remove the skillet from the heat.

3 Drain the pasta and transfer to a warmed serving dish. Add the smoked salmon and arugula mixture, toss lightly, and serve, garnished with lemon halves.

macaroni & seafood bake

ingredients

SERVES 4

12 oz/350 g dried
    short-cut macaroni
6 tbsp butter, plus extra for
    greasing
2 small fennel bulbs,
    thinly sliced
6 oz/175 g mushrooms,
    thinly sliced
6 oz/175 g cooked
    shelled shrimp
pinch of cayenne pepper
1¼ cups Béchamel Sauce
    (see below)
½ cup freshly grated
    Parmesan cheese
2 large tomatoes, sliced
olive oil, for brushing
1 tsp dried oregano
salt and pepper

béchamel sauce

10 fl oz/300 ml/1¼ cups milk
1 bay leaf
6 black peppercorns
slice of onion
mace blade
2 tbsp butter
3 tbsp all-purpose flour
salt and pepper

method

1 To make the Béchamel sauce, pour the milk into a pan and add the bay leaf, peppercorns, onion, and mace. Heat to just below boiling point, then remove from the heat, cover, let infuse for 10 minutes, then strain. Melt the butter in a separate pan. Sprinkle in the flour and cook over low heat, stirring constantly, for 1 minute. Gradually stir in the milk, then bring to a boil and cook, stirring, until thickened and smooth. Season with salt and pepper.

2 Bring a large pan of lightly salted water to a boil. Add the pasta, return to a boil, and cook for 8–10 minutes, or until tender but still firm to the bite. Drain and return to the pan. Add 2 tablespoons of the butter to the pasta, cover, shake the pan, and keep warm.

3 Melt the remaining butter in a pan. Add the fennel and cook for 3–4 minutes. Stir in the mushrooms and cook for 2 minutes. Stir in the shrimp, then remove the pan from the heat. Stir the cayenne pepper into the Béchamel sauce and add the shrimp mixture and pasta.

4 Grease a large ovenproof dish with butter, then pour the mixture into the dish and spread evenly. Sprinkle over the Parmesan cheese and arrange the tomato slices in a ring around the edge. Brush the tomatoes with olive oil, then sprinkle over the oregano. Bake in a preheated oven, 350°F/180°C, for 25 minutes, or until golden brown. Serve immediately.

crab ravioli

ingredients

SERVES 4

6 scallions

12 oz/350 g cooked crabmeat

2 tsp finely chopped
   fresh gingerroot

$1/8$–$1/4$ tsp chili or Tabasco
   sauce

1 lb 9 oz/700 g tomatoes,
   peeled, seeded, and
   coarsely chopped

1 garlic clove, finely chopped

1 tbsp white wine vinegar

1 quantity basic pasta dough
   (see below)

all-purpose flour, for dusting

1 egg, lightly beaten

salt

2 tbsp heavy cream

shredded scallion, to garnish

pasta dough

7 oz/200 g/1 cup all-purpose
   flour, plus extra for dusting

pinch of salt

2 eggs, lightly beaten

1 tbsp olive oil

method

1 To make the pasta dough, sift the flour into a food processor. Add the salt, eggs, and olive oil and process until the dough begins to come together. Knead on a lightly floured counter until smooth. Cover and let rest for 30 minutes.

2 Thinly slice the scallions, keeping the white and green parts separate. Mix the green scallions, crabmeat, gingerroot, and chili sauce to taste in a bowl. Cover and let chill.

3 Process the tomatoes in a food processor to a purée. Place the garlic, white scallions, and vinegar in a pan and add the puréed tomatoes. Bring to a boil, stirring, then let simmer gently for 10 minutes. Remove from the heat.

4 Thinly roll out half of the pasta dough on a lightly floured counter. Cover with a dish towel and roll out the other half. Place small mounds of the filling in rows $1^1/2$ inches/4 cm apart on one sheet of dough and brush in between with beaten egg. Cover with the other half of dough. Press down between the mounds, cut into squares, and let rest on a dish towel for 1 hour.

5 Bring a large pan of lightly salted water to a boil. Add the ravioli, in batches, return to a boil, and cook for 5 minutes. Remove with a slotted spoon and drain on paper towels. Meanwhile, gently heat the tomato sauce and whisk in the cream. Serve the ravioli with the sauce poured over and garnished with shredded scallion.

spaghetti with clams

ingredients

SERVES 4

2 lb 4 oz/1 kg live clams,
scrubbed under cold
running water*

6 fl oz/175 ml/³/₄ cup water

6 fl oz/175 ml/³/₄ cup dry
white wine

12 oz/350 g dried spaghetti

5 tbsp olive oil

2 garlic cloves, finely chopped

4 tbsp chopped fresh
flat-leaf parsley

salt and pepper

* discard any clams with
broken or damaged shells
and any that do not shut
when sharply tapped

method

1 Place the clams in a large, heavy-bottom pan, add the water and wine, cover, and cook over high heat, shaking the pan occasionally, for 5 minutes, or until the shells have opened.

2 Remove the clams with a slotted spoon and let cool slightly. Strain the cooking liquid into a small pan through a strainer lined with cheesecloth. Bring to a boil and cook until reduced by about half, then remove from the heat. Meanwhile, discard any clams that have not opened, remove the remainder from their shells, and reserve until required.

3 Bring a large pan of lightly salted water to a boil. Add the pasta, return to a boil, and cook for 8–10 minutes, or until tender but still firm to the bite.

4 Meanwhile, heat the olive oil in a large, heavy-bottom skillet. Add the garlic and cook, stirring frequently, for 2 minutes. Add the parsley and the reduced clam cooking liquid and let simmer gently.

5 Drain the pasta and add it to the skillet with the clams. Season with salt and pepper and cook, stirring constantly, for 4 minutes, or until the pasta is coated and the clams have heated through. Transfer to a warmed serving dish and serve immediately.

fish curry with rice noodles

ingredients

SERVES 4

2 tbsp vegetable or peanut oil

1 large onion, chopped

2 garlic cloves, chopped

3 oz/85 g white mushrooms

8 oz/225 g monkfish, cut into
1-inch/2.5-cm cubes

8 oz/225 g salmon fillets, cut
into 1-inch/2.5-cm cubes

8 oz/225 g cod fillets, cut into
1-inch/2.5-cm cubes

2 tbsp Thai red curry paste

14 oz/400 g/1^3/4 cups canned
coconut milk

handful of fresh cilantro,
chopped

1 tsp jaggery or brown sugar

1 tsp Thai fish sauce

4 oz/115 g dried rice noodles

3 scallions, chopped

2 oz/50 g/scant ^{1}/2 cup bean
sprouts

few fresh Thai basil leaves

method

1 Heat the oil in a preheated wok or large skillet over medium heat, add the onion, garlic, and mushrooms and cook, stirring frequently, for 5 minutes until softened, but not browned.

2 Add the fish, curry paste, and coconut milk and bring gently to a boil. Let simmer for 2–3 minutes before adding half the cilantro, and the sugar and fish sauce. Keep warm.

3 Meanwhile, soak the noodles in enough boiling water to cover in a heatproof bowl for 3–4 minutes until tender, or cook according to the package instructions. Drain well through a metal colander. Put the colander and noodles over a pan of simmering water. Add the scallions, bean sprouts, and most of the basil and steam on top of the noodles for 1–2 minutes until just wilted.

4 Pile the noodles onto warmed serving plates and top with the fish curry. Sprinkle the remaining cilantro and basil over the top and serve at once.

cod with spiced noodles

ingredients

SERVES 4

1 tbsp peanut or corn oil

finely grated rind and juice of
1 large lemon

4 cod or haddock steaks,
about 5 oz/140 g each,
skinned

paprika, to taste

salt and pepper

spiced noodles

9 oz/250 g dried medium
Chinese egg noodles

1 tbsp peanut or corn oil

2 garlic cloves, chopped

1-inch/2.5-cm piece fresh
gingerroot, peeled and
finely chopped

2 tbsp very finely chopped
fresh cilantro roots

1 tbsp kecap manis (sweet
soy sauce)

1 Thai chile, seeded and
finely chopped

1 tbsp nam pla
(Thai fish sauce)

method

1 Put the noodles in a pan of boiling water and boil for 3 minutes, until soft, or cook according to the package instructions. Drain, rinse with cold water to stop the cooking, and drain again, then set aside.

2 Mix 1 tablespoon of the oil with the lemon juice and brush over one side of each fish steak. Sprinkle with the lemon rind and a dusting of paprika and add a little salt and pepper. Lightly brush a broiler rack with oil, then place the fish on the rack and broil under a broiler preheated to high, about 4 inches/ 10 cm from the heat, for 8–10 minutes, until the flesh flakes easily.

3 Meanwhile, heat a wok or large skillet over high heat. Add 1 tablespoon oil and heat until it shimmers. Add the garlic and gingerroot and stir-fry for about 30 seconds. Add the cilantro and kecap manis and stir round. Add the noodles and stir thoroughly so they are coated in the kecap manis. Stir in the chopped chile and nam pla. Serve each broiled fish steak on a bed of noodles.

teriyaki salmon fillets with chinese noodles

ingredients

SERVES 4

4 salmon fillets, about
   7 oz/200 g each, any
   scales wiped off
4 fl oz/125 ml/^{1}/$_2$ cup
   teriyaki marinade
1 shallot, sliced
^{3}/$_4$-inch/2-cm piece fresh
   gingerroot, finely chopped
2 carrots, sliced
4 oz/115 g closed-cup
   mushrooms, sliced
40 fl oz/1.25 liters/5 cups
   vegetable stock
9 oz/250 g dried medium egg
   noodles
4 oz/115 g/1 cup frozen peas
6 oz/175 g Napa cabbage,
   shredded
4 scallions, sliced

method

1 Arrange the salmon fillets, skin-side up, in a dish just large enough to fit them in a single layer. Mix the teriyaki marinade with the shallot and gingerroot and pour over the fish. Cover and let marinate in the refrigerator for 1 hour, turning the salmon over once.

2 Put the carrots, mushrooms, and stock into a large pan. Arrange the salmon, skin-side down, on a shallow cookie sheet. Pour the fish marinade into the pan of vegetables and stock and bring to a boil. Reduce the heat, cover, and let simmer for 10 minutes.

3 Meanwhile, cook the salmon under a broiler preheated to medium for 10–15 minutes, until the flesh turns pink and flakes easily. Remove from the broiler and keep warm.

4 Add the noodles and peas to the stock and return to a boil. Reduce the heat, cover, and let simmer for 5 minutes, or until the noodles are tender. Stir in the Napa cabbage and scallions and heat through for 1 minute.

5 Drain off 10 fl oz/300 ml/1^1/$_4$ cups of the stock into a heatproof pitcher and set aside. Drain and discard the remaining stock. Divide the noodles and vegetables among 4 warmed serving bowls and top each with a salmon fillet. Pour over the reserved stock and serve.

thai fisherman's catch

ingredients

SERVES 4

20 cooked jumbo shrimp

20 cooked mussels in their
    shells*

2 oz/55 g oyster mushrooms,
    wiped

2 scallions, finely sliced

3 kaffir lime leaves,
    thinly sliced

1 lemongrass stalk, center
    part only, finely chopped

$^1/_2$ red onion, very thinly sliced

$3^1/_2$ oz/100 g dried medium
    rice noodles

thai coconut dressing

4 fl oz/125 ml/$^1/_2$ cup
    creamed coconut

3 tbsp lime juice

$1^1/_2$ tbsp nam pla (Thai fish
    sauce)

$1^1/_2$ tbsp brown sugar

1–2 fresh red chiles, to taste,
    seeded and thinly sliced

1 small garlic clove, crushed

* discard any mussels that
remain closed after cooking

method

1 To make the dressing, stir all the ingredients together in a large bowl until the sugar dissolves. Add the shrimp, mussels, mushrooms, scallions, lime leaves, lemongrass, and red onion, then cover and let chill until required.

2 Meanwhile, soak the noodles in a bowl with enough lukewarm water to cover for 20 minutes, until soft, or cook according to the package instructions. Drain well.

3 To serve, divide the noodles among 4 bowls. Spoon the seafood salad over them, adding any extra dressing.

malaysian-style coconut noodles with shrimp

ingredients

SERVES 4

2 tbsp vegetable oil

1 small red bell pepper, seeded and diced

7 oz/200 g bok choy, stalks thinly sliced and leaves chopped

2 large garlic cloves, chopped

1 tsp ground turmeric

2 tsp garam masala

1 tsp chili powder (optional)

4 fl oz/125 ml/^{1}/$_2$ cup hot vegetable stock

2 heaping tbsp smooth peanut butter

12 oz/350 ml/1^1/$_2$ cups coconut milk

1 tbsp soy sauce

9 oz/250 g thick rice noodles

10 oz/280 g cooked shelled jumbo shrimp

2 scallions, finely shredded and 1 tbsp sesame seeds, to garnish

method

1 Heat the oil in a preheated wok or large, heavy-bottom skillet over high heat. Add the red bell pepper, bok choy stalks, and garlic and stir-fry for 3 minutes. Add the turmeric, garam masala, chili powder, if using, and bok choy leaves, and stir-fry for 1 minute.

2 Mix the hot stock and peanut butter together in a heatproof bowl until the peanut butter has dissolved, then add to the stir-fry with the coconut milk and tamari. Cook for 5 minutes over medium heat, or until reduced and thickened.

3 Meanwhile, immerse the noodles in a bowl of just boiled water. Let stand for 4 minutes, then drain and refresh the noodles under cold running water. Add the cooked noodles and shrimp to the coconut curry and cook for an additional 2–3 minutes, stirring frequently, until heated through.

4 Serve the noodle dish sprinkled with scallions and sesame seeds.

shrimp laksa

ingredients

SERVES 4

20–24 large raw unshelled
    shrimp
16 fl oz/450 ml/2 cups
    fish stock
pinch of salt
16 fl oz/450 ml/2 cups
    coconut milk
2 tsp nam pla (Thai fish sauce)
1/2 tablespoon lime juice
4 oz/115 g dried medium
    rice-flour noodles
4 oz/115 g/1/2 cup
    bean sprouts
fresh cilantro, chopped,
    to garnish

laksa paste

6 fresh cilantro stalks with
    leaves
3 large garlic cloves, crushed
1 fresh red chile, seeded and
    chopped
1 lemongrass stalk, center
    part only, chopped
1-inch/2.5-cm piece fresh
    gingerroot, peeled and
    chopped
1 1/2 tbsp shrimp paste
1/2 tsp ground turmeric
peanut oil

method

1 Remove the heads and shells from the shrimp, leaving the tails intact, and devein. Reserve the heads and shells. Put the fish stock, salt, and the shrimp heads and shells in a pan over high heat and slowly bring to a boil. Lower the heat and let simmer for 10 minutes.

2 Meanwhile, make the laksa paste. Put all the ingredients, except the oil, in a food processor and blend. With the motor running, slowly add up to 2 tablespoons of peanut oil just until a paste forms. (If your food processor is too large to work efficiently with this small quantity, use a mortar and pestle.)

3 Heat 1 teaspoon of peanut oil in a large pan over high heat. Add the paste and stir-fry until it is fragrant. Strain the fish stock through a strainer lined with cheesecloth. Stir the stock into the laksa paste, along with the coconut milk, nam pla, and lime juice. Bring to a boil, then cover and let simmer for 30 minutes.

4 Meanwhile, soak the noodles in a large bowl with enough lukewarm water to cover for 20 minutes, until soft. Drain and set aside.

5 Add the shrimp and bean sprouts to the soup and continue simmering just until the shrimp turn opaque and curl. Divide the noodles among 4 bowls and ladle the soup over. Garnish with chopped cilantro and serve.

scallops on noodles

ingredients

SERVES 4

4 oz/115 g dried green tea
noodles, or the thinnest
green noodles you can find

1 oz/30 g butter

1 garlic clove, crushed

pinch of paprika

1 tbsp peanut or corn oil, plus
a little extra for cooking
the scallops

2 tbsp bottled mild or medium
Thai green curry paste

2 tbsp water

2 tsp light soy sauce

2 scallions, finely shredded,
and extra scallions, sliced,
to garnish

12 fresh scallops, shucked,
with shells reserved, if
possible

salt and pepper

method

1 Boil the green tea noodles for about $1^{1}/_{2}$ minutes, until soft, then rinse with cold water and drain well. For any other noodles, follow the package instructions. Drain and set aside. Meanwhile, melt the butter in a small pan and cook the garlic in it for about 1 minute. Add the paprika and set aside.

2 Heat a wok over high heat. Add the oil. Stir in the curry paste, water, and soy sauce and bring to a boil. Add the noodles and stir around to reheat. Stir in the scallions, then remove from the heat and keep warm.

3 Heat a ridged, cast-iron grill pan over high heat and brush lightly with a little oil. Add the scallops to the pan and cook for 3 minutes on the first side, then no more than 2 minutes on the second, brushing with the garlic butter, until just cooked (the center shouldn't be totally opaque if cut open). Season with salt and pepper. Divide the noodles among 4 serving plates and top with 3 scallops each. Garnish with spring onions and serve immediately.

salads & stir-fries

Salads and stir-fries are two of the most healthy ways to eat vegetables, and adding a first-class protein in the form of fish and seafood makes an ideal combination. This chapter is filled with inspiring ideas for those who have health problems, or who believe that prevention is better than cure!

Salmon & Avocado Salad, Smoked Salmon, Asparagus & Avocado Salad, Tuna & Two-bean Salad, Shrimp & Papaya Salad, and Monkfish Stir-fry are excellent options for maintaining a healthy heart, and diabetics can enjoy Tuna & Avocado Salad and Coconut Shrimp with Cucumber Salad. Avocado, rather like oil-rich fish, is often viewed with suspicion because of its high fat content, but the fat is almost entirely monounsaturated and is excellent for the circulatory system. It also has a fabulous, smooth texture that goes very well with fresh or smoked salmon and fresh tuna, so recipes with these ingredients have a recklessly indulgent air about them and feed the soul as well as the body!

If you are not on a restricted diet and simply love salads and stir-fries, Smoked Salmon & Wild Arugula Salad has an irresistible lime-mayonnaise dressing, and Salmon & Scallops with Cilantro & Lime is packed with flavor for a special occasion.

salmon & avocado salad

ingredients

SERVES 4

1 lb/450 g new potatoes

4 salmon steaks, about
   4 oz/115 g each

1 avocado

juice of $1/2$ lemon

2 oz/55 g baby spinach
   leaves

$4^1/2$ oz/125 g mixed small
   salad greens, including
   watercress

4 tomatoes, cut into fourths

2 oz/55 g/scant $1/2$ cup
   chopped walnuts

dressing

3 tbsp unsweetened clear
   apple juice

1 tsp balsamic vinegar

pepper

method

1 Cut the new potatoes into bite-size pieces, put into a pan, and cover with cold water. Bring to a boil, then reduce the heat, cover, and let simmer for 10–15 minutes, or until just tender. Drain and keep warm.

2 Meanwhile, preheat the broiler to medium. Cook the salmon steaks under the preheated broiler for 10–15 minutes, depending on the thickness of the steaks, turning halfway through cooking. Remove from the broiler and keep warm.

3 While the potatoes and salmon are cooking, cut the avocado in half, remove and discard the pit, and peel the flesh. Cut the avocado flesh into slices and coat in the lemon juice to prevent discoloration.

4 Toss the spinach leaves and mixed salad greens together in a large serving bowl until combined. Arrange the greens and the tomato fourths on individual serving plates.

5 Remove and discard the skin and any bones from the salmon. Flake the salmon and divide among the plates along with the potatoes. Sprinkle the walnuts over the salads.

6 To make the dressing, mix the apple juice and vinegar together in a small bowl or pitcher and season well with pepper. Drizzle over the salads and serve at once.

smoked salmon, asparagus & avocado salad

ingredients

SERVES 4

7 oz/200 g asparagus spears

1 large avocado

1 tbsp lemon juice

large handful of arugula leaves

8 oz/225 g smoked salmon

1 red onion, finely sliced

1 tbsp chopped fresh flat-leaf
    parsley, plus extra sprigs
    to garnish

1 tbsp snipped fresh chives

lemon wedges, to garnish

whole wheat bread, to serve

dressing

1 garlic clove, chopped

4 tbsp extra-virgin olive oil

2 tbsp white wine vinegar

1 tbsp lemon juice

pinch of sugar

1 tsp mustard

method

1 Bring a large pan of salted water to a boil, add the asparagus, and blanch for 4 minutes. Drain and plunge into cold water, then drain again. Set aside to cool.

2 To make the dressing, combine all the dressing ingredients in a small bowl and stir together well.

3 Halve, peel, and pit the avocado and cut into bite-size pieces. Brush with the lemon juice to prevent discoloration.

4 To assemble the salad, arrange the arugula leaves on individual serving plates and top with the asparagus and avocado. Cut the smoked salmon into strips and arrange over the top of the salads, then sprinkle over the onion and herbs. Drizzle over the dressing, then garnish with parsley sprigs and lemon wedges. Serve with whole wheat bread.

smoked salmon & wild arugula salad

ingredients

SERVES 4

1³/₄ oz/50 g wild arugula
   leaves
1 tbsp chopped fresh flat-leaf
   parsley
2 scallions, finely diced
2 large avocados
1 tbsp lemon juice
9 oz/250 g smoked salmon
lime wedges, to serve

lime mayonnaise

5 fl oz/150 ml/²/₃ cup
   mayonnaise
2 tbsp lime juice
finely grated rind of 1 lime
1 tbsp chopped fresh flat-leaf
   parsley, plus extra sprigs
   to garnish

method

1 Shred the arugula and arrange in 4 individual salad bowls or on 4 small plates. Sprinkle over the chopped parsley and scallions.

2 Halve, peel, and pit the avocados and cut into thin slices or small chunks. Brush with the lemon juice to prevent discoloration, then divide among the salad bowls. Mix together gently. Cut the smoked salmon into strips and sprinkle over the top.

3 Put the mayonnaise in a bowl, then add the lime juice and rind and the chopped parsley. Mix together well. Spoon some of the lime mayonnaise on top of each salad, garnish with parsley sprigs, and serve with lime wedges for squeezing over.

smoked fish salad

ingredients

SERVES 4

12 oz/350 g smoked haddock
    fillet, skinned
4 tbsp olive oil
1 tbsp lemon juice
2 tbsp sour cream
1 tbsp hot water
2 tbsp snipped fresh chives,
    plus extra to garnish
salt and pepper
1 plum tomato, peeled,
    seeded, and diced
8 quails' eggs
4 thick slices whole grain or
    multigrain bread
4 oz/115 g mixed salad greens

method

1 Fill a large skillet with water and bring to a boil. Add the smoked haddock fillet, cover, and remove the skillet from the heat. Let stand for 10 minutes until the fish is tender. Remove with a slotted spoon and drain on a plate. Flake the fish, removing and discarding any small bones. Set aside. Discard the cooking liquid.

2 Meanwhile, whisk the oil, lemon juice, sour cream, hot water, chives, salt, and pepper together in a pitcher. Stir in the tomato. Set aside.

3 Bring a small pan of water to a boil. Carefully lower the quails' eggs into the water and cook for 3–4 minutes from when the water returns to a boil (3 minutes for a slightly soft center, 4 minutes for a firm center). Drain at once and refresh under cold running water. Carefully shell the eggs, cut in half lengthwise and set aside.

4 Toast the bread and put a slice on each of 4 serving plates. Top with the salad greens, then the flaked fish and finally the quails' eggs. Spoon over the dressing and garnish with a few extra chives.

pasta niçoise

ingredients

SERVES 4

4 oz/115 g green beans, cut
into 2-inch/5-cm lengths

8 oz/225 g dried fusilli tricolore

3½ fl oz/100 ml/generous
⅓ cup olive oil

2 tuna steaks, about
12 oz/350 g each

salt and pepper

6 cherry tomatoes, halved

2 oz/55 g/⅓ cup black olives,
pitted and halved

6 canned anchovies, drained
and chopped

3 tbsp chopped fresh
flat-leaf parsley

2 tbsp lemon juice

8–10 radicchio leaves

method

1 Bring a large, heavy-bottom pan of lightly salted water to a boil. Add the green beans, reduce the heat, and cook for 5–6 minutes. Remove with a slotted spoon and refresh in a bowl of cold water. Drain well. Add the pasta to the same pan, return to a boil, and cook for 8–10 minutes, or until tender but still firm to the bite.

2 Meanwhile, brush a grill pan with some of the olive oil and heat until smoking. Season the tuna with salt and pepper and brush both sides with some of the remaining olive oil. Cook over medium heat for 2 minutes on each side, or until cooked to your liking, then remove from the grill pan and reserve.

3 Drain the pasta well and tip it into a bowl. Add the green beans, cherry tomatoes, olives, anchovies, parsley, lemon juice, and remaining olive oil and season with salt and pepper. Toss well and let cool. Remove and discard any skin from the tuna and slice thickly.

4 Gently mix the tuna into the pasta salad. Line a large salad bowl with the radicchio leaves, spoon in the salad, and serve.

tuna & two-bean salad

ingredients

SERVES 4–6

7 oz/200 g green beans

14 oz/400 g canned small
    white beans, such as
    cannellini, rinsed and
    drained

4 scallions, finely chopped

2 fresh tuna steaks, about
    8 oz/225 g each and
    ³/₄ inch/2 cm thick

olive oil, for brushing

9 oz/250 g cherry tomatoes,
    halved

lettuce leaves

fresh mint and parsley sprigs,
    to garnish

country-style crusty bread,
    to serve

dressing

handful of fresh mint leaves,
    shredded

handful of fresh parsley
    leaves, chopped

1 garlic clove, crushed

4 tbsp extra-virgin olive oil

1 tbsp red wine vinegar

salt and pepper

method

1 First, make the dressing. Put the mint leaves, parsley leaves, garlic, olive oil, and vinegar into a screw-top jar, add salt and pepper, and shake until blended. Pour into a large bowl and set aside.

2 Bring a pan of lightly salted water to a boil. Add the green beans and cook for 3 minutes. Add the white beans and cook for another 4 minutes until the green beans are tender-crisp and the white beans are heated through. Drain well and add to the bowl with the dressing and scallions. Toss together.

3 To cook the tuna, heat a stovetop ridged grill pan over high heat. Lightly brush the tuna steaks with oil, then season with salt and pepper. Cook the steaks for 2 minutes, then turn over and cook on the other side for an additional 2 minutes for rare or up to 4 minutes for well done.

4 Remove the tuna from the grill pan and let rest for 2 minutes, or until completely cool. When ready to serve, add the tomatoes to the bean mixture and toss lightly. Line a serving platter with lettuce leaves and pile on the bean salad. Flake the tuna over the top. Serve warm or at room temperature with plenty of bread, garnished with the herbs.

tuna & avocado salad

ingredients

SERVES 4

2 avocados, pitted, peeled, and cubed

9 oz/250 g cherry tomatoes, halved

2 red bell peppers, seeded and chopped

1 bunch fresh flat-leaf parsley, chopped

2 garlic cloves, crushed

1 fresh red chile, seeded and finely chopped

juice of $\frac{1}{2}$ lemon

6 tbsp olive oil

pepper

3 tbsp sesame seeds

4 fresh tuna steaks, about 5$\frac{1}{2}$ oz/150 g each

8 cooked new potatoes, cubed

arugula leaves, to serve

method

1 Toss the avocados, tomatoes, red bell peppers, parsley, garlic, chile, lemon juice, and 2 tablespoons of the oil together in a large bowl. Season with pepper, cover, and let chill in the refrigerator for 30 minutes.

2 Lightly crush the sesame seeds in a mortar with a pestle. Tip the crushed seeds onto a plate and spread out. Press each tuna steak in turn into the crushed seeds to coat on both sides.

3 Heat 2 tablespoons of the remaining oil in a skillet, add the potatoes, and cook, stirring frequently, for 5–8 minutes, or until crisp and brown. Remove from the skillet and drain on paper towels.

4 Wipe out the skillet, add the remaining oil, and heat over high heat until very hot. Add the tuna steaks and cook for 3–4 minutes on each side.

5 To serve, divide the avocado salad among 4 serving plates. Top each with a tuna steak, then sprinkle over the potatoes and a handful of arugula leaves.

seafood & spinach salad

ingredients

SERVES 4

1 lb 2 oz/500 g live mussels,
   prepared (see page 38)
3¹/₂ oz/100 g raw shrimp,
   shelled and deveined
12 oz/350 g live scallops,
   shucked and cleaned
1 lb 2 oz/500 g baby spinach
   leaves
4 tbsp water
3 scallions, sliced
lemon wedges, to garnish

dressing

4 tbsp extra-virgin olive oil
2 tbsp white wine vinegar
1 tbsp lemon juice
1 tsp finely grated lemon rind
1 garlic clove, chopped
1 tbsp grated fresh gingerroot
1 small fresh red chile,
   seeded and sliced
1 tbsp chopped fresh cilantro,
   plus extra sprigs to garnish
salt and pepper

method

1 Put the mussels in a large pan with a little water and cook, covered, over high heat, shaking the pan occasionally, for 3–4 minutes, or until the mussels have opened. Discard any mussels that remain closed. Strain the mussels, reserving the cooking liquid.

2 Return the reserved cooking liquid to the pan and bring to a boil, add the shrimp and scallops, and cook for 3 minutes. Remove from the heat and drain. Remove the mussels from their shells. Refresh the mussels, shrimp, and scallops under cold running water, drain, and put them in a large bowl. Let cool, then cover with plastic wrap and let chill in the refrigerator for 45 minutes.

3 Meanwhile, rinse the spinach leaves and put them in a pan with the water. Cook over high heat for 1 minute. Transfer to a colander, refresh under cold running water, and drain.

4 To make the dressing, combine all the dressing ingredients in a small bowl. Divide the spinach among 4 serving dishes, then sprinkle over half the scallions. Top with the mussels, shrimp, and scallops, then sprinkle over the remaining scallions. Drizzle over the dressing, garnish with cilantro sprigs and lemon wedges, and serve.

coconut shrimp with cucumber salad

ingredients

SERVES 4

7 oz/200 g/1 cup brown
    basmati rice

$^1/_2$ tsp coriander seeds

2 egg whites, lightly beaten

3$^1/_2$ oz/100 g/generous
    $^3/_4$ cup dry unsweetened
    coconut

24 raw jumbo shrimp, shelled
    and tails left intact

$^1/_2$ cucumber

4 scallions, thinly sliced
    lengthwise

1 tsp sesame oil

1 tbsp finely chopped fresh
    cilantro

1 lime, cut into wedges,
    to garnish

method

1 Bring a large pan of water to a boil, add the rice, and cook for 25 minutes, or until tender. Drain and set aside in a strainer covered with a clean dish towel to absorb the steam.

2 Meanwhile, soak 8 wooden skewers in cold water for 30 minutes, then drain.

3 Crush the coriander seeds in a mortar with a pestle. Heat a nonstick skillet over medium heat and cook the seeds, turning, until they start to color. Tip onto a plate and set aside.

4 Put the egg whites into a shallow bowl and the coconut into a separate bowl. Roll each shrimp first in the egg whites, then in the coconut. Thread onto a skewer. Repeat so that each skewer is threaded with 3 coated shrimp.

5 Using a potato peeler, peel long strips from the cucumber to create ribbons, put into a strainer to drain, then toss with the scallions and oil in a bowl, and set aside.

6 Cook the shrimp under a broiler preheated to high for 3–4 minutes on each side, or until pink and slightly browned. Mix the rice with the coriander seeds and cilantro, press into 4 dariole molds and invert each mold onto a serving plate. Serve with cucumber salad and shrimp skewers, garnished with lime wedges.

shrimp & rice salad

ingredients

SERVES 4

6 oz/175 g/generous $^3/_4$ cup
    mixed long-grain
    and wild rice

12 oz/350 g cooked shelled
    shrimp

1 mango, peeled, pitted,
    and diced

4 scallions, sliced

1 oz/25 g/$^1/_4$ cup slivered
    almonds

1 tbsp finely chopped fresh
    mint

pepper

dressing

1 tbsp extra-virgin olive oil

2 tsp lime juice

1 garlic clove, crushed

1 tsp honey

salt and pepper

method

1 Bring a large pan of lightly salted water to a boil. Add the rice, return to a boil, and cook for 35 minutes, or until tender. Drain, then transfer to a large bowl and stir in the shrimp.

2 To make the dressing, combine the olive oil, lime juice, garlic, and honey in a large pitcher, season with salt and pepper, and whisk until well blended. Pour the dressing over the rice and shrimp mixture and let cool.

3 Add the mango, scallions, almonds, and mint to the salad and season with pepper. Stir thoroughly, transfer to a large serving dish, and serve.

shrimp & papaya salad

ingredients

SERVES 4

1 papaya, peeled

12 oz/350 g large cooked
    shelled shrimp

assorted baby salad greens,
    to serve

dressing

4 scallions, chopped finely

2 fresh red chiles, seeded
    and chopped finely

1 tsp fish sauce

1 tbsp vegetable or peanut oil

juice of 1 lime

1 tsp jaggery or soft light
    brown sugar

method

1 Scoop the seeds out of the papaya and slice thinly. Stir gently together with the shrimp.

2 Mix the scallions, chiles, fish sauce, oil, lime juice, and sugar together.

3 Arrange the salad greens in a bowl and top with the papaya and shrimp. Pour the dressing over and serve immediately.

monkfish stir-fry

ingredients

SERVES 4

2 tsp sesame oil

1 lb/450 g monkfish steaks, cut
into 1-inch/2.5-cm chunks

1 red onion, sliced thinly

3 cloves garlic, chopped finely

1 tsp grated fresh gingerroot

8 oz/225 g fine tip asparagus

6 oz/175 g/3 cups
mushrooms, sliced thinly

2 tbsp soy sauce

1 tbsp lemon juice

lemon wedges, to garnish

cooked noodles, to serve

method

1 Heat the oil in a skillet over a medium-high heat. Add the fish, red onion, garlic, gingerroot, asparagus, and mushrooms. Stir-fry for 2–3 minutes.

2 Stir in the soy sauce and lemon juice and cook for another minute. Remove from the heat and transfer to warmed serving dishes.

3 Garnish with lemon wedges and serve immediately on a bed of cooked noodles.

stir-fried rice noodles with marinated fish

ingredients

SERVES 4

1 lb/450 g monkfish or cod, cubed

8 oz/225 g salmon fillets, cubed

2 tbsp vegetable or peanut oil

2 fresh green chiles, seeded and chopped

grated rind and juice of 1 lime

1 tbsp fish sauce

4 oz/115 g wide rice noodles

2 tbsp vegetable or peanut oil

2 shallots, sliced

2 garlic cloves, chopped finely

1 fresh red chile, seeded and chopped

2 tbsp Thai soy sauce

2 tbsp chili sauce

sprigs of cilantro, to garnish

method

1 Place the fish in a shallow bowl. To make the marinade, mix the oil, green chiles, lime juice and rind, and fish sauce together and pour over the fish. Cover and let chill for 2 hours.

2 Put the noodles in a bowl and cover with boiling water. Leave for 8–10 minutes (check the package instructions) and drain well.

3 Heat the oil in a wok or large skillet and sauté the shallots, garlic, and red chile until lightly browned. Add the soy sauce and chili sauce. Add the fish and the marinade to the wok and stir-fry gently for 2–3 minutes until cooked through.

4 Add the drained noodles and stir gently. Garnish with cilantro and serve immediately.

shrimp, snow pea & cashew nut stir-fry

ingredients

SERVES 4

3 oz/85 g/generous $^1/_2$ cup
   dry roasted cashew nuts

3 tbsp peanut oil

4 scallions, finely sliced

2 celery stalks, sliced thinly

3 carrots, sliced finely

100 g/3$^1/_2$ oz baby corn cobs,
   halved

6 oz/175 g/3 cups
   mushrooms, sliced finely

1 clove of garlic,
   chopped coarsely

1 lb/450 g raw shrimp,
   shelled

1 tsp cornstarch

2 tbsp soy sauce

2 fl oz/50 ml/$^1/_4$ cup
   chicken stock

8 oz/225 g/2 cups savoy
   cabbage, shredded

6 oz/175 g/1$^3/_4$ cups
   snow peas

cooked rice, to serve

method

1 Put a skillet over a medium heat and add the cashew nuts; toast them until they begin to brown. Remove with a slotted spoon and reserve.

2 Add the oil to the pan and heat. Add the scallions, celery, carrots, and baby corn cobs and cook, stirring occasionally, over medium-high heat for 3–4 minutes.

3 Add the mushrooms and cook until they become brown. Mix in the garlic and shrimp, stirring until the shrimp turn pink.

4 Mix the cornstarch smoothly with the soy sauce and chicken stock. Add the liquid to the shrimp mixture and stir. Then add the savoy cabbage, snow peas, and all but a few of the cashew nuts and cook for 2 minutes.

5 Garnish with the reserved cashew nuts and serve on a bed of rice.

salmon & scallops with cilantro & lime

ingredients

SERVES 4

6 tbsp peanut oil

10 oz/280 g salmon steak, skinned and cut into 1-inch/2.5-cm chunks

8 oz/225 g scallops

3 carrots, sliced thinly

2 celery stalks, cut into 1-inch/2.5-cm pieces

2 orange bell peppers, sliced thinly

6 oz/175 g/3 cups oyster mushrooms, sliced thinly

1 clove garlic, crushed

6 tbsp chopped fresh cilantro

3 shallots, sliced thinly

2 limes, juiced

1 tsp lime zest

1 tsp dried red pepper flakes

3 tbsp dry sherry

3 tbsp soy sauce

cooked noodles, to serve

method

1 In a wok or large frying pan, heat the oil over medium heat. Add the salmon and scallops, and stir-fry for 3 minutes. Remove from the pan, then set aside and keep warm.

2 Add the carrots, celery, bell peppers, mushrooms, and garlic to the wok and stir-fry for 3 minutes. Add the cilantro and shallots, and stir.

3 Add the lime juice and zest, dried red pepper flakes, sherry, and soy sauce and stir. Return the salmon and scallops to the wok and stir-fry carefully for another minute.

4 Serve immediately on a bed of cooked noodles.

scallops in black bean sauce

ingredients

SERVES 4

2 tbsp vegetable or peanut oil

1 tsp finely chopped garlic

1 tsp finely chopped fresh
gingerroot

1 tbsp fermented black beans,
rinsed and lightly mashed

14 oz/400 g scallops

$1/2$ tsp light soy sauce

1 tsp Shaoxing rice wine

1 tsp sugar

3–4 red Thai chiles,
finely chopped

1–2 tsp chicken stock

1 tbsp finely chopped
scallions

method

1 In a preheated wok or deep pan, heat the oil. Add the garlic and stir, then add the gingerroot and stir-fry together for about 1 minute, or until fragrant.

2 Mix in the black beans, then toss in the scallops and stir-fry for 1 minute. Add the light soy sauce, Shaoxing, sugar, and chiles.

3 Lower the heat and simmer for 2 minutes, adding the stock if necessary. Finally add the scallions, then stir and serve.

squid & red onion stir-fry

ingredients

SERVES 4

1 lb/450 g squid rings
2 tbsp all-purpose flour
$^{1}/_{2}$ tsp salt
1 green bell pepper
2 tbsp peanut oil
1 red onion, sliced
5$^{3}/_{4}$-oz/160-g jar black
    bean sauce

method

1 Rinse the squid rings under cold running water and pat dry with paper towels.

2 Place the all-purpose flour and salt in a bowl and mix together. Add the squid rings and toss until they are finely coated.

3 Using a sharp knife, seed the bell pepper and slice into thin strips.

4 Heat the peanut oil in a large preheated wok. Add the bell pepper and red onion to the wok and stir-fry for 2 minutes, or until the vegetables are just beginning to soften. Add the squid rings to the wok and cook for an additional 5 minutes, or until the squid is cooked through.

5 Add the black bean sauce to the wok and heat through until the juices are bubbling. Transfer to warmed bowls and serve at once.

sweet chile squid

ingredients

SERVES 4

1 tbsp sesame seeds

2 tbsp sesame oil

10 oz/280 g squid, cut into
strips

2 red bell peppers, sliced thinly

3 shallots, sliced thinly

3 oz/85 g/1^{1}/$_{2}$ cups
mushrooms, sliced thinly

1 tbsp dry sherry

4 tbsp soy sauce

1 tsp sugar

1 tsp hot chile flakes, or to
taste

1 clove of garlic, crushed

1 tsp sesame oil

cooked rice, to serve

method

1 Place the sesame seeds on a cookie sheet and toast under a hot broiler, then set aside. Heat 1 tablespoon of oil in a skillet over a medium heat. Add the squid and cook for 2 minutes. Remove from the skillet and set aside.

2 Add the other tablespoon of oil to the skillet and cook the bell peppers and shallots over a medium heat for 1 minute. Add the mushrooms and cook for another 2 minutes.

3 Return the squid to the skillet and add the sherry, soy sauce, sugar, chile flakes, and garlic, stirring thoroughly. Cook for an additional 2 minutes.

4 Sprinkle with the toasted sesame seeds, then drizzle over the sesame oil and mix. Serve on a bed of rice.

Also by Lee Bacon

The
JOSHUA
DREAD
Series

Joshua Dread
Joshua Dread: The Nameless Hero

A Mutant Named Mizzie

(A Digital Original Short Story)

Book Level : 5.0

Points : 7.0

Quiz # : 166361

The Dominion Key

JOSHUA DREAD

The Dominion Key

LEE BACON

DELACORTE PRESS

Text copyright © 2014 by Lee Bacon
Jacket and interior illustrations copyright © 2014 by Brandon Dorman

Visit us on the Web! randomhouse.com/kids

Educators and librarians, for a variety of teaching tools, visit us at RHTeachersLibrarians.com

Library of Congress Cataloging-in-Publication Data
Bacon, Lee.
The Dominion Key / Lee Bacon. — First edition.
pages cm. — (Joshua Dread ; [3])
Summary: When Alabaster Academy, a school for students with superpowers, comes under attack, Joshua and his friends race to stop evil Phineas Vex from finding a mysterious key that will enable complete world domination for whoever possesses it.
ISBN 978-0-385-74382-2 (hc) — ISBN 978-0-375-99130-1 (glb) —
ISBN 978-0-385-37127-8 (ebook)
[1. Supervillains—Fiction. 2. Superheroes—Fiction. 3. Friendship—Fiction.] I. Title.
PZ7.B13446Do 2014
[Fic]—dc23
2013024860

Printed in the United States of America

10 9 8 7 6 5 4 3 2 1

First Edition

For my grandparents
James and Sue Greek

1

Our trip to the mall started off normal enough. I should've known it wouldn't stay that way.

I was with my friends Milton, Sophie, and Miranda. Milton and I had gotten to know the girls a while back (long story). Then we were all nearly killed by a super-villain in an indestructible suit (even *longer* story).

"I hate back-to-school sales," Milton complained, looking at a BACK-TO-SCHOOL SALE! sign as we wandered into a store. "They should call them summer's-about-to-be-over-and-there's-nothing-you-can-do-about-it sales."

"That's not quite as catchy," I said. But I totally knew what he meant. Seventh grade was starting in a few days, and I wished there were a way to slow down time, to keep things exactly the way they were. Long days with nothing to do but hang out with friends. No classes, no homework, no evil maniacs trying to kill you.

"Hey, check it out!" Miranda said. "It's *you*!"

Nearby was a rack of T-shirts, all with the same picture on the front. My picture. Except hardly anybody outside our group would recognize me. My identity was hidden by a uniform and a mask. Superheroic letters stretched behind me, spelling out THE NAMELESS HERO.

It was hard to believe that I'd briefly been the most famous kid on the planet. That I'd appeared on TV shows and in commercials, had my face plastered across all kinds of products. It had only been a couple of months since the hype over the Nameless Hero had died down, but to me it felt like a couple of decades.

And apparently, I wasn't the only one who was moving on. The store was obviously trying to get rid of all its Nameless Hero inventory. A sign on top of the rack read

85% OFF!!!
ALL NAMELESS HERO MERCHANDISE MUST GO!!!

Sophie nudged me with her elbow. "That's a pretty good deal. Maybe I should get one."

"Or fifty," I said. "They'll be collector's items someday."

"And every time I see it, I'll remember the good old days."

"Like getting chased around Times Square by clones?"

Our conversation came to a sudden stop when I noticed Joey and Brick coming our way. Just seeing the two biggest bullies in Sheepsdale knocked my mood down a few notches.

Joey had red hair and a pointed face that reminded me of a rat with an attitude problem. Brick looked like . . . well, a *brick*.

Joey gave Miranda a harsh look. "Who's the new girl?" He turned his sneer on Sophie. "Is she a freak like you?"

Sophie stepped toward Joey and Brick. "Leave us alone."

Even though Brick was about twice Sophie's size, a shadow of fear passed over his face. He was probably remembering how Sophie had dismantled a hallway of lockers and sent him and Joey to the nurse's office last year.

See, Sophie has the power of superhuman strength. But it comes with a slight . . . side effect. Whenever she uses her Gyft, it causes her skin to radiate in a way that makes her look like Tinker Bell. Except much bigger, and a whole lot stronger.

"What're you gonna do?" Joey asked. "Show off your freaky glow-in-the-dark trick for everyone in the mall?"

He gestured to the crowds of shoppers moving through the aisles around us. As much as I hated to admit it, Joey had a point. If Sophie used her Gyft right now, it would draw a lot of unwanted attention.

And believe me, for kids like us, unwanted attention can be a *very* bad thing.

"Let's just go," I said to Sophie in a low voice. "They're not worth it."

"Speaking of freaky . . ." Joey turned toward Milton and me. "It's the Amazing Exploding Dork and his trusty sidekick."

My hands curled into fists. I could feel my own Gyft—spontaneous combustion—crackling inside me. It always starts off the same: A tingling in my fingertips. A pounding heartbeat. Energy pulsing through my veins. It wouldn't take much to make these two regret ever messing with us.

But a few shoppers were looking in our direction. I wasn't sure how they'd react if I blasted Joey and Brick all the way to the underwear department.

"Come on," I said to my friends. "Let's hit the food court."

𝄐

"I sure could go for some cheese fries!" Milton was at the front of our group, an excited look on his face. He gets that way whenever cheese fries are an option.

Sophie didn't look nearly so thrilled. I could see that the confrontation was still weighing on her.

"Everything okay?" I asked.

She shrugged. "Sometimes I just wish I could be—"

"Like everyone else?"

Sophie let out a deep breath. "Exactly."

I definitely knew how she felt. I'd spent my life trying to blend in, to be normal. But that's basically impossible when you've got parents like mine.

"Those guys are jerks," I said. "They pick on everyone. It'd be weird if they *didn't* mess with you."

"I guess you're right." A slight smile formed on Sophie's

lips. Her blue-gray eyes shone a little brighter. She looked like she was about to say something else when a voice cut into our conversation.

"Are we getting cheese fries or not?"

Milton was standing next to a cell-phone kiosk, tapping his foot. Sophie and I hurried to catch up.

The food court was bustling. We grabbed one of the last available tables, setting down the large plate of cheese fries in the middle so we could all share.

"I wish we didn't have to go to school on Monday," Milton said between bites.

"I'm just glad to be starting off the year with friends." Miranda smiled at us. Below her right eye, a birthmark in the shape of a star stood out against her olive skin. "That's a first for me."

"Me too," Sophie said. "Besides, at least at school I don't have to be around my dad and that redheaded bimbo."

Sophie's dad was the world-famous superhero Captain Justice. And as for the "redheaded bimbo" . . . that was Sophie's nickname for her dad's new girlfriend, Scarlett Flame. Ever since their romance went public, hardly a day passed by when I didn't see photos of the two of them cuddling on the cover of *Super Scoop* magazine or battling zombies on the evening news.

"You should see them together." Sophie made a gagging noise. "It's disgusting. She comes over to watch Dad's show with him. The only thing Scarlett *Lame* likes more than my dad is seeing herself on TV."

Captain Justice's reality show, *Hangin' with Justice,* had

become a national sensation. Maybe Sophie didn't like witnessing the romance between her dad and Scarlett Flame, but apparently the rest of the country did.

I reached for a handful of cheese fries, but the plate was gone.

"You already finished the fries?" I frowned at Milton. "Thanks for leaving some for the rest of us."

"What do you mean?" Milton stared at the center of the table. All that remained was a glob of cheese where the plate had been. "They were just here a second ago."

"Guys—look." Miranda pointed beneath the table. On the floor was our plate of cheese fries.

"How the heck did they get *there*?" Sophie asked.

"Dunno." Milton shrugged.

"Well, they couldn't have just teleported," I said. "Someone must've—"

I went silent when something hit my forehead with a wet *splat*. My hand shot up to wipe away a thick substance that looked like blood. Except it wasn't blood. It had to be—

"Ketchup," Miranda said. "Why do you have ketchup on your face?"

"Good question." I spotted a bottle of ketchup behind Sophie. It seemed to be . . . drifting in midair. And suspended in the air beside it was a bottle of mustard.

Pffft!

Another stream of ketchup squirted from the bottle. This time it landed on the table in a looping shape that looked

6

something like a *W*. The mustard came next, writing out an *E* beside the other letter.

Sophie gawked at the floating bottles. "Did someone order a magic show without telling me?" she asked in a shaky voice. "Because otherwise, I'm starting to get nervous."

"Oh, man!" Milton scrambled out of his seat, pointing a trembling finger. "The food court's possessed!"

I watched as the floating ketchup and mustard squirted out an apostrophe onto the table, followed by an *R* and an *E*.

"What's doing this?" I asked.

"Not what," Miranda said. "*Who*. Someone's controlling the bottles."

She turned in her seat, her eyes searching. Miranda is a Senser, which is another way of saying she has superpowered intuition. Her Gyft gives her insight into things normal people can only guess about.

"We're not the only Gyfted kids here." Her voice was slow and measured. "There are . . . others. Don't know who, but one of them has the power of telekinesis—"

"Tele-ki-*what*-sis?" Milton asked.

"The ability to control objects with the mind."

"I'm guessing that includes bottles of ketchup and mustard," I said.

Miranda nodded. "Whoever these people are . . . they're sending us a message."

"Yeah," Sophie said. "And they're spelling it out with condiments."

She pointed at the table. There in gloppy red and yellow letters were four words:

WE'RE COMING FOR YOU

It was right around this time that chaos broke out across the food court.

2

I'd been so caught up watching the ketchup and mustard practice their spelling that I hadn't noticed what was going on around the rest of the food court. A group of high school girls squealed when a strawberry smoothie exploded against their table like a pink grenade. Close by, I spotted a family covered in kung pao chicken.

A food fight had broken out in the Sheepsdale Mall. And the food seemed to have a mind of its own.

As if that weren't bad enough, other objects were getting in on the action. A bunch of DVDs looked like they'd floated over from the electronics store and were now whizzing across the food court like Chinese throwing stars. The pinball machine had escaped from the arcade. I watched with a growing sense of fear as it chased a group of old ladies.

Screams filled the air. Swarms of people were running for the exits.

"Any guesses what this is all about?" Sophie asked. She used a plastic tray as a shield against an incoming slice of pizza.

A look of concentration passed over Miranda's face. After a moment, she let out an exasperated breath. "There's too much going on right now. It's like static. I can't pick up on any one thing."

"What about that message?" Milton looked down at the words scrawled on our table in mustard and ketchup. "*Who is coming for us?*"

"No idea." Miranda ducked just in time to avoid getting smacked in the face by an airborne phone. "Whoever it is, it looks like they're driving everyone else out of here."

She was right. A battalion of plastic dolls had ventured from the toy store and were herding people through the exits. Anyone lagging behind got a kick in the butt from a floating tennis shoe. A mall security guard tried to restore order—until a flock of books flew at him, their pages flapping like wings, chasing him toward the open doors.

"That guy's got the right idea," Milton said, watching the security guard bolt. "Let's go!"

I broke into a run. But obstacles kept getting in our way. When we tried to reach the emergency exit, a set of kitchen knives darted into our path, their gleaming points aimed at our chests. Turning around, we were met by a dozen baseball bats from the sporting goods store. They floated in midair, swinging at any of us who got too close.

With her superpowered intuition, Miranda usually knows what's coming next. But even SHE couldn't predict the chaos that was about to hit the food court.

Whoever was controlling the mall might have been driving the rest of the people out, but they were doing everything to keep us *in*.

Before long, we were the only ones left.

WHAM!

All at once, the doors slammed shut. And just to make sure they stayed that way, arcade games scooted across the floor, sealing the exits closed. Mountains of TVs, stereo equipment, and computers piled up across the broad corridors that led to other parts of the mall, creating a barrier that trapped us into the food court.

Knives drifted closer. Baseball bats circled.

There was no way out.

A shadow fell across the food court. My eyes were drawn to the ceiling, where the blazing August sunlight poured through a glass roof. Staring down from above was a girl, perched at the edge of the glass. She looked about our age, with a pixie haircut and a smirk on her face, the kind of expression you'd see on a kid sneaking out of detention.

"That's her!" Miranda said, pointing at the girl.

"The one with tetanus?" Milton asked.

"Telekinesis," Miranda corrected him. "She's the one controlling everything!"

The girl held out one hand, fingers outstretched. A flick of her wrist and the glass shattered, sending hundreds of shards crashing down.

Clenching her hand into a fist, the girl yanked her arm back like she was pulling on an invisible string. Suddenly, a TV rose from the messy floor, its cable dangling beneath it like a tail. The TV drifted steadily through the air until it was only a foot below the shattered ceiling.

The girl repeated the same motion—clench fist, pull back—with her right hand, then her left. A laptop burst into the air, followed by a plastic serving tray. More objects began drifting toward the ceiling—a computer monitor, a DVD player, a coffee-table book—each coming to a stop a little below the one before it.

She was building a spiral staircase.

The girl stepped through the hole in the ceiling, one foot landing on the flat-screen TV that was levitating beneath her. Her other foot came down on the laptop, then the plastic tray. She descended to our level using the mall's merchandise as her own personal stairway. Even with the pit of nerves twisting inside me, it *was* impressive.

As soon as she reached the floor, a movement above distracted me. Someone else was peering down at us through the gaping hole in the ceiling. A guy who looked a couple of years older than us—and a whole lot *bigger*. Square jaw, no neck, muscular arms. And his size wasn't even the most remarkable thing about him. The dude had skin the color of concrete. I stared up at him with equal parts fear and awe. He was like a boulder in an XXL T-shirt.

Big Boy uncrossed his arms, went into a crouch, and . . .

Jumped.

I staggered backward, too distracted by the sight to give much thought to the knives and baseball bats circling us. The guy plummeted to the ground and landed like a ton of bricks—which is probably about what he weighed. The impact shook the entire food court. The floor cratered beneath him. But Big Boy looked unfazed. As he rose to his full height, his concrete face broke into a crooked grin and he brushed the dust and debris off his supersized clothes.

Ten feet away, the girl with the pixie haircut looked up at him.

"You call *that* an entrance?" she said. With a snap of her fingers, her staircase of consumer goods went crashing to the ground. "Where's the skill? Where's the precision and elegance?"

"Yeah, but my way's faster," replied the gray-skinned behemoth in a gravelly voice.

Milton looked from one to the other. "W-what do you want with us?" he asked. "Who are you?"

"Leave the introductions to me."

The voice came from above. Hearing it was like a claw gripping my heart. And right away, I knew who the voice belonged to.

nFinity.

He'd been the fifth member of the Alliance of the Impossible, the superhero group we'd formed at the start of the summer. nFinity had once been a teenage supercelebrity. But that was before he betrayed us and joined up with Phineas Vex, the evil billionaire who'd attempted to kill or kidnap me and my friends on multiple occasions.

So I guess you could say I wasn't thrilled to be seeing him again.

After vanishing with Vex, nFinity had gone missing.

14

Until now. I stared up at him, watching as he drifted toward us on his sleek hover scooter. He had the same tousled brown hair, the same blue and red uniform with the same *n* logo on his chest. But he looked different now. Changed. His eyes were bloodshot, ringed with dark circles, as though he hadn't slept over the past couple of months. His face was pale and gaunt. It was like his time with Vex had scrubbed away every last trace of the heart-throb he'd once been.

I nervously searched the food court for an escape route, but all exits had been blocked. And there was little chance that we could get that far anyway. Not with floating knives bearing down on us like bayonets and baseball bats waiting for us to make a false move.

"This is Grifter." nFinity pointed to the girl. "Found her in Vegas, using her Gyft as a street magician."

"Distract folks with a nice show," Grifter said, "and it's a lot easier to lift their wallets."

"And my concrete friend here goes by the name Lunk."

"S'up," said the massive guy. "I'm looking forward to squashing you."

"Patience, Lunk," nFinity said. "You'll have your chance soon enough. Just give us a moment to get reacquainted. It's been a while since I've seen my old teammates."

"Teammates?" I spat the word back at him. "You handed us over to Vex. You nearly got us killed."

"No, I nearly got *them* killed." nFinity's bloodshot eyes flickered to my friends. "Vex wouldn't let me harm a hair on your head. As much as I may have wanted to. He had something entirely different in mind for the all-important Joshua Dread."

"And what was that?"

nFinity's jaw clenched. "I don't know."

"That's because you're just his minion," Milton said. "His unpaid intern."

nFinity flung out his arm, and a flame burst loose from the palm of his hand. It took the shape of a pit bull that snapped its fiery jaws. Milton tumbled backward, falling to the ground. If nFinity's fire show had come any closer, it would've been stop-drop-and-roll time for Milton.

"I serve the most powerful being on this planet!" nFinity's fire dog bared its teeth and clawed the air in front of Milton. "So you'd be wise to show some respect."

"Why are you doing this?" Sophie asked. She'd been the closest to nFinity during our time in the Alliance of the Impossible, and I could tell how much it still pained her to see him this way. "This isn't like you. You're better than this."

nFinity's eyes fell on Sophie, and for a moment I saw a glimpse of the guy he'd once been. The ultracool super-hero everyone had looked up to. The star who had ap-peared in commercials and on the covers of magazines. But then it was gone. Replaced by the new-and-definitely-*not*-improved nFinity 2.0. The traitor. The villain.

"You don't know me," he hissed. "You never did. All I was to you—to everyone—was a product. A face on TV. Someone to sell cereal and zit cream. But now I have *real*

16

power. And before long, the entire world will see who I really am."

nFinity clasped his hand into a fist and the flaming dog vanished.

"Enough talk." He turned to face Grifter and Lunk. "You know the orders. Vex wants Dread—alive. As for his friends?" nFinity's scowl deepened. "Kill them."

3

I really didn't want to watch my friends die in the food court, but it was starting to look like that was the way things were going. Grifter glared at us with a dark smile. Beside her, Lunk cracked his enormous gray knuckles.

"Watch out!" Miranda screamed. Her superpowered intuition let her know about dangers before they even materialized. She dove, knocking Milton out of the way just as Lunk slammed his massive fist against the floor, leaving a crater in the spot where Milton had been standing.

"Th-thanks," Milton spluttered, staring wide-eyed at the cracked tiles.

Miranda was already on the move again. Lunk growled, trying to keep up with her. He took another swing, but she darted away from him.

"Over here, big guy!" Miranda taunted him. She performed an acrobatic sideways flip, barely avoiding the next hit. "That the best you got?"

"You know, teasing him only makes him angrier," Milton called.

"Exactly." Miranda jumped backward.

"Playtime's over!" Lunk boomed. "Now it's *squash* time!"

"Gotta catch me first."

Miranda leaped backward. Suddenly, she was dangerously close to a baseball bat. The wooden bat swung, but Miranda was ready for that too. She dropped and rolled sideways as Lunk closed in for his next attack. And instead of Miranda, the brute's massive gray fists slammed the bat. It exploded into a thousand splinters.

"RAAARGH!"

Lunk took another wild swing—and *another*. But Miranda was always one move ahead. Like they were in a game of Whac-a-Mole, Lunk trailed behind her, shattering bats and swatting knives out of the air.

"She's getting Lunk to destroy his own weapons!" Milton said excitedly.

Miranda's strategy nearly collapsed when she slipped on some spilled water and wiped out between a trio of tables. Lunk skidded to a stop. As he gazed nervously at the water, his gray features transformed from brute anger to fear.

A moment later, Miranda was back on her feet and running again. Lunk carefully sidestepped the water and rumbled after her, smashing everything in his path. Milton bolted in the opposite direction, trailed by nFinity.

I surged after them but immediately tumbled to the floor. Glancing down, I saw an extension cord wrapped around my ankles. Another slithered forward like a snake, twisting around my arms and binding my wrists together.

"Going someplace?"

Grifter shot me a mischievous grin. She clenched her hand into a fist and the cords tightened around my wrists and ankles. She flung out her other hand and the swarm of knives darted in Sophie's direction.

Sophie ducked and dodged, but how long could she keep it up? How long could any of us last?

The extension cord dug into my wrists. As the fight raged around me, I stopped struggling to free myself and took a deep, calming breath. It was the only way to use my Gyft. Focus. Control your emotions. Not always the easiest things to do when you're being attacked by accessories from an electronics store.

But within seconds, I felt it—the energy surging through my chest, down my arms and legs. The extension cords began to sizzle, melting away from my wrists and ankles.

Shaking off the severed cords, I climbed to my feet and sprinted toward Grifter. Along the way, I grabbed hold of the ketchup and mustard bottles that had been floating around our table earlier. With a bottle in each hand, I called out, "Hey, Grifter!"

She whirled around just as I squeezed the bottles. Globs of ketchup and mustard splattered her face. Grifter reeled back, clutching at her eyes. The knives she'd been controlling stopped pursuing Sophie and clattered to the ground.

"She can't control what she can't see," I said, catching up with Sophie.

"Then let's make sure she can't see *anything*." Sophie hopped behind a fast-food counter, pouring a jumbo milk shake. "Hope you like strawberry swirl!" she called, hurling the shake into Grifter's face.

"How 'bout some spaghetti and meatballs to go with that?" I grabbed a half-eaten plate from the table beside me and let loose.

With an all-you-can-eat buffet of food (not to mention free drink refills) hitting her in the face, Grifter's telekinesis was worthless. We threw everything we could find—nachos, mashed potatoes, refried beans. As she staggered blindly, I opened a door marked STORAGE and Sophie gave her a push. Grifter stumbled into the storage closet. I slammed the door shut and Sophie sealed it closed with a couple of arcade games.

"One down," I said. "Two to go."

"We'd better make it quick. Milton and Miranda are in trouble."

Even with the intense glow that radiated from her skin, I could see concern in Sophie's eyes. And when I followed her gaze, I saw why. At the other end of the wrecked food court, nFinity and Lunk had our friends cornered. Milton had his back against the wall, a baseball bat clutched in his hand. Miranda was beside him, her face drawn with exhaustion. Her shirt was ripped, and blood trickled down her knee.

Sophie heaved a sofa above her head, taking aim.

"Hold on." I spotted a water gun on the floor. "No offense, but I don't think furniture's gonna do the job."

Balancing the sofa on one hand, Sophie gave me a confused look. "You have a better idea?"

I grabbed the water gun. "How 'bout we give this a try?"

"You're kidding, right?"

"Nope." Something about the way Lunk had hesitated in front of the pool of water told me he wasn't a fan of liquids. Not that there was any time to explain my theory at the moment. All I said was, "Just trust me. And keep them distracted."

Sophie looked skeptical, but she nodded anyway. As she launched the sofa at Lunk, I hopped behind one of the food counters and filled up the water gun.

By the time I caught up with the others, the situation was looking grim. Nothing Sophie used against Lunk had worked. She was backed against the wall beside Milton and Miranda. While nFinity watched, Lunk stomped toward my friends, his enormous concrete fists raised.

"Hey, doofus," I called. "You thirsty?"

Lunk stopped and turned toward me, his eyes widening when he saw what I had in my hands. I pumped the handle and pulled the trigger.

Splooosh!

As soon as the water hit him, Lunk began to . . . melt. Or at least, that was the way it looked at first. His concrete skin turned to sludge—his features dripping away, his arms and legs becoming gray mush.

It was like concrete being made—except the opposite.

22

Instead of water causing the cement mixture to harden, it liquefied the concrete.

I could barely believe what was left after the concrete washed away. Standing in a pool of gray sludge was a skinny kid with a pencil neck and braces. All he had on was a pair of flowery boxer shorts.

"Well, that's just *great*!" he complained in a squeaky voice. "I was just starting to have some fun!"

But that still left nFinity. With his goons taken out of the equation, he was on his own. Not that he lacked firepower. He thrust out his hand, and the flaming pit bull once again sprang from his palm, snapping its jaws fiercely.

All I could bring to the fight was my water gun, and I seriously doubted that would do much against nFinity's pet dog. Unless . . .

Concentrating again, I tossed the water cannon at nFinity. A surge of energy pulsed through me. As the plastic gun left my fingers, it buzzed with spontaneous combustion. It flew high into the air, and then . . .

BOOOOOOM!

The water cannon exploded a few feet from nFinity, splattering him with water and melted plastic. Without slowing down, I grabbed a stereo speaker and then a teddy bear and tossed them nFinity's way. Waves of spontaneous combustion passed through my veins. One by one, each object exploded in nFinity's face. He staggered backward. His fiery dog faded, then vanished.

But it was Sophie who delivered the finishing blow. She ripped a table loose from the floor, bolts and tiles flying everywhere. nFinity tried to get out of the way, but he wasn't quick enough. The table grazed his shoulder, tearing a pouch loose from his uniform. As nFinity crumpled to the floor, a slip of paper fell from the pouch.

I rushed forward to grab it, then turned to follow the others toward the exit.

nFinity's voice echoed behind me. "You can't run forever! Vex will find you!"

Reaching the exit, Sophie grabbed hold of the arcade game that blocked the door and tossed it over her shoulder like it weighed nothing at all. Milton flung open the door and we ran outside.

Once we were a safe distance from the mall and sure we weren't being followed, I looked at the slip of paper.

"What is that?" Sophie asked.

"Don't know." I gulped a mouthful of air. "nFinity lost it in the food court."

With the others reading over my shoulder, I scanned the words on the paper:

PLATINUM-SEALED ALPHA CAPACITOR

NEUTRON FLOW REVERSAL CHAMBER

OSCILLATING PARTICLE IMMOBILIZER

THE DOMINION KEY

Staring at the list, I got the feeling we'd found a clue. I just didn't know what the heck it meant.

4

"All right, people! We've got a serious situation. Lives are at stake. Now . . . who wants snacks?"

I'd never seen our living room so crowded before. But the really remarkable thing was who'd shown up. Milton, Sophie, and Miranda were in the corner. Dad was perched on the edge of the couch, nervously polishing his customized eyeglasses. And sitting beside him, looking extremely uncomfortable, was Captain Justice.

It wasn't every day that a famous superhero hangs out in the home of the world's most horrible supervillains. Throughout most of their careers, the only reason for the Dread Duo to get this close to Captain Justice had been because they were trying to kill, maim, or grievously injure him.

But this was an extreme circumstance. After Sophie and I told our parents about the attack, they'd insisted that we

SOPHIE

After the attack by Vex's goons,
Sheepsdale is no longer safe. Even for
a girl with superhuman strength.

meet immediately. And because my parents' house was the closest to the Sheepsdale Mall—not to mention equipped with state-of-the-art security and surveillance features—it had become the improvised meeting place.

At least Captain Justice hadn't brought along his camera crew this time. That didn't mean he'd come alone, though. Standing nearby was his robot butler, Stanley. Tall and dignified, with metallic skin and glowing eyes, Stanley stepped forward.

"If you would like, I would be glad to prepare a light meal for anyone who wants it," Stanley volunteered in a crisp electronic voice.

"No need," my dad replied.

"You sure?" Captain Justice asked. "Stanley's a whiz in the kitchen."

"Thank you, but I've got *my own* robot butler," Dad said defensively. "And Elliot happens to be a terrific cook—"

Dad was interrupted when the door to the dining room burst open. In stumbled what appeared to be an aluminum trash can with paddles for feet.

"I haaave made mini-pizzzas!" slurred Elliot, bumping into a framed picture of Mom on the wall. The picture fell, glass shattering across the floor. "Sooorrry! I will take caaare of that!"

As Elliot bent over to scoop up the broken glass, the mini-pizzas spilled off his tray. Not that it was a huge loss. Pizza isn't supposed to be green.

Elliot was Dad's invention. And even though he would never admit it, I was positive Dad had built Elliot as a way of keeping up with his former archnemesis. Unfortunately, Elliot was a long way from perfect. But despite his flaws, Elliot had saved my life a couple of months back. Ever since then, I'd kept my complaints to a minimum.

Elliot wasn't the only one of my parents' inventions making a scene. There was also Micus, the mutant ficus that my mom had developed several months back. Micus may have looked like an ordinary houseplant, but there was one slight difference.

He had a mind of his own.

At the moment, the ficus seemed a little disgruntled that he was stuck in the dining room, away from all the action. Using his leafy branches as hands, he kept grabbing clumps of soil from his pot and tossing them into the living room. And for some reason, the dirt usually ended up hitting me.

One other thing you should know about Micus . . . he has a serious grudge against me.

"Let's just get to business," Mom said, doing her best to ignore the soil that was sailing across the room. "nFinity and two of his minions were able to track you kids to the Sheepsdale Mall this afternoon. You did an excellent job of defending yourselves, but it's only a matter of time until they come after you again."

"And next time it could be at your school. Or . . ." Dad shivered. "Or even here."

Captain Justice clenched his muscular jaw. "We can't let that happen. Sophie—you're all I've got."

"What about Scarlett?" Sophie muttered.

It was tough, to be sure, but I think Captain Justice may have blushed a little at the comment. "Scarlett Flame is my . . . er . . . lady friend. But she could never replace you, honey. You're my daughter. And I won't let anything happen to you."

"I know you kids like it here in Sheepsdale," Mom began, "but it's no longer safe for you."

My stomach twisted into a knot. I'd been a part of this conversation enough over the years to know what was coming next. When you've got internationally feared supervillains as parents, you get used to a life on the move. I'd spent my entire childhood being shuffled around from town to town, school to school. Every time a superhero started sniffing around our backyard or the FBI tracked down my parents' aliases, we were forced to pack up and start over someplace else. New names, new identities, new lives.

And now it was all happening again. I glanced at my friends. Sophie, Milton, Miranda—was this the last time we were going to see each other? The thought of starting the seventh grade without them was unbearable.

"There's gotta be some other way," I pleaded. "You can't separate us."

"I just convinced my mom to let me stay in Sheepsdale." Miranda stared miserably at the floor. "What am I supposed to tell her now? Never mind? Oh, and by the way, you need to set me up with a fake name?"

"School's gonna be super-lame if you guys all leave," Milton complained.

"We're in a lot more danger on our own," Sophie said. "Look at what happened today. The only reason we survived that attack was because we were together."

"I understand the points you kids are making," Dad said, "but we're out of options here."

"Perhaps not." Captain Justice gazed into the distance as if he'd just spotted an idea fluttering around our living room. "I may have a solution. A way to keep the children safe without separating them."

He paused, considering. A tense silence settled over the living room. Even Elliot took a break from his attempt to "clean" and chewed on the dustpan nervously.

"What if . . . ," Captain Justice began, "we sent them to . . . Alabaster?"

The word meant nothing to me. But it seemed as if my parents knew exactly what Captain Justice was talking about. And whatever Alabaster was, they didn't like it.

"Not a chance!" Dad said loudly.

"We want to keep them safe," Mom added. "*Not* warp them for life."

"Aren't you being a little dramatic?" Captain Justice eyed my parents. "Alabaster is a very prestigious institution. The children could benefit greatly from a little time there."

"Would someone please tell me what you guys are talking about?" I asked.

"Yeah." Milton glanced from my parents to Captain Justice, confused. "Why the heck do you want to send us to Alabama?"

"Not Alabama," Mom replied. *"Alabaster.* It's a school."

"Alabaster Academy is the country's oldest and best boarding school for Gyfted youth," Captain Justice explained. "It's where I spent six of the best years of my life."

"We're well aware of your glory years," Dad grumbled. "But not *everyone* had such a grand experience."

Dad's comment sparked a faint memory. I turned to my parents. "Wait a second . . . I remember Alabaster Academy—that's where *you guys* went to school!"

Mom nodded, although she didn't look too eager to stroll down memory lane. "That was a long time ago."

"You never told me the Dread Duo were your classmates!" Sophie said to her dad.

"We ran with different crowds," Captain Justice explained.

Dad crossed his arms. "Yeah, he was in the too-cool-for-everyone-else-and-totally-stuck-up crowd," he muttered.

"What's that supposed to mean?"

"It means you were antisocial and aggressive. Not to mention dangerous to those around you."

"At least I didn't go around acting like I was the king of middle school." Dad rose from the couch. For a second there, I thought the two of them were going to break out the weapons, just like old times.

"Everyone calm down." Mom stepped between them. "I

think we've had enough reminiscing for one day. We're not here to talk about school. We're here to find a way to keep our children safe."

"And I say Alabaster is the best way to do that." Over Dad's grumbling, Captain Justice went on: "The principal there owes me a favor. I'll make sure the children are enrolled under fake names. Nobody will know who their parents are or where they came from. And among so many other Gyfted kids, they'll totally blend in."

Mom still didn't look thrilled about the idea, but she nodded anyway. "They *do* have excellent security at Alabaster. . . ."

Dad faced her, shocked. "You're actually *considering* this?"

"I know we didn't have the best experience there, but Alabaster *is* a top-notch school. And more important, it's our best chance to protect Joshua from Phineas Vex."

Dad grudgingly accepted her point. "All right, then. Just until Vex is behind bars . . . or dead."

I could see worry spreading across Milton's face. "So this school is for Gyfted kids, huh?" he began in an unsteady voice.

"No need for concern, Marlon." Captain Justice gave Milton a kind look (even if he *had* just called Milton by the wrong name). "I'll have a talk with the principal, tell him you're still waiting on your Gyft. We'll say you're a late bloomer."

"Thanks, but . . . I seriously doubt my mom will let me

go to some school she's never heard of. She doesn't know anything about all of . . . *this*." Milton gestured to the odd gathering in our living room—three superpowered kids, one celebrity hero, two fiendish villains, a couple of robot butlers, and one mutant houseplant. "If I try to explain this to her, she'd probably have a heart attack."

"Your mom will let you come." Miranda gazed at Milton with a look of certainty. "Trust me."

Milton took a relieved breath. "Any hints about how I'm supposed to convince her?"

"Captain Justice will talk her into it."

"I will?" The superhero looked just as surprised by Miranda's comment as Milton did. But that didn't last long. Clearing his throat, he turned to Milton with a confident smile. "I mean—I *will*!"

I wasn't sure about leaving my home behind. Especially if it meant going to some preppy school for superpowered kids. Did I really want to *live* at school? It sounded to me like a prison with textbooks. But if that was the only way my friends and I could stay together, then I wasn't arguing.

And just like that, it was decided. The four of us would be starting the seventh grade at Alabaster Academy.

f

There wasn't much time to prepare. If nFinity could track us to the mall, then nowhere in Sheepsdale was safe. Not even my parents' house. But just as everyone began discussing plans for getting to Alabaster, the conversation was drowned out by a noise from outside. Whatever it was, it was getting closer.

"What *is* that?" Dad asked.

Mom listened for a moment. "It sounds like . . . a helicopter."

She was right. The *thwump*ing of propellers grew louder and louder. It sounded like the helicopter was directly above us. Ignoring the warnings of my parents, I rushed to the window. Cracking open the blinds, I peered outside just in time to see a bright red helicopter landing in our front yard.

And that was only the *second*-biggest surprise.

The doors swung open and out stepped Scarlett Flame.

5

So much for keeping a low profile.

With a cherry-red helicopter parked in your front yard and an internationally famous superhero standing beside it, you're bound to draw a little attention. But drawing attention was one of Scarlett Flame's specialties. It's part of the reason why she'd become the most recognizable female superhero on the planet. You could spot her on morning talk shows discussing her latest battle with Tesla the Terrible, or on the covers of fashion magazines. She had her own line of signature lipsticks. ("Scarlet isn't just a hue," she said in the commercials. "It's an *attitude*.") Once she'd begun dating Captain Justice, her fame had only grown.

And now she was standing on our front lawn.

Her mane of red hair swirled in the wind from the propellers. Sunlight glistened across her golden one-piece uniform.

Mom glared out the window, gritting her teeth at the new arrival. "What the heck is *she* doing here?"

"Uh, well . . ." Captain Justice tugged at his cape. "I invited her."

"You invited your superhero girlfriend to our house?"

"I wouldn't say that she's my *girlfriend*, exactly. We're dating, but we're trying not to use that label until we've fully—"

Captain Justice went quiet when he noticed the angry looks my parents were giving him.

"It's bad enough that *you're* here!" Dad flung up his arms, pacing back and forth. "Now *Scarlett Flame* knows our address!"

"I thought you'd met before?"

"Yeah. We did. She disrupted our death satellite and captured a few of our best zombies!"

"Pardon me, but my daughter is in danger!" Captain Justice stepped forward, flexing his biceps. "We can use all the help we can get."

Sophie turned on her dad. "I don't need your girlfriend to protect me."

"She's *not* my girlfriend!"

Everyone was talking at once, raising their voices to be heard over the thrum of the helicopter outside. My parents' relationship with Captain Justice had been shaky enough *before* Scarlett Flame's arrival. The way things were going, it wouldn't be long before they were back to being mortal enemies.

"WOULD EVERYONE JUST SHUT UP!"

SCARLETT FLAME

Superhero, tabloid sensation,
girlfriend to Captain Justice.
But Sophie definitely ISN'T a fan.

The sound of my voice silenced the argument. My parents turned on me, shocked. They had a rule against using the words "shut up"—which always struck me as kind of strict, coming from two people who'd tried to destroy the world more times than I could count—but by this point, I really didn't care.

Stepping forward, I looked from my parents to Captain Justice. "Phineas Vex is on the loose, nFinity is trying to kill us, and Scarlett Flame is standing in our front yard. But all you guys do is fight. The longer she stands outside with that helicopter, the more people are going to notice."

Dad sighed. "He's right. We've got more important things to think about. Like keeping our children safe. And the best way to do that right now is to get the superhero—and her helicopter—off our lawn."

Captain Justice opened the front door just wide enough to wave Scarlett Flame inside. As the door closed behind her, the red helicopter rose back into the air and disappeared into the blue sky.

"Sorry I'm late, everyone!"

Scarlett swept into the living room. If anything, she looked even more beautiful and glamorous in real life than in all the commercials and magazines.

"Whoa!" Milton whispered, staring.

Sophie elbowed him. "Might want to wipe the drool off your chin."

"Your dad's the luckiest guy in the world."

Scarlett gazed at her surroundings. Dropping her red

handbag on the sofa, she exclaimed, "What a quaint house! So tiny and disheveled! I *love* it!"

"Just make yourself at home," Mom grumbled.

Scarlett didn't seem to hear the comment. Smiling radiantly at my mom, she exclaimed, "Emily Dread! So nice to see you again!"

Scarlett leaned forward to plant an air kiss on each of my mom's cheeks. It was probably a good thing Mom was too surprised to react. Otherwise, I'm pretty sure she would've karate-chopped Scarlett across the room.

Releasing my mom, Scarlett whirled to face my dad.

"And Dominick! How long has it been? You look terrific!"

"Uh . . . well . . . th-th-thanks," Dad stammered. He adjusted his glasses. "Er . . . so do you."

This last comment didn't go over too well with Mom. Her scowl shifted from Scarlett Flame to Dad. Not that Scarlett noticed. She was too busy crossing the room, arms outstretched toward Captain Justice. "Honey-poo! I missed you *sooo* much!"

"Greetings, sweetie pie!" Captain Justice took hold of Scarlett's hands, pulling her in for a kiss.

Sophie turned away like she was searching for the nearest barf bag. "Let's not forget that everyone's life is in danger. Save the mushy stuff for later."

One thing was for sure: Scarlett Flame knew how to make an entrance. I'd been so distracted by her arrival that I'd momentarily forgotten about the current crisis. And by the look of it, so had almost everyone else. It was up to Sophie to fill Scarlett Flame in on the situation at hand.

"Right before you caught the attention of everyone in town," Sophie remarked in an annoyed voice, "we decided that my dad would help us enroll under fake identities at Alabaster Academy."

"How wonderful!" Scarlett gushed. "My alma mater!"

"Your alma *what*?" Milton asked.

"It means she went to Alabaster too," Miranda explained.

"She was a couple of years behind us," Captain Justice explained.

"*Several* years behind them," Scarlett said quickly. "But yes—I had an absolutely marvelous time at Alabaster. You'll love it there—"

Mom stepped forward, clearing her throat. "As much as we appreciate your school spirit, Ms. Flame, we aren't sending the kids to Alabaster for the pep rallies. We're doing this to keep them safe."

"The first thing to consider is transportation," Dad said. "Alabaster is hundreds of miles from here—"

"Three hundred fifty-seven miles," Miranda said.

"Exactly. Getting there could be problematic. We can't risk being followed. Or attacked along the way."

"You're welcome to ride in my helicopter," Scarlett volunteered.

"Ooh, yeah!" Milton hopped up and down eagerly. "Can we?"

My parents were already shaking their heads. "Your helicopter would draw unwanted attention," said Mom.

"And there wouldn't be enough room for other passengers," Dad pointed out.

I glanced at my dad. "What other passengers?"

"Your mother and I will be traveling with you. Just in case something *does* happen on the way."

"We're coming too! Aren't we, honey-poo?" Scarlett reached for Captain Justice's hand.

"Certainly, sweetie pie. And of course Stanley will be joining us."

Dad puffed out his chest defensively. "If your robot gets to come, then so does mine."

"Roooaaad triiip!" Elliot squealed.

"That's quite a lot of people," Mom said. "Where are we going to find a vehicle big enough to fit everyone?"

Captain Justice reached for his utility belt and removed his phone. "If it's space you need, I have the perfect solution. Just let me make a quick call."

We had a lot to do, and not much time. Luggage to pack, birth certificates to forge. Miranda went home to tell her mom the news. Meanwhile, Captain Justice paid a visit to Milton's house. And it went just like Miranda had predicted. Milton's mom was so astounded to see Captain Justice in her living room, it didn't matter that she'd never even *heard* of Alabaster Academy, or that Captain Justice kept referring to her son as "Marlon." By the time the superhero was through charming her, she agreed: Alabaster was a terrific opportunity for her Milton.

Early the next morning, we loaded into three cars, making sure that each kid had at least one superhero or

41

supervillain escort. I crammed into the Volvo with my parents and Elliot. Miranda traveled with her mom and Scarlett Flame. Captain Justice and Stanley went with Sophie and Milton. Each car took a different route (in case we were being followed), but we all ended up at the same place.

A warehouse on the outskirts of Sheepsdale.

Inside, the warehouse was stuffed with promotional items for *Hangin' with Justice*. T-shirts, posters, coffee mugs, trading cards, baseball caps, action figures.

"Wow!" Milton whispered, gazing at the endless racks of Captain Justice–themed merchandise.

My parents weren't nearly as impressed. For years, they'd considered Captain Justice a "super-sellout" more interested in his own celebrity than saving the world. Since getting to know him a little better, their opinions had mellowed. But now their lips curled with disgust as they looked at box after box of "worthless junk" (Mom's words) and "cheap throwaway items to be hoisted onto the unwitting masses" (that part came from Dad).

I was taking a closer look at a stack of mouse pads— each plastered with an identical image of Captain Justice's grinning face—when I heard the sound of brakes groaning outside.

Our footsteps echoed across the vast warehouse as we hurried toward the loading dock. Heavy steel doors rose to reveal a gigantic silver and blue tour bus. On its side was the same grinning picture of Captain Justice that I'd just been looking at on the mouse pad—only bigger. *Way* bigger. My eyes scanned the splashy words emblazoned beside his picture:

HANGIN' WITH JUSTICE—
NATIONAL TOUR!!!

"Looks like our ride's here," Captain Justice said.

6

I'll admit, at first it didn't seem like the best idea.

Our goal was to travel more than three hundred miles without anyone noticing. And so what did we do? Join a national publicity tour with a couple of world-famous superheroes. Yeah, that's not gonna get attention.

"Tell me again why we agreed to do this," Mom said, stepping hesitantly onto the tour bus.

"It's called hiding in plain sight," Captain Justice said. "Phineas Vex and his minions assume you're in a secret location. Which is why they'll never expect you to be hidden in the middle of a publicity extravaganza."

"Yeah, because who would be idiotic enough do that?" Dad muttered, following my mom onto the bus.

"The kids will never leave the bus. Nobody will even know they're coming along. And this way, we can all be there to protect them."

As soon as I climbed onto the bus, my jaw dropped. It was like a four-star hotel on wheels. Leather sofas stretched along both sides of the vehicle. Flat-screen TVs were attached to the walls. Beneath a row of tinted windows was a mini-kitchen that came equipped with a sink, microwave, and refrigerator. And past all that was a bathroom, six bunk beds concealed behind curtains, and a door that led into *another* room, with a king-sized bed.

"Forget Alabaster Academy." Milton plopped down on the sofa, gazing at his surroundings. "I say we hide out in *here* for the next year or two."

Miranda sat down beside him. "This is a big step up from the buses I *usually* take to school."

"And unlike your average tour bus, this one comes with state-of-the-art security features," Captain Justice said. "Just in case anyone *does* attempt to mess with us."

Once everyone was on board, Stanley took a seat behind the steering wheel—Elliot was strapped into the passenger seat beside him—and closed the door. A moment later, the bus lurched into motion.

We were on our way to Alabaster.

ꝭ

But first we had a couple of stops to make.

"People will get suspicious if we don't do any publicity on our publicity tour," Captain Justice said.

And so, after an hour of driving, Stanley navigated the bus off the highway and pulled into a parking lot. Nearby was an outdoor stage where thousands of fans were already awaiting an appearance from Captain Justice and Scarlett Flame. The door opened and the two superstars stepped out.

Captain Justice poked his head back through the door. "We shall return soon."

"Take your time," said Milton, kicking back on the sofa. He plucked the remote off a foldout table beside him and flipped on the TV. "We'll be fine."

Sophie popped a frozen pizza into the microwave and we cracked open a few drinks from the fridge. After the stress of the past two days, it was great to just relax and watch a little brainless TV. Even Elliot joined us, taking a seat on the sofa and munching on a pizza box.

The game show switched to a live shot of a news reporter. She was holding a microphone and standing in front of a building that was roped off with police tape.

"I'm coming to you live from the headquarters of Pulse Dynamics . . . ," the reporter began.

"*Bor*ing!" Milton reached for the remote.

Miranda batted his hand away. "Hold on!"

". . . the site of a stunning burglary," the reporter continued. "Two culprits allegedly broke into the high-security facility and stole a Platinum-Sealed Alpha Capacitor—"

I nearly fell off the sofa. Scrambling sideways, I reached into my pocket and dug out the paper that had fallen out of nFinity's shoulder pouch.

PLATINUM-SEALED ALPHA CAPACITOR

NEUTRON FLOW REVERSAL CHAMBER

OSCILLATING PARTICLE IMMOBILIZER

THE DOMINION KEY

"Guys!" I said. "The Platinum-Sealed Alpha Capacitor—that's on nFinity's list!"

"But what is it?" Sophie asked. "What does it—"

"Shhh!" Miranda pointed at the TV.

"We have obtained exclusive security footage from the facility." The live feed of the reporter disappeared, replaced by grainy black-and-white video of two people.

I recognized them immediately.

7

"They're the ones who attacked us at the food court!" I leaned closer to the TV. There was no mistaking the two figures in the security footage: The girl with the pixie haircut. And her massive cement friend.

"Grifter and Lunk," Milton said. "But what do they want with a Platypus-Stuffed Alphabet Container?"

"It's a Platinum-Sealed Alpha Capacitor," Miranda corrected. "They must've stolen it for nFinity."

"Which means they're really working for Vex," Sophie said.

Just hearing the name made my insides curl. After nearly dying, Phineas Vex had bribed and threatened the world's top scientists and engineers to build him a bionic body that wouldn't just keep him alive, it would make him *invincible*. And unfortunately, I'd been one of the first to see it in action. Ten feet tall, bulging with body armor and equipped with more devious gadgetry than you can imagine, the suit gave Vex the powers of the world's most fearsome villains.

But what did he want with the items on nFinity's list?

Dad must've seen the worry in my face. Taking a seat on the sofa beside me, he said, "Don't let it get you too upset. Supervillains are always scheming to track down dangerous technology. It's part of our job description."

"Your father has a point," Mom added. "I discovered a list like that when I took your father's coat to the dry cleaner the other day. You shouldn't make too much of it."

"But this is Vex we're talking about."

"Tell you what. As soon as we get back, your mother and I will do some asking around. See if anyone in the villain community has heard anything about any of these items."

"Uh . . . speaking of the villain community"—Milton was peering through the windows with a fearful expression—"looks like we've got visitors."

Two men in tights were crossing the parking lot in the direction of our bus. The first was wearing a swamp-green uniform that was stretched to the breaking point over his bulging stomach. The man beside him was thin and ragged, outfitted in an orange one-piece that made him look like a deflated pumpkin.

"Do you think they're working for Vex too?" Sophie asked.

My mom shook her head. "No way Vex would hire these two rejects. They look more like D-Listers to me."

"D-Listers?"

"The bottom of the barrel in the supervillain world. The worst of the worst—and not in a good way."

"D-Listers are wannabes," Dad explained. "People who lack the talent to make it as big-time villains but keep trying anyway."

"They turn up at high-profile events like this, hoping to get the attention of everyone who came out to see Captain Justice and Scarlett Flame. Most of the time, they're too chicken to actually engage big-name superheroes in a fight. They're just looking to do something that will get their picture in *Super Scoop*."

"In other words, meaningless self-promotion," Dad sneered. "No skill, no finesse."

Miranda pressed a finger to her temple, concentrating. "The guy in the ugly orange spandex calls himself Bubble Boy."

"Sounds terrifying," Sophie said sarcastically.

"And the guy in green goes by the name StinkBomb. His power is . . . well, you'll smell it in a second."

"Smell *what*?" Milton sniffed. "I don't smell any—" Suddenly, Milton's nose wrinkled and his eyes began to water. "Okay, now I—*ACK!*—get what you mean."

"Ugh!" Sophie clapped a hand over her nose. "That's horrible!"

At first, I had no idea what they were talking about. And then it hit me. A putrefying wave of stink. Like a skunk with a really bad case of indigestion had just climbed onto the bus. It was the worst thing I'd ever smelled in my life. And I've been in the boys' locker room on Taco Tuesday.

By now, everyone was coughing and gagging. While I struggled to breathe without choking on the stink fumes, Sophie staggered across the bus. She pulled open drawers and cabinet doors, knocking down bags of chips and cans of instant coffee until she found what she was looking for.

"Gas masks," she said, tossing one to each of us. "Let's hope they work against really nasty smells too!"

Holding my breath, I fastened the rubber mask over my nose and mouth. Once it was tightly secured, I inhaled and . . . the stink was gone.

"I'm glad we've solved our odor problem," I said, my voice muffled by the mask. "But what do we do about *them*?" I pointed out the window. The D-Lister duo was getting closer.

"Just like your parents said—they're here for attention." Miranda focused on the two men, her eyes narrowing. "They aren't here for a fight. They came for . . . something else. They're planning to do something to the bus."

"You mean the bus we're currently sitting in?" Milton adjusted his mask nervously. "The bus we're not allowed to leave?"

"You may be confined to the bus," Dad said. "But we're not."

My parents were in their "civilian" clothes, which meant nobody would recognize them as the Dread Duo if they stepped outside—especially with gas masks covering their faces. But since they didn't have their uniforms, they also didn't have most of their gear. Luckily, they'd packed some deadly weapons for the drive.

Dad scrambled out of his seat, glancing at Mom. "Honey, where'd you put my portable plasma refractometer?"

"Check my handbag."

Dad stumbled across the bus and grabbed Mom's bag. I watched through the window as the villain who called himself Bubble Boy thrust out his arms. A quivering sphere took shape between his hands, drifting in our direction.

"Ooh, real scary!" Milton snickered through his gas mask. "The big bad villain just blew a bubble at us!"

But this was no ordinary bubble. The closer it got to us, the more it expanded, like a balloon inflating in midair. Soon it was enormous—bigger than any bubble I'd ever seen. By the time it reached my window it was twice the size of the tour bus. The edge of the bubble pressed against the glass. And then—

Flooop!

Just like that, the bus was *inside* the bubble. I felt a gentle floating movement as the bus rose into the air.

Dad was too busy rummaging through Mom's handbag to notice that we were drifting higher and higher. "I can never find anything in this—AAAGH!"

Okay, *now* he noticed.

"We're inside the bubble!" he shrieked.

"Duh!" Milton yelled back. "Can't you do something?"

Dad clenched his jaw. "Yes. Of course." He turned Mom's handbag upside down. Everything fell onto the floor. Sunglasses, a pen, a bottle of water. And a portable plasma refractometer.

Dad grabbed the device and sprang to his feet. He started for the door but didn't get very far. The bus lurched and he stumbled into a counter.

Elliot swung his extendable arms like a kid on a roller coaster. "This is fuuun!"

Staring out the window, I watched the inner surface of the bubble glisten and wobble. Beyond that, it was like looking up from the bottom of a swimming pool. The world outside our floating bubble had become a smear of blobs and colorful shapes.

I could still see the vague forms of Bubble Boy and StinkBomb on the ground. Two squiggly figures getting smaller and smaller as we drifted higher and higher.

Miranda gasped. "Their plan," she said in a strained voice. "The D-Listers are going to float the bus out over the stage where Captain Justice and Scarlett Flame are performing for the crowd. And then . . ."

I didn't need superpowered intuition to know what would come next. I could see it in Miranda's expression. The bubble pops. The bus falls. Hundreds of people injured or killed.

"I might have a solution." Pulling off her gas mask, Mom climbed to her feet. She clutched the wall for support as she moved closer to where Dad was standing. "On the count of three, I want you to blast the inside of the bubble with the refractometer."

"You sure about that, honey?" Dad asked.

Mom nodded. My parents had worked together long enough—that was all the explanation Dad needed.

"Okay, then," he said. "On three."

"Hang on a second." Milton looked around uncertainly. "Have you *seen* how high we are right now? There's no way we'd survive a fall."

"You're going to have to trust us, Milton," Dad commanded, as Mom began to count.

"One . . ."

"Uh . . . guys." My voice cracked. "I have to say, I'm with Milton here. This seems kind of dangerous. Isn't there some other way?"

"Your mother has a plan," Dad said. "Now, I recommend everyone find a secure place and hold on tight."

"Two . . ."

My heart was performing a drum solo in my chest. Sweat trickled down my forehead. In the front, Stanley checked his seat belt and Elliot buzzed with excitement. I looked at Miranda, wondering if she already knew how this was going to turn out, but she was too busy scrambling for a better handhold to give any predictions. Sophie was on the other side of me, gripping the edge of the sofa. A faint glow radiated from her skin—a sign that heightened emotions had triggered her Gyft. When she caught my eye, there was something in her expression that made me think things weren't quite as bad as they could've been. As if to say, *Sure, we're about to plummet to our deaths, but at least we're together.*

I gripped the back of the sofa until my knuckles turned white. Mom called out—

"Three!"

Dad fired the refractometer. A flash of red. Followed by a sudden—

POP!

The bubble exploded around us. For a split second, the bus seemed to hover in midair. Then gravity took over and we began to fall.

8

AAAGGHH!

That was what went through my head as our Tour Bus of Death tumbled toward the earth. My arms were clamped around the back of the sofa, but my legs flew out behind me. The world was a blur. Screams filled the bus. I shut my eyes tight, preparing for impact. But instead, the bus came to a gentle stop. It felt like we'd landed on the world's biggest feather mattress.

My eyes flickered open. The bus was suspended a hundred feet in the air by a tangle of roots. Vegetation wrapped around the bus like tentacles. Peering through the window, I could see where the parking lot had cracked far below and the roots had burst from the earth to catch us.

So *that* was my mom's plan. Mom was also known as the Botanist; her superpower gave her the ability to control plants. I'd seen her ensnare superheroes in the branches of trees and use vines to do her bidding. But I'd never witnessed her power on such a huge scale.

Her face was tight with concentration. The roots gradually sank, lowering the bus toward the earth. It wasn't until we were safely resting in the parking lot and the plants had slithered back below the ground that Mom showed just how much the act had taken out of her. Her face slack, she slumped against the wall.

Ripping off my gas mask, I crossed the bus as quickly as my wobbly legs would carry me. "You saved us!" I said, helping my mom onto the sofa.

When Mom finally managed to speak, her voice came out as a cracked whisper.

"This is why I don't do publicity tours."

There was no sign of Bubble Boy or his stinky accomplice. They must've escaped when they noticed that the local vegetation had a mind of its own.

In the background, I could hear the amplified voices of Captain Justice and Scarlett Flame among the roar of electric guitars and the applause of the crowd. They had no idea how close their promotional event had come to turning into a disaster zone.

A little later, the two superheroes finally returned to the bus. They climbed aboard without even noticing the cracked cement outside and the mess that had been strewn across the bus during our fall.

"Greetings, everyone!" Captain Justice grinned, holding the door open for Scarlett Flame. "Hope the wait wasn't too boring!"

After a few more hours of driving, Stanley navigated the tour bus through a security gate and pulled into an airplane hangar.

"This is as far as we can go," Captain Justice said. "You children will have to travel the rest of the way on your own. But not to worry, I've made all the arrangements. Principal Alabaster is expecting you."

Surprise passed over Milton's face. "The principal is named after the *school*?"

"Actually, the school is named after the principal. Or to be more precise, it's named after his great-great-grandfather. Herman Alabaster founded Alabaster Academy nearly two hundred years ago. When he stepped down, his son took over, and when his son retired, the position went to his grandson. This was repeated again and again over the years, generation after generation of Alabasters. And now Edwin Alabaster is in charge of the school. But not even *he* will be aware of your true identities. So make sure you familiarize yourselves with your fake names and backgrounds."

"Does that mean none of this will go on our permanent transcript?" Miranda asked.

"We'll have to work out all the details later," Captain Justice said. "For now, we have only a few minutes until departure, so let's keep our goodbyes brief."

My parents pulled me into a suffocating group hug.

"We'll miss you!" Mom's voice shook as she gripped

me a little tighter. "You sure you'll be okay away from home?"

"Mfff," I said into her shoulder.

"That's the spirit, Joshua!" Dad gave me a firm pat on the back. "You'll do great at Alabaster!"

When they finally released me, Elliot wobbled in my direction, his eyes glowing. "Goood luck at yourrr new schoool!"

"Thanks, Elliot," I said. "Take care of my mom and dad while I'm gone."

"Hurry up!" Milton called from the backseat of the SUV. "Don't want to miss our boat!"

After a quick goodbye to Captain Justice and Scarlett Flame, I climbed into the back next to Sophie, Milton, and Miranda. On the seat were four folders with information about our new identities. While Stanley drove, we read through our files, memorizing the details. Sophie and I had been through this enough times in the past, but for Milton, this was a new experience.

"What if I can't remember everything about myself?" He gripped his folder nervously. "What if I forget my name, or where I was born?"

"Just relax," I said. "You'll get used to it."

"The idea of a false identity was a lot cooler before I had all this stuff to remember." Milton was still grumbling as the SUV pulled to a stop at a pier that looked out on the Atlantic Ocean. Stanley informed us that Alabaster was located on an island about twenty miles off the coast of Massachusetts.

"You will be traveling the rest of the way by ferry," said the robot.

The afternoon sky had turned dark. Storm clouds loomed in the distance, and fog drifted over the gray water. The mist opened like a curtain and our ferry emerged.

"Guess that's our ride," Miranda said.

We dragged our luggage and backpacks onto the ferry. When it was clear we would be the only passengers, a horn sounded and the boat lurched back out onto the dark water. The four of us stood by the railing and looked back at the shore as the pier vanished into the fog.

Except for the crew, we were alone on the deck. We listened to the sound of waves knocking against the sides of the ferry and seagulls crying overhead. Sophie, Miranda, and I took turns quizzing Milton on the details of his new life story. A faint rain pattered against my cheeks.

Gradually, a shadowy shape emerged from the fog. A chill gripped me as I got my first glimpse of Alabaster Academy.

9

"**N**obody informed me that we'd be starting the seventh grade at a haunted castle," Sophie said.

Alabaster Academy was perched on top of a rocky island. Gray stone walls rose out of the tumbling waves, towering high into the air. Crooked turrets loomed over the ocean, disappearing into the mist. At the top of the tallest tower was a lighthouse that sent its beam swiveling through the fog.

By the time we reached the island, the light drizzle had transformed into a heavy rain. Dragging our luggage behind us, we hurried onto a dock. A grim, hooded figure was waiting up ahead. His raincoat flapped in the wind. His features were shrouded in shadows, so all I could see was a thick silver beard and a pair of dark eyes staring back at me.

Milton hesitated, gripping his jacket tighter. "I-is it too late to turn back?"

I glanced at the ferry behind us. It was already pulling away from the dock. "Afraid so."

"You sure this is a good idea?"

At that exact moment, I wasn't. Maybe it was the storm. Or the waves crashing around us. Or the forbidding fortress rising from the rocks. Or the dark figure waiting on the steps, looking like the Grim Reaper with a beard. But right then, I was beginning to wonder whether we'd live long enough to see the first day of school.

Then something unexpected happened. The figure in the raincoat threw back his hood and called out in a jolly voice, "Greetings! I'm Principal Alabaster!"

He had bushy silver eyebrows to match his beard. Rain streamed down his pudgy red cheeks. He was more Santa Claus than Grim Reaper.

"I hope you had safe travels." The man had to yell to be heard over the sounds of wind and waves. "You must be . . ."

And here he listed off our fake names. But since I wouldn't want to put us in any more danger, I'll just leave that part out of the story.

As we climbed the steps, Principal Alabaster looked us over with a huge grin. "It's an honor to welcome you to Alabaster!" he said. "A real honor. You must be very proud!"

"Proud?" Milton blurted out. "Of what?"

Principal Alabaster chuckled. "No need for modesty. Captain Justice himself called to let me know that you four have qualified for the first Captain's Kiddos Scholarship Award. And he's even offered to make a very generous donation to our endowment fund. Now, let's get inside before we wash away."

Our feet splashed against the wooden dock as we trailed Principal Alabaster toward the tall front doors. "Education is a top priority at Alabaster Academy," he said, inserting a huge iron key into the lock. "And so is safety. When my great-great-grandfather founded this school, society feared and misunderstood Gyfted children. That's why our fine institution was built on this isolated island, with walls that can withstand the most fearsome attacks. Not to mention top-notch security features."

Principal Alabaster pressed his hand against a fingerprint recognition pad. With a *click* the doors swiveled open.

I took one last look up at the gloomy towers of Alabaster Academy. Then I followed the others inside.

The entry hall was enormous. An iron chandelier hung from the high ceiling, casting a glow across two marble stairways that spiraled up into the shadows. On the stone walls were flags with the years of different classes stitched into them.

"For nearly two centuries, Alabaster has been home to many of the most remarkably Gyfted youngsters from around the country," Principal Alabaster explained. "It's a nurturing environment where you will receive a quality education while also honing your other—shall we say—*skills*."

A pair of footsteps drew my attention to the far end of

the entryway. I noticed a tall, slender girl with skin the color of porcelain and long, silver hair that shone in the light of the chandelier.

The girl looked at us with curiosity. "Are these the newbies?" she asked.

Principal Alabaster grinned affectionately at the girl. "Now, Cassie, surely you're aware that the official term is 'incoming seventh graders.'"

The girl—Cassie—rolled her eyes. "Thanks for the update, Dad."

"You're welcome to leave your luggage here," Principal Alabaster said to us. "Cassie will show you to your rooms."

"I'll take it from here." The girl motioned for us to join her. "Well, newbies? What are you waiting for? Dinner's in an hour, and we've got a big school to cover."

Cassie spun and headed through an open doorway. My friends and I jogged to catch up. We entered a hall that looked more like a museum than a school. Instead of lockers, the walls were lined with framed paintings. Turning a corner, I nearly bumped into a suit of armor.

Cassie listed off the sights as we went. "Classroom, classroom, stuffed rhinoceros, classroom."

"Excuse me . . . er, Cassie," Milton called after her. "So you're Principal Alabaster's—"

"Daughter? Yes."

"So does that mean you're next in line to be principal?"

"Not in a million years."

"How come?"

Cassie came to a stop beside a tall window. With her

64

CASSIE

For Cassie, Alabaster Academy is a family tradition. Her great-great-great-grandfather founded the school. Her dad's the principal. But she has other plans for her future.

ghostly pale skin and grandmother hair, it was tough to pin down her age. For a moment, she looked no older than thirteen. But a shift of the light suddenly made her appear twice that age.

Gazing at the rain and the tumbling waves outside, she said, "I've basically spent my entire life on Alabaster Island. Dad's the principal, Mom's a teacher. They decided to homeschool me."

"But your home *is* a school," Miranda pointed out.

"Exactly. And that school happens to be located on an island where there are two kinds of weather: rainy and *very* rainy. Don't get me wrong. It's an interesting place to grow up. But if I took over as principal, I'd spend the *rest* of my life here. No thanks."

Cassie started walking again. Our next stop was the library, where a girl was scaling the tall shelves like a spider. Plucking a book off the top shelf, she leaped, performing a backflip on the way down.

"You know there are ladders, right, Veronica?" Cassie called out, leading us into a hallway.

We walked past a kid admiring his reflection in a tarnished old mirror. But as we passed, the boy actually stepped *into* the mirror. And instead of bumping his head, the two reflections merged and the kid disappeared.

"Okay, that was awesome," Milton said.

"You get a lot of that kind of thing here," Cassie said. "In regular society, Gyfted kids are treated like freaks when they use their powers. But here, they don't have to hide who they are."

We followed Cassie up a flight of stairs. A kid zipped past us, down the banister, squealing. With a yelp, he collided with another kid, who was sliding *up* the banister. The two boys tumbled onto the steps, cackling with laughter.

Cassie rolled her eyes. "As you can see, everyone's a little restless with classes starting tomorrow."

At the end of the hall, we reached a massive steel door. Cassie pressed her face close to a retina scanner. An automated voice droned through speakers above the door: *"Access granted."*

Cassie led us into a recreation room. In the corners, kids were sprawled on beanbag chairs, playing video games or watching TV. A group was gathered around a card table. Ten feet above them, a girl was lying in a hammock tied to the ceiling beams, reading a book. In the center of the room, a couple of teenagers were playing Ping-Pong—at least until one of them slammed the ball so hard it exploded.

As my friends and I entered the room, all the activities came to a stop. Everyone turned in our direction. The girl in the hammock peered down at us. The guy who'd just caused a Ping-Pong ball to explode gripped his paddle a little tighter, as if he was thinking about doing the same thing to our heads.

I felt like someone had tied my vocal cords in a knot. Luckily, Cassie took care of the introductions.

Sort of.

"All right, everyone. These are the newest newbies. I won't bother telling you their names, 'cause you probably won't remember them anyway. They're starting seventh grade. Apparently, they've been personally recommended by Captain Justice. So feel free to tease, torment, or torture them, as long as you don't mind risking a butt-kicking from a superhero."

The entire room gaped at us for a few seconds longer. And then everyone went back to what they'd been doing before.

"Okay, then," Cassie said. "This concludes your tour. The boys' dorms are to the left. Girls' are on your right. And don't even think about sneaking from one to the other. The RHMs can be ruthless."

"RHMs?" Sophie asked.

"Robotic hall monitors. They maintain law and order around here. Believe me, you *don't* want to upset them."

We decided to meet in the rec room in half an hour to get dinner together. While Cassie led Sophie and Miranda to the girls' dorms, Milton and I headed to our left, down a bright hallway that seemed to go on forever.

On either side of the hall were students' rooms, the doors decorated with messages scribbled on dry-erase boards, photographs, and pages cut out of *Super Scoop*. Halfway down the hall, we passed a wrinkled poster that showed me dressed up as the Nameless Hero. Someone had drawn a mustache on my masked face and scribbled THE NAMELESS NERD.

"Check it out." Milton tugged at my sleeve and pointed. "One of those RHM thingies."

Whizzing in our direction was an all-white robot with a pair of treads for legs and glowing slits for eyes. It had a downturned speaker where its mouth should've been, giving it a permanent frown.

"Greetings, new students," the RHM said in a formal electronic voice. "My identification code is Epsilon-45736, but you can call me Bob."

"Hey, Bob!" Milton waved. "Nice to m—"

"Proceed this way," the RHM interrupted. It whirled and began rolling back the way it had come. We hurried after it, passing a few students who were hanging out in the hallway, chatting about their summers and throwing a Frisbee around.

"No tossing objects in the hallway," the RHM said. Without slowing down, it snatched the Frisbee midflight and crushed it in its metallic claws.

With cries of protest trailing us, we jogged after the robot. At the very last door, it came to a stop.

"This is your room," it said. "Before entering, you must submit security protocols."

Zipping forward, the RHM plugged its claw into a slot. A panel opened beside the door. At the robot's command, Milton and I pressed our hands against the panel. Once it had scanned our handprints, we did the same with our eyes.

Milton squirmed, his face pressed against the panel. "It's tickling my eyeball!"

The RHM removed its claw from the slot. "You now have security authorization clearance. Goodbye."

With that, the robot turned and rolled away.

"See ya later, Bob!" Milton called.

I pressed my hand against the panel again, and this time the door slid open. Milton and I stepped inside.

I paused just inside the doorway. Everything seemed to be smaller than in my bedroom at home. A wooden bunk bed. Two tiny desks, each with a small computer monitor perched on top. A mini-fridge. A couple of squat dressers. A thin window at the other end of the room looked out on the ocean—rain and gray waves as far as I could see.

Our luggage was waiting for us at the foot of the beds. By the time Milton and I were done putting away all our stuff, it was time to meet the others for dinner. We hurried back down the hallway, jumping sideways to avoid getting run over by Bob along the way.

10

The cafeteria was a madhouse. Grabbing a tray, I joined the line along with Milton, Sophie, and Miranda.

"Have you guys seen Cassie?" Milton asked.

Miranda shook her head. "She said she'd meet us here. But I haven't—"

A cloud of silver smoke drifted into line beside us. The cloud whirled into a human form, tendrils of smoke solidifying into fingers, a face forming from the silver blur. And suddenly, Cassie was standing next to us.

As the four of us stared, speechless, she flipped her silver hair over her shoulder and picked a tray off the stack.

"Thanks for saving my spot," she said.

After being served our food by a line of surly cafeteria drones, we set out to find a table. On the way, we passed a group of tough-looking kids. The burliest of them shot us a nasty glare. Even though he looked about our age, the guy already had stubble on his cheeks and hair on his arms. I guess puberty had hit him especially hard.

"Looks like we got us some newbies," he said in a low growl. "Fresh off the boat."

I tried to sidestep the guy, but he lumbered into my path.

"I heard you got a sissy scholarship from Captain Justice," he snarled. "You think that makes you special?"

Cassie pushed between us. "What's the matter, Winston?" she asked. "Swallow a hair ball?"

"Very funny, daddy's girl." His lips curled back, showing off a set of long, sharp fangs that looked like they were made for ripping apart large animals. I felt sorry for his dentist.

The guy—Winston—shot the rest of us a malicious grin and moved aside.

"See ya around, newbies," he said. It sounded like a threat.

"What's *his* problem?" Sophie asked once we were out of earshot.

Cassie shrugged off the question. "If you thought that was bad, you should see him when he's angry."

She set down her tray near the end of a table. A group of other kids our age were already eating. As we took our seats, Cassie introduced us. Fortunately, they were a lot more welcoming than Winston.

A guy with eyes that changed color from green to blue to purple asked, "How was the ferry ride over here?"

"Wet," Miranda replied.

"It always is."

Beside him was the girl we'd seen earlier, scaling the shelves of the library like a climbing wall. Veronica.

"Did Cassie tell you about the ghost?" she asked.

Milton dropped his fork. "What ghost?"

"Some people say the ghost of my great-great-great-grandfather haunts the school," Cassie said.

"The ghost of Herman Alabaster," said Veronica in a spooky voice. "People claim he lives in the walls. You can sometimes hear him rattling around at night."

"Pass the salt," called a kid at the other end of the table. The guy with color-shifting eyes pointed a finger at the saltshaker. It zipped across the table.

"Has anyone ever seen the ghost?" I asked.

"Tons of people."

"Really?" Milton glanced around like he might see the ghost of Herman Alabaster drifting through the cafeteria, munching on a sloppy joe. "What's he look like?"

"You can see for yourself," Veronica said. "There's a painting of Herman Alabaster on the second floor. Some people say he emerges from his painting in the middle of the night to roam the hallways."

A mixture of disbelief and curiosity stirred inside me. I wondered if there was any truth in what they were saying. Of course, in the past forty-eight hours, I'd been attacked by mall merchandise, taken a ride in the world's biggest bubble, and changed my identity to enroll in a school full of superpowered kids.

Maybe a ghost wasn't such a strange idea after all.

𝓕

"I call top bunk!" Milton said, pulling his eye away from the retina scanner. The door to our room slid open and he raced inside.

I followed him into the room. "Do you think all that stuff is true? About Herman Alabaster being a ghost?"

"I wouldn't be surprised." Milton grabbed his laptop and scrambled up the bunk-bed ladder. "There's all sorts of crazy stuff going on in this place. Why *not* a ghost?"

"I guess you're right. It's like everyone and everything at Alabaster is extraordinary in some way."

"Yeah, well . . . *almost* everyone."

"What's that supposed to mean?"

Milton didn't say anything. Instead, he opened his laptop and hunched behind the screen, as if he was trying to hide his face.

"Everything okay?" I asked.

"It's just"—a sigh came from behind the laptop—"I don't belong at a school like this. You said yourself, everyone's extraordinary. Except me."

"That's not what I said."

"Might as well have. All the kids here are special. Even the paintings have ghosts living in them."

MILTON

Milton's always loved the world of superheroes
and supervillains. But how will he fit in as the
only unGyfted kid at Alabaster?

"You don't know that."

"The point is I don't fit in here. And before long, everyone else is gonna realize it."

I'd felt the same way as Milton most my life. Like I didn't fit in. Like the rest of the world was on the verge of finding out the truth about me. Like a fake. In every new town, in every new school, I was constantly wondering if my classmates would realize my true identity, or my parents would embarrass me by trying to destroy the world again.

Things had only gotten tougher in the last year. As my Gyft started to kick in, I was always on edge. Middle school is hard enough *without* a freaky superpower. Believe me, when your gym shorts catch on fire during PE, you get some weird looks from the other kids.

All of a sudden, everything had flipped upside down. Everyone at Alabaster had superpowers.

Except Milton.

"Don't let it get to you," I said. "How many of the kids here can say that they've been part of a famous superhero team? How many have saved the world?"

"Yeah . . . I guess." Milton leaned backward, his face emerging from behind the laptop. In the glow of the screen, I could see a slight smile forming on his lips.

By the time I brushed my teeth and climbed into the bottom bunk, the only sounds in the room were the patter of rain against the windows and the *click-click* of Milton on his laptop above me. Just as I was starting to drift off, the bed creaked. A second later, Milton's head appeared next to me, upside down.

"Dude!" he said. "You've gotta see what I just found!"

"Is it more photos of Scarlett Flame in a bikini?"

"Not that." Milton lowered his laptop. "Take a look at this."

I leaned forward. The screen showed the website for *Super Scoop*. A headline was splashed across the top of the page in big, bold letters:

RARE COMPONENT GOES MISSING!

"Okay?" I squinted drowsily at the screen. "And?"

"Just read it."

"Fine." I took the computer and began reading.

Officials are scratching their heads in the wake of another bold burglary. Mere hours ago, a duo of dangerous desperadoes stole a Neutron Flow Reversal Chamber from the high-security research facility where it was being kept—

Suddenly, I was wide awake. I reached for the side table, where I'd emptied my pockets earlier. Loose change, cell phone—and a slip of paper. The same paper that had fallen out of nFinity's shoulder pouch in the food court. I scanned the list until I saw what I was looking for. *Neutron Flow Reversal Chamber.*

It was the second object on the list to be stolen in a twenty-four-hour period. And I could already guess who was behind it. Scrolling down, my eyes scanned words in the article—*only device of its kind in the world* . . . *scene of de-struction* . . . *motive unknown*—until I got to a black-and-white security photo of the thieves.

Grifter and Lunk.

There were a total of four items on the list. And now they'd stolen two of them. Staring at the grainy photo of the telekinetic pixie and her enormous concrete buddy, I wondered what they planned to steal next.

And why?

11

*B*AM! BAM! BAM! BAM!
        I was startled awake by a pounding at the door.
Bolting up in bed, I could hear Milton snoring.

"Extra cheese on those nachos, *por favor*," he mumbled.

Gradually, the details of my new life came back to me.
I was in a dorm, at Alabaster. Today was our first day of
classes.

I'd been up half the night thinking about the article
Milton showed me on his laptop. I still had no idea what
Grifter and Lunk were up to. But if they were working for
Phineas Vex, it had to be something wicked.

Whoever was at the door began banging again. Looking at the digital clock on the bedside table sent a flurry of
panic through my chest.

I banged on the top bunk. "Milton, wake up!"

The bed creaked and Milton let out a sleepy groan. "Huh? Whu?"

"We're late. First class is in twenty minutes."

As another round of knocking shook the door, I jumped out of bed. But that was about as far as I got. The sheets were still tangled around my legs and I landed face-first on the floor. Kicking my legs free, I staggered across the room and swung open the door—

And there was the RHM. Bob. Balanced on his metal hands was a stack of clothes.

"Your uniforms," droned the robot.

"Uniforms?" I repeated.

"Students are required to wear a school-mandated uniform to all classes."

I grabbed the pile of clothes. "Thanks, Bob."

The RHM swiveled and made his way back down the hall.

I slammed the door closed and began sorting through the clothes. "Here." I tossed a white shirt and khakis in Milton's direction. Then I held up a long strip of blue fabric. "We're supposed to wear . . . a *tie*?"

I had no idea how to *tie* a tie. And neither did Milton. But that was something we'd have to figure out later. Because by the time we'd put on the rest of our uniforms, we had less than ten minutes until our first class. Knotting the tie sloppily around my neck, I grabbed my backpack and burst into the hallway.

We rushed down the hall, through the empty rec room, and down the stairs. Luckily, Milton and I had the same class for first period. Unluckily, neither of us had any idea how to get there.

Most other students must've already been in class, because the halls were nearly vacant. We ran down one corridor, then another, searching for the classroom, until a voice stopped us in our tracks.

"There you are! We've been looking everywhere for you!"

Sophie was standing in the center of the hall, her arms crossed. She was wearing a blue-checked skirt and a white polo.

"What *happened* to you guys?" she asked.

Milton was doubled over, trying to catch his breath. Between huge gulps of air, he managed to get out the basic info. "Overslept." *Pant, pant.* "Robot woke us." *Wheeze.* "Looking for"—*gasp*—"room one twenty-one."

"Miranda and I are in that class too. She's saving us a seat."

"Great!" I said. "Let's go."

"Uh . . . you're not showing up to class like that, are you?"

I glanced down. My tie looked like it'd been twisted around my neck by a gorilla.

Sophie rolled her eyes. "Here, let me do it." She reached out and loosened the tie, pulling the end between a fold. With her standing so close, I was suddenly unsure what to do with my hands.

"Um . . . so, where'd you learn to do this?" I asked, more to break the silence than anything.

"My dad's completely clueless when it comes to tying a tie," she said. "It's not a skill a superhero needs very often. So whenever he has a fancy awards ceremony, I end up doing it for him."

Sophie pulled at the tie and straightened the knot.

"There. That should do the trick."

Sophie remained where she was standing, and so did I. Her face inches from mine, her hands resting on my collar. It felt like we stood like that for a half hour, but it was probably closer to a half second before Milton's voice broke in.

"Uh . . . I could use a little help too."

I stumbled backward, jamming my hands into my pockets. Sophie turned away from me, clearing her throat. Beside us, Milton watched with a quizzical expression on his face and a tie wrapped around his forehead.

Hurrying to first period, I filled Sophie in on Milton's discovery from the night before. The break-in at the high-security research facility and the stolen Neutron Flow Reversal Chamber.

"That's the second item on nFinity's list," Sophie said breathlessly. "But why?"

"No idea."

I jumped sideways just in time to dodge an older kid on a hover skateboard. A teacher's voice called from a doorway. "No hover vehicles in the hallway, Mr. Cooper."

"All we know so far is that Grifter and Lunk committed both robberies," I said. "And that they're working for nFinity—"

"In other words, Phineas Vex," Milton added.

"There are two more items on the list," Sophie pointed out.

"An Oscillating Particle Immobilizer. And the Dominion Key." I still had no idea what either object was. But I'd spent enough time staring at the list that the strange words practically rolled off my tongue.

"I bet it's only a matter of time before they try to steal those too." Sophie speed-walked around the corner. Milton and I followed. Our room was up ahead. A few other kids were also hustling to class. One was running on the ceiling.

"I just wish I knew what Vex was up to," Milton said.

"Same here."

The bell rang just as we entered the room. Our conversation would have to wait.

Milton and I paused in the doorway, looking around the room. Rows of lab stations, two students seated at each. The gray stone walls were decorated with diagrams of bombs and illustrations of missiles. A poster near the back was headlined WHAT TO DO IF YOUR HAIR CATCHES ON FIRE.

What kind of class was this?

I got an answer to my question a second later when the teacher stood and called out in an English accent, "Welcome to Introduction to High-Grade Weaponry."

In the back corner was an empty lab station. I trailed Milton across the room and took a seat.

"My name is Dr. Nigel Fleming," said the teacher. "The previous High-Grade Weaponry teacher was horribly injured in a heat-seeking-missile incident. I couldn't be more thrilled to take over the position!"

Dr. Fleming was tall, with graying brown hair. He looked like the kind of guy who would play the cool dad on a TV show. Stacks of notes were scattered across his desk. Behind him on the blackboard was a blizzard of calculations.

"Your presence at Alabaster Academy implies that you are among the nation's most gifted Gyfted children," Dr. Fleming announced. "Many of you will grow up to become superheroes, supervillains, secret agents, spies, scientists. . . . Therefore, it's imperative that you learn how to deploy and defuse the world's deadliest weapons. In this class, you will each be working with a partner to gain practical experience dealing with highly explosive materials. So make sure you wear lab goggles."

I glanced sideways at Milton. He was grinning like a maniac.

Dr. Fleming grabbed a cardboard box from his messy desk and moved around the room, carefully handing each set of partners a small gadget. The thing looked like one of my dad's unfinished inventions: a jumble of circuit boards and batteries entangled in a nest of multicolored wires. On top of it was a blank digital display.

"You have each been given a simple time bomb," Dr. Fleming said.

Time bomb? I scooted back on my stool.

The teacher continued. "Your first assignment is to disable the bomb before detonation. On page fourteen of your textbook, you'll find a list of instructions on how to do this. You have five minutes."

Dr. Fleming pushed aside a pile of paperwork, revealing a laptop. Flipping it open, he jabbed the keyboard a few times. The digital display on our bomb thingy suddenly flashed a string of red numbers:

$$00{:}05{:}00$$

"Please open your textbooks and begin." Dr. Fleming pressed another key on the laptop and the numbers began counting down.

$$00{:}04{:}59$$
$$00{:}04{:}58$$

"This has to be a joke," I whispered to Milton. "I thought the first day was supposed to be a breeze."

"It's gonna be more like an explosion if we don't figure this out," Milton replied.

I flipped open our book. On page fourteen was a labeled illustration of the bomb, followed by a list of detailed steps. I scanned the page. *Remove the blue wire and replace with the teal wire. . . . Give the half-inch battery a quarter-turn in a counter-clockwise direction. . . . Make sure you don't touch the purple wire—doing so will detonate the bomb. . . .*

Glancing from the page to the bomb, I felt my brain starting to melt. There must've been twenty different wires, and at least five of them looked purple to me.

At the lab station beside us were Sophie and Miranda. They seemed to be making a lot more progress. Miranda's fingers plucked at the bomb, pulling at wires like she'd done this a thousand times before, while Sophie watched. Must have been nice to have a Senser as a lab partner.

I tried to reread the page, but my eyes kept skipping to the digital clock. Time was ticking away.

00:03:25
00:03:24

"We've gotta do something. Let's start by removing this wire." Milton reached for the bomb.

"No!" I warned. "That's purple."

"Looks bluish to me."

I shook my head, pointing. "*This* is the blue wire."

"No, that's teal."

I tugged at my safety goggles. How were we supposed to defuse a bomb when we couldn't even agree on colors? At least we weren't the only ones struggling with our first assignment. Except for Sophie and Miranda, the rest of the class looked just as lost as we did.

00:02:42
00:02:41

"All right, fine," Milton said, exasperated. "We'll try it your way. You think this is the blue wire?"

I nodded.

"You sure about that?"

"Definitely."

"Okay, then." Milton reached out. His fingers pinched the wire. "Here goes."

Milton pulled the wire and—

POP!

My vision filled with dark smoke. I let out a hacking cough, waving away the cloud. Next to me, Milton's face was covered in black soot. He looked like he'd just gone bungee jumping down a chimney. I would've laughed, except I probably looked the same.

"If this were a real bomb, our entire classroom would be rubble right now," Dr. Fleming said in a grim tone. "But don't be dismayed, gentlemen. It's exceedingly rare for a student to get it right on the first—"

"Done!"

At the next lab station, Miranda was beaming with pride. The clock on her time bomb had stopped.

"Excellent work." Dr. Fleming examined the defused bomb. "Excellent work indeed."

Miranda shrugged. "Beginner's luck, I guess." Even as she tried to feign modesty, I could see the gleam in her eye.

Dr. Fleming reset our bomb and we gave it another try— with the same result. Our third, fourth, and fifth attempts were no better. By the time we left class, everyone was covered in black soot. Well, *almost* everyone. Sophie and Miranda were as spotless as when they'd walked in.

"That was fun!" Sophie chirped.

"Yeah!" Miranda gushed. "I can't wait to see what Dr. Fleming gives us tomorrow!"

"Teacher's pet," Milton muttered.

Our next class was PE. After trading our ties and khakis for T-shirts and gym shorts, Milton and I met up with Sophie and Miranda in the center of the basketball court. Lots of other seventh graders were milling around waiting for class to begin—including the tough-looking group we'd seen the day before in the cafeteria. The biggest (and hairiest) was the guy Cassie had called Winston.

As I approached, he shot me an unfriendly smile, offering another glimpse of his sharp fangs.

The PE teacher was Coach Stillwell, a middle-aged guy with a massive mustache and a tiny pair of shorts. "Today's activity," he said, "is dodgeball."

Winston's deadly grin widened. "This is gonna be fun."

Tugging at his undersized shorts, Coach Stillwell selected Winston as one team captain. And for some reason, he singled me out as the other.

For his team Winston chose his posse from the cafeteria. Which basically included anyone who looked eager for the chance to knock someone's head off with a rubber ball.

My picks were Sophie, Milton, Miranda, Cassie, and a bunch of the kids who'd shared our table at dinner.

"The rules are simple." Coach Stillwell shuffled across the court, placing rubber balls on the centerline. "You get hit, you're out. Throw a ball that your opponent catches before the first bounce, you're out. First team to eliminate the other side wins. Have fun, and try not to get killed."

Stepping to the sideline, Stillwell blew the whistle. The game began.

12

I'd played dodgeball a few times before, but never like *this*.

Winston and the rest of his team rushed forward like an attacking army. I was still standing there like an idiot when the first ball was launched in my direction. It was radiating an eerie green glow, as if someone had just dipped it in a pool of radioactive sludge. I would've started the game off with a faceful of toxic rubber if I hadn't hit the deck just in time.

Rising to my hands and knees, I caught a glimpse of a red-eyed girl on Winston's team. She was holding a ball in front of her chest. When she removed her hands, the ball remained in place, drifting between her palms, surrounded by waves of red light. It was a disturbing sight, and it only grew worse when she trained her red eyes on me. The energy field crackled and sparked. And even though the girl's hands never moved, the ball shot forward like it had been fired out of a cannon.

I rolled sideways, feeling a rush of wind sweep past as the ball missed me by less than an inch.

"You can run!" Winston screamed from across the court. "But you can't hide!"

Glancing around, I realized that several of my teammates had already been eliminated. And more were dropping like flies. A scrawny kid was pegged in the back as he tried to escape to the bleachers. Veronica hung from the ceiling rafters—at least until a fastball from Winston brought her back to earth.

By the time Sophie got her hands on a ball, her skin was glowing like a fluorescent bulb. She lunged and threw the ball. It ripped through the air and slammed into Red Eyes with the force of an eighteen-wheeler, knocking her into the bleachers.

"Lucky shot," Winston snarled. As he reached for a ball, hair sprouted from his arms and neck. His fingernails grew into ultrasharp claws. His bulging biceps ripped the sleeves of his T-shirt. His eyes had turned into yellow canine slits, and slobber dripped down his long fangs.

He was becoming a . . . wolf.

One look at him made me miss the bullies back in Sheepsdale. This guy wasn't even the same *species* as Joey and Brick.

Releasing a piercing howl, Winston reared back and launched the ball at Cassie. One second she was standing there like an easy target; the next she was gone, replaced

WINSTON

This bully has some serious anger-management issues. Not to mention sharp claws, deadly fangs, and a whole lot of hair.

by a pillar of silver smoke. As the ball flew harmlessly past, the smoke whipped a few feet to the left and re-formed into Cassie.

"What's the matter?" Cassie shot a sarcastic grin across the court. "Hair get in your eyes?"

"Real funny!" Winston growled. "Too bad yer gonna be leaving this court on a stretcher."

Winston yanked a ball out of a teammate's hands and hurled it straight at Cassie. Another near miss. His next shot was aimed at Miranda. But she was ready for the throw before it even left his hand. She leaped sideways, performing a one-handed cartwheel-flip combo. Only Miranda could make dodgeball look like a professional acrobatics display.

The ball bounced off the bleachers and right into my hands. Before the other team had a chance to react, I took aim and threw. A wave of energy surged through my entire body. The ball burst into flames and shot across the court like a comet. It grazed a kid near the sideline. The kid trudged off the court, wiping his charred sleeve.

The game raged on. Eventually, the only one left on the other side of the court was Winston. He was hunched over, panting. The best part: all the ammunition was on our side. Everyone on our team had a dodgeball (Sophie had two) and Winston was empty-handed.

"Let's give this hairball a taste of rubber," Cassie said.

"What're you wimps waiting for?" Winston screamed. Slobber sprayed all over the free-throw line. "Afraid I'll bite? You couldn't hit me with a—"

The rest of his speech was silenced by a barrage of dodgeballs that knocked him clear out of his gym socks.

"I could get used to this!"

Miranda looked like she'd won the lottery. On top of the skills she'd shown with time bombs and dodgeballs, she'd impressed everyone during sixth-period Basics of Antigravity.

The same couldn't be said for me and Milton. He'd spent most of the class upside down, and I was still dizzy from head-butting the ceiling.

"Anyone up for some Ping-Pong?" Sophie asked as we exited the cafeteria.

"Sure!" Miranda said.

Milton sized up the competition: one person who could smash the ball into oblivion and another who could predict where Milton would hit his shot before *he* did.

"All right, but no superpowers." He glanced at Sophie. "If you start glowing, I quit." He turned to Miranda. "And if you're a Senser, you have to play with . . . uh . . . with your eyes closed."

"Fine with me," Sophie said.

"Same here." Miranda glanced my way. "How about you?"

"I'll pass," I said.

"You sure?"

I nodded. My last experience with Ping-Pong had ended with a flaming paddle and lots of apologies.

"I think I'll do a little looking around," I said.

"Suit yourself."

The others rushed off toward the rec room. I went the other way. Past windows that looked out on the dark sea. Outside, sheets of rain pounded the inky-black water. At the end of the hall was a trophy case. I paused long enough to scan the gleaming golden awards. *First Place: Hover Scooter Relay . . . Sixteenth Annual Zombie Roundup Award . . . National Champion: 50,000-Yard Dash.*

My footsteps echoed up the stairway. At the top was the tall wooden door that led into the Alumni Hall, followed by a display of antique superhero uniforms. The sounds of other students had faded. I was completely alone in the dark hallway.

I walked past a few empty classrooms and then came to a tall, framed portrait of a stern-looking man with a headful of silver hair and a matching mustache. The golden nameplate at the bottom of the frame read HERMAN ALABASTER, FOUNDER AND FIRST HEADMASTER OF ALABASTER ACADEMY.

So this was the ghost everyone was talking about. Looking at the painting, I remembered what the others had said in the cafeteria yesterday. That you could sometimes hear footsteps through the stone walls. That Herman Alabaster emerged from his painting in the middle of the night to roam the hallways.

I could see why the guy might spook people. Herman

Alabaster's features looked as craggy and gray as the island that was named after him.

Then I heard a noise. A faint shuffle from somewhere behind the painting. I looked both ways, but there was nobody around. The noise grew louder. Closer.

I staggered backward a step. Herman Alabaster's gray eyes seemed to follow me.

Suddenly, my palms were covered in sweat.

A draft blew through the hallway, sending a chill down my neck and raising goose bumps along my arms. Then the frame started to rattle and shake.

All my curiosity turned to paranoia. Before I could give it a second thought I spun around and took off running. The hallway was a gray blur. My heartbeat and footsteps pounded in my ears.

But as soon as I rounded the corner, my fear began to melt away and I heard a voice in the corner of my brain saying, *There's no such thing as ghosts. The shuffle you heard behind the wall was the echoing footsteps of students somewhere else in the school. And the rattling frame? Just the wind.*

I slowed to a walk. Glancing around, I was glad that at least nobody had seen me running away from a painting of some old dude.

At the other end of the stairway, I came to a stop by a wall of black-and-white photographs showing students from years past. Sixth-grade class pictures. The first was more than a hundred years old. A scratchy black-and-white image of boys in suits and ties and girls in old-fashioned dresses, all posed with severe expressions, as if they knew that by the time I looked at their picture, they'd all be dead.

As my eyes moved from one framed class to the next, the photos became more recent. Seventy years ago. Sixty-five. Fifty. I paused in front of one from thirty years ago. The clothes weren't as stuffy and the students didn't look quite so uptight. Many of them were smiling—especially a tall blond boy in the center. When I leaned in a little closer, I saw that he was floating a few inches off the ground.

But it was a couple of other kids who really grabbed my attention. A boy and a girl perched at the far edge of the crowd, as if they couldn't wait to get away from the group. The girl had long, dark hair and looked like she was practicing her supervillainous scowl for the camera. Beside her was a skinny kid with thick glasses. His arms were crossed, and he was staring sourly at the ground.

I didn't need to scan the fine-print list of names at the bottom of the photo to know. . . . These were my parents.

It was strange to think that Mom and Dad had *ever* been my age, but there they were. I wondered what they'd been like back then, and why they never talked about Alabaster Academy.

"Taking a trip through time, I see!"

I nearly jumped out of my skin. Especially when I spun around and saw the ghost of Herman Alabaster looming over me.

13

Okay, maybe I *was* still a little freaked out. Because an instant later, I realized it wasn't a ghost after all. It was Principal Alabaster. With his silver hair and gray eyes, he looked a lot like the painting of his great-great-grandfather.

"I'm terribly sorry," he said. "Didn't mean to startle you."

"Th-that's okay," I said. "It's just—for a second, I thought you were . . . someone else."

"I noticed you looking over our old class photos." Principal Alabaster leaned in, squinting at the photograph. "Aha. So *that's* why you're so interested!"

His remark set off alarm bells in my mind. Had he seen the way I was looking at my parents? What if he made the connection between me and the Dread Duo? Nobody was supposed to know my real identity. Not even Principal

Alabaster. We'd been at the school for two days. What if I'd already blown my cover?

"I wasn't looking at anybody," I mumbled. "I swear."

The principal gave me a funny look. "Captain Justice. Didn't you recognize him? He's front and center."

It took me another second to figure out what he was talking about. Then my vision snagged on the kid I'd first noticed. The blond boy, floating in the front row . . .

Captain Justice.

It was easy to see how he would grow up to become a world-famous superhero. Tall, good-looking, with a beaming smile. Even in the sixth grade, he was obviously the center of attention.

"Captain Justice has been very generous to this school over the years," said Principal Alabaster. "Of course, he's just one of *many* distinguished alumni from this class. There's also . . ." He squinted again. "Hmm, unfortunately, I can't see much without my glasses. Just one moment . . ."

Principal Alabaster reached out with one hand, pinching his forefinger and thumb together. His silver eyebrows furrowed with concentration.

Then he pulled his fingers apart.

What happened next is tough to describe. It was sort of like he . . . unzipped the universe. As his fingertips spread, a gash seemed to open in the air in front of him. Once his finger and thumb were as far apart as they would go, Alabaster turned his hand sideways and spread the two edges of the weird portal thingy the way you might open an envelope.

My jaw dropped. The opening was like a window into someplace completely different. Through the sliver, I could see a dark mahogany desk, a pile of books, a lamp. An office. Just floating there, smack in the middle of the hall.

Principal Alabaster did all this with remarkable ease. Like it was the most ordinary thing in the world. *No big deal—just slashing open a paranormal hole in space. I'll be with you in a sec.*

The principal reached into the portal, so that his arm was in one place and the rest of him was in another. He clicked on the lamp and fumbled around the desk until he found what he was looking for—a pair of eyeglasses.

He removed his arm and placed the glasses on his nose. He positioned both hands at the edges of the opening. When he brought his hands together, the portal vanished. The opening into his office was gone.

"As I was saying . . ." The principal blinked behind his glasses, examining the photo. "This was quite a remarkable class. A number of superheroes and supervillains who would go on to experience fame and infamy. The future U.S. Secretary of Mutant Affairs. A couple of—"

"Uh . . . Principal Alabaster," I interrupted. "How'd you do that?"

The principal tilted his head. "Do *what?*"

"Create an opening in space. Grab your glasses off your desk when you're nowhere near your office. That kind of thing."

"Ah yes. I can see how that might be a little perplexing to those unfamiliar with IGF."

"IGF?"

"Interspatial gateway fabrication. My power. If I focus my mind on a single location, I'm able to generate a 'door' "—he put the word in air quotes—"that opens directly onto that location. In other words, a 'shortcut' "—more air quotes— "from one place to another."

"Whoa." I tried to wrap my brain around what he'd just told me. "Can you step through the . . . uh . . . the door?"

Principal Alabaster nodded. "It definitely cuts down on travel time."

"That's incredible! You can go anywhere you want!"

"Not quite *anywhere*. The location must be anchored in my mind. IGF works only if I have a strong connection with the place. That means I can't just pop over to Tokyo for sushi unless I've spent a significant amount of time there. Which I haven't."

All of a sudden, an idea occurred to me.

"Would it be possible . . ." I hesitated. "I mean—would you let *me* go through the gateway?"

The principal stroked his silver beard, considering. "And where would you go?"

I gave this some thought. "How about . . . a pyramid in Egypt?"

"Never been there."

"A movie premiere? Red carpet?"

The principal shook his head.

"The Eiffel Tower?"

"Nope. However, I just thought of the perfect place. A location where I spent countless hours when I was your age."

"Where?"

"The rec room."

My shoulders drooped. This was a once-in-a-lifetime chance to skip through space, to get transported across the globe in the blink of an eye—and I was going . . . upstairs? I could *walk* there in about the same amount of time!

"I know it's not quite what you had in mind," the principal said, a note of apology in his voice. "But unfortunately, we can't have you zapping to the other end of the earth right before curfew."

My disappointment faded as soon as Alabaster created the portal—an opening in space that was just big enough for me to step through. Maybe it wasn't very far, but it was still pretty amazing. The rec room glowed on the other side of the portal. Students lounged in beanbag chairs, played video games, listened to headphones. And in the center of it all were Milton and Miranda, caught up in a game of Ping-Pong. It looked like Milton was losing, despite the fact that Miranda was blindfolded.

A dozen different conversations trickled through the opening. The entire room seemed oblivious.

I glanced sideways at Principal Alabaster and he gave me a reassuring smile. Taking a deep breath, I stepped forward. I wasn't sure what I expected. An electric shock? A sudden gravitational shift? But it turns out the feeling you get when you pass through an interspatial gateway is . . . nothing.

It feels just like walking through an open door.

Milton was the first to notice me. He was gearing up for a serve when his eyes flicked in my direction.

"BWAAAGH!" The paddle flew out of his hand and he tumbled butt-first onto the ground. He pointed up at me with a trembling finger. "You just—? But how—? Where'd you come from?"

Miranda pulled off her blindfold and gasped. On the other side of the table, Sophie was staring my way with surprise.

"Hey, guys." I picked Milton's paddle up off the floor. "Drop something?"

14

After a few days at Alabaster, I was starting to get used to the place. I'd even learned to tie a tie. Although I still hadn't mentioned that to Sophie. I admit, I sort of liked her tying it for me every morning.

On Thursday, Milton and I arrived at Introduction to High-Grade Weaponry just as the bell rang. Before we even reached our lab station, Dr. Fleming announced, "Please follow me, class. I have something extremely dangerous to show you."

Then he stepped out the door and into the hallway.

I glanced at Sophie and Miranda, wondering if they had any clue what was going on. They just shrugged. I joined the rest of the class and trailed Dr. Fleming through the empty hallway. When he reached a door marked NOT AN EXIT, he pushed it open and stepped inside.

"Didn't he say he has something *dangerous* to show us?" Sophie asked.

I nodded. "What do you think it is?"

"Another bomb?" Milton guessed.

"It's not that." Miranda squinted. "It's something else. Something with a . . . a really big nose."

"How is that dangerous?" Milton asked. "What's it gonna do? Sneeze on us?"

We followed the others through the door and into a twisting stairwell. Thirty pairs of stomping feet echoed in the cramped space as we rose higher and higher. After about twelve floors, we entered a room with walls made of glass. In the center of the room was the biggest lightbulb I'd ever seen. The thing was about twice my height. It rotated slowly, its beam directed through the glass walls so that it pierced the fog outside.

We were in the lighthouse tower. I'd seen it from the ferry on the day we arrived, though at the time it hadn't looked nearly so big.

"You may want to avert your eyes as the light passes by," Dr. Fleming warned us. "Otherwise you'll be seeing stars for the next week."

I took his advice. As the massive light swiveled in my direction, I turned the other way and let it pass over me.

"Right this way," Dr. Fleming said. Opening my eyes again, I saw him crossing the room toward a ladder. "Daisy's right up here."

I glanced at the others. "Daisy?"

Dr. Fleming was taking us to see something extremely dangerous . . . that had a really big nose . . . and was named Daisy.

Yeah, that made a lot of sense.

Dr. Fleming climbed the ladder and disappeared through a hatch in the ceiling. The rest of us followed one by one.

As I popped my head through the opening, I was slammed by a rush of wind. Bracing myself, I climbed the rest of the way. We were on the rooftop. My tie flapped in the wind. Beyond the school, the gray ocean stretched out on all sides.

It was the first time I'd been outside since we arrived. Dark clouds loomed overhead. A heavy mist clung to the rooftop. Far below, waves crashed against jagged rocks. Not the kind of weather that makes you want to go out and toss around a football.

SQUAWK!

I jumped at the hideous sound. Whirling, I saw something that sent my heart into my throat.

A metal bird the size of a fighter jet was descending on us.

Its enormous wings pounded the air as its silver webbed feet slapped down onto the rooftop just a few feet from where I was standing. I staggered backward, staring up at the thing. It looked like . . . like . . .

"A duck," Milton murmured, gaping up at the bird in wide-eyed amazement. "A humongous robotic duck."

He was right. The metallic bird was shiny green with matching wings that clicked into place at its sides as it came to rest on the rooftop. Between its glowing eyes was a huge silver bill that opened and closed on smooth hinges.

I glanced at Miranda. "So it has a huge nose, huh?"

"Nose, beak . . . ," Miranda said. "Same difference."

Dr. Fleming approached the robotic duck, speaking loudly to be heard above the wind. "Ladies and gentlemen, meet Daisy!"

15

"**G**ather round, class," Dr. Fleming said. "She won't bite . . . unless I command her to."

In one hand he was holding what looked like a black game controller. When Dr. Fleming punched a button on it, the massive bird opened its bill and let out a skull-rattling *QUACK!*

"People tend to forget what a magnificent creature the duck is," Dr. Fleming said over the rushing wind. "It is extremely versatile, able to go from land to air to water with complete ease. It takes flight to hunt insects and dives beneath the waves to eat fish. That's why I used the duck as a model for Daisy."

Dr. Fleming gazed admiringly at the giant robot.

"I took the duck's natural advantages and made a few modifications to design the ideal multifunctional airborne-aquatic-submergible machine. Daisy represents the top of the line in high-grade weaponry."

I was having trouble believing that Daisy was some kind of superweapon. If she'd been a giant robotic eagle or a hawk, then maybe I could see it. But a *duck*? Standing there on the rooftop, Daisy looked like a much bigger version of something you'd see paddling around a pond or begging for scraps of bread—not exactly the most threatening sight.

At least, that was what I thought *before* seeing Daisy in action.

Dr. Fleming fiddled with the controller. Suddenly, Daisy began to flap her massive wings. With another booming *QUACK!* she launched into the air. Daisy sliced through the sky with remarkable speed, maneuvering gracefully around the stone walls of Alabaster. Afterward, the duck glided out over the ocean and plunged into the water.

Just as I was starting to wonder whether she would ever come back up, Daisy popped above the waves, bobbing on the surface with a huge fish dangling from her bill. Gulping down the fish, the robot skimmed across the water like a motorboat before taking flight again. She was far out over the ocean when Dr. Fleming punched a button on the controller and a supersized egg dropped from the duck's metal tail feathers. The egg tumbled a hundred feet and exploded like the world's biggest grenade when it hit the water.

Okay, so maybe Daisy wasn't such a bad weapon after all.

DAISY

Daisy is capable of executing midair acrobatics, launching underwater attacks, and laying enormous exploding eggs. This is one duck that doesn't migrate when danger's around.

You'd think meeting a huge robotic duck would be the highlight of my day, but the excitement was just beginning.

That evening, Milton and I were on our way to dinner when we saw Sophie and Miranda waiting for us in the rec room.

"We need to talk," Miranda said.

"Now," Sophie added.

"What's going on?" I asked.

Sophie cast a glance across the room. Kids lounging around, watching TV or working on assignments for tomorrow. "Not here. Let's find someplace more private."

It wasn't so easy to find a spot where we wouldn't be overheard. We attempted to sneak Sophie and Miranda into our room, but it turned out Cassie wasn't kidding about the robotic hall monitors—they *really* weren't cool about girls in the boys' dorms. When Bob the RHM spotted us, the robot's eyes flashed red and it chased us down the hallway, shrieking, "FEMALE INTRUDER ALERT!"

"Okay, then," Miranda said, once we'd bolted from the boys' dorm. "Maybe we should try someplace else."

We headed up a spiral staircase to the third floor. On the way, we passed a purple rabbit hopping from one step to another. Milton bent down to pet it, then lurched away when the rabbit transformed into a teenage girl with purple hair.

"Back off, buddy," the girl said in an annoyed voice.

"Sorry!" Milton jogged the rest of the way up, taking the stairs two at a time.

At the top of the stairwell, we saw the tall wooden door marked ALUMNI HALL.

Sophie pulled the heavy door open and we all stepped inside. The Alumni Hall was empty. It looked like the kind of place to hold parties or dances: a vast room with high ceilings and dark mahogany walls lined with paintings of adults who must've been former students. Portraits of scientists, politicians, superheroes, and villains, all gazing down gloomily from their ornate frames.

"Hey, Sophie, there's your dad!" Milton pointed.

Sure enough, one of the largest paintings showed Captain Justice, muscular arms crossed. His shining blue cape perfectly matched his shining blue eyes. The superhero peered into the distance as if he'd just spotted a wounded puppy in need of rescuing.

Next to that was a painting of a gorgeous woman with fiery red hair and a golden one-piece uniform. Scarlett Flame.

Not surprisingly, Sophie insisted that we sit in a corner as far from the two portraits as possible.

"Okay, so what's going on?" I asked as we settled into four comfy leather chairs. "Why the secret meeting?"

"There's been another burglary." Sophie reached into her pocket and removed her phone. Handing it to me, she said, "Grifter and Lunk broke into a lab in Boston. They stole an Oscillating Particle Immobilizer."

I looked down at the phone. Sophie had pulled up the mobile website for *Super Scoop*. A headline filled the screen in big, bold letters:

BRAZEN BADDIES PULL OFF ANOTHER HEIST—
MOTIVE REMAINS A MYSTERY

Beneath the headline was a grainy security shot of the evil pixie teenager and her gigantic concrete friend.

A dark shadow rolled over my thoughts. I didn't need to read any more. I passed the phone to Milton and unzipped my backpack to remove a slip of paper. nFinity's list. I'd crossed off the first two stolen items. Now I pulled out a pen and drew a line through the most recent object to go missing.

~~PLATINUM-SEALED ALPHA CAPACITOR~~
~~NEUTRON FLOW REVERSAL CHAMBER~~
~~OSCILLATING PARTICLE IMMOBILIZER~~
THE DOMINION KEY

"There's only one left," I said.

"The Dominion Key." Miranda shivered, wrapping her arms around her shoulders. "And I know exactly where Grifter and Lunk are planning to steal it from."

Milton glanced up from the phone. "What? How?"

"When we were on the roof this morning with Daisy, I felt something—"

"Heavy winds?" Milton guessed. "Torrential rainfall? Fear of death?"

"Intuition," Miranda said. "Like a spark in my brain. At first, I wasn't sure what it meant. But then Sophie showed me the article from *Super Scoop* and it got stronger. I knew where I needed to look."

Miranda reached into her backpack and pulled out our textbook for Introduction to High-Grade Weaponry. She set it down on the table with a heavy *thud*.

"Okay, we get it," Milton said. "You're doing better in class than us. No need to brag about it."

Miranda ignored the comment. "Did you ever notice who *wrote* the book?"

I realized I hadn't. Not only that, I'd never noticed the author of any of my textbooks—*ever*. It wasn't the kind of thing that showed up on the test, so I never bothered to pay attention.

But now my eyes moved to the bottom of the thick book. And in a small font was a name.

DR. NIGEL FLEMING, PHD.

I pointed at the name. "*The* Dr. Fleming?"

Miranda nodded.

"The teacher of our first-period class?"

"Yep," Miranda said.

"The guy with the British accent and the gigantic duck?"

"That's the one."

It seemed strange that a teacher could assign his own book to his students. I guess if he was an expert, then why not? But the more important question was, "What does this have to do with the Dominion Key?"

Miranda flipped the book open to one of the last pages. "Take a look."

My eyes landed on a block of text in the middle of the page. With the steady rhythm of rain washing down the window outside, I began to read. . . .

ABOUT THE AUTHOR

NIGEL FLEMING received a PhD in Physics at the University of Cambridge and has since gained a reputation as one of the world's foremost experts in—

I skimmed the next couple of lines, stumbling over words like "experimental atomic fusion" and "particle beam neutralization." Looking up from the page, I said, "I'm sure this is fascinating for nerds like you. But I still don't get what this has to do with anything."

Sophie sighed. "Just read the last sentence."

Taking Sophie's advice, I skipped to the end.

Before taking a teaching position at the prestigious Alabaster Academy, Fleming became known for his work in developing the Dominion Key.

I gripped the edges of my chair. The sound of thunder rumbled in the distance, rattling the windows.

"Dr. Fleming created the Dominion Key," I said.

Miranda nodded. "And I have a hunch Phineas Vex is sending his goons here to steal it."

I glanced out the rain-smudged window as a blade of nerves twisted my insides. Miranda's hunches had a nasty habit of coming true.

16

"We have to find Dr. Fleming!" I stood from my chair. "We have to warn him!"

The four of us bolted out of Alumni Hall and down the stairs. Most of the school was at dinner and the hallways were nearly empty. On the second floor, we ran past the portrait of Herman Alabaster. His eyes seemed to follow us. His expression was grim, as if he already knew something bad was headed our way.

I remembered the last time I'd been this close to Herman Alabaster's painting. The shuffling in the stone walls. The rattling frame. But this was no time to think about ghosts. We had other things to worry about.

"Fleming might be in his classroom," Milton suggested.

"It's worth a shot," Sophie said.

But when we got there, the door to Fleming's classroom was locked. A sign on the door read:

DO NOT ENTER!!!
UNAUTHORIZED ACCESS TO THIS ROOM MAY RESULT IN:
-PROPERTY DAMAGE-
-INJURY-
-DISMEMBERMENT-
-DEATH-
-ALL OF THE ABOVE-

Milton gulped. "Maybe we should try somewhere else."

Peering through the slim window in the door, Miranda said, "He's not there anyway."

Over the sound of my friends' voices, I heard footsteps. I turned, hoping to see Dr. Fleming. Instead, Principal Alabaster was walking our way. He tugged at his bow tie, considering us with a kindly smile.

"Looking for someone?" he said.

"Do you know where we can find Dr. Fleming?" I asked.

"What's this about?"

I hesitated, trying to think of an explanation that *wouldn't* risk revealing our true identities or the real reason why we'd come to the school.

I was still struggling to come up with something when Milton spoke. "Extra credit," he blurted out. "Dr. Fleming assigned us extra credit and it's . . . uh . . . due tomorrow. We had a couple of questions. Do you know where he is?"

"You might want to check his office," the principal said. "It's on the fourth floor. Take a right at the top of the staircase. Past the hologram chamber. Through the tropical greenhouse. When you see a stuffed Siberian tiger, take a left. Or is it a *right*?" Principal Alabaster stroked his silver beard. "Now that I think about it, the tiger might not even be *Siberian*. Perhaps it's albino?"

"Uh, Principal Alabaster . . . ," Sophie began.

The principal's gray eyes flashed. "On second thought, I have another solution."

He brought his hands together, concentrating. And when he pulled them apart, a portal appeared. IGF—that was the name for his power to unzip the universe. *Interspatial gateway something-that-starts-with-F.* Fluctuation? Fabrication? It didn't matter at the moment. Because now there was a shimmering opening in front of us.

What I saw on the other side of the portal made me stagger back a step. A snarling white tiger with massive teeth and ultrasharp claws.

"Not to worry." Principal Alabaster reached through the portal and tapped the perfectly still tiger on its nose. "Like I said, it's a *stuffed* Siberian tiger. Or is it an albino?"

The principal was still puzzling over this when the four of us stepped cautiously through the IGF opening. Just like the last time, it felt like nothing at all. Like walking through a door.

"Say hello to Nigel for me!" Principal Alabaster cheerily called. He pulled his hands together and the portal closed.

And just like that—we were in the hallway, on the fourth floor, standing next to a huge stuffed tiger.

"That way!" Miranda pointed.

We followed her past a few other rooms before reaching

a door with Dr. Fleming's name on it. Miranda was about to knock when something made her pause.

An explosion.

The sudden boom came from inside the office, a rumble that shook the door.

"What was that?" Sophie turned my way. Worry strained her expression. A faint glow radiated at the edge of her eyes. "What if we're too late? What if Vex got to him first?"

She gasped when the door swung open. On the other side was Dr. Fleming. He didn't look hurt. Although he *was* covered in brown and purple globs of something that looked like . . .

Peanut butter and jelly?

Running a finger along his forehead, he wiped off a smudge of the gooey substance, then stuck his finger in his mouth. He seemed to notice us for the first time. "Ah, hello, kids. Glad you're here. Allow me to pose a question—"

"Actually," Miranda began, "we came to talk to you about something. Something important."

Dr. Fleming ignored her urgent tone. "What do you think of when you see a peanut butter and jelly sandwich?"

"Uh . . . lunch?" Milton said.

"Precisely! An innocuous meal to satisfy your cravings!"

"Dr. Fleming!" Miranda said in a louder voice. "We just heard something explode inside your office. What *was* that?"

"I'll show you," Dr. Fleming replied. "Come inside! Quickly!"

He spun around and rushed back into his office. The four of us stood at the edge of his door, trying to make sense of what we'd just witnessed. Finally, Milton shrugged and stumbled inside. Miranda, Sophie, and I followed.

Dr. Fleming's office would've been a mess even if it *weren't* covered in sticky globs of peanut butter and jelly. Bookshelves were overflowing. The floor was crammed with boxes of materials that looked highly dangerous. His desk was covered with discarded circuit boards, tangles of wire, and scraps of paper.

And on top of everything, a fresh layer of peanut butter and jelly. Yum.

Dr. Fleming grabbed a wet rag from a rusted sink and wiped down four chairs.

"Have a seat," he said.

I cautiously stepped over a crate that was filled with dynamite and PB&J. My friends and I settled into our chairs as Dr. Fleming began to explain.

"I wanted to devise an explosive apparatus that wouldn't raise suspicions. Something ordinary, plain, unthreatening. And what's more ordinary, plain, and unthreatening than a peanut butter and jelly sandwich?" He opened a drawer in his desk and removed a sealed plastic bag. Inside was a PB&J sandwich. "As you see, this object has the look, weight, and texture of a common sandwich. However, unsealing the plastic bag activates a timed detonation. It's much like a grenade. Except . . . well, much more delicious."

He scooped a glob of peanut butter off his elbow and

120

licked it. With a nod of approval, Dr. Fleming grabbed three more sandwich bags and handed one to each of us.

"Here. Take these. Try them out. Let me know what you think."

"Uh . . . thanks?" Sophie was holding the bag as far from her as possible.

"Not to worry. It's nonlethal. At worst, your victim will need a long shower and a fresh set of clothing. Nevertheless, it can be quite useful if you're in a jam." Dr. Fleming chuckled. "Get it? *Jam?*"

Nobody else laughed.

Cautiously placing the sandwich in my backpack, I said, "Dr. Fleming, there's something important we need to talk to you about." I lowered my voice. "The Dominion Key. We think someone's about to steal it."

All of a sudden, Dr. Fleming's carefree smile vanished. He turned in his chair and gazed toward the window. The storm outside had worsened. Rain pounded the glass. I wasn't sure if it was the gray light streaming through the window or the shift in his mood, but Dr. Fleming's face looked as pale as ice.

"What do you know about the Dominion Key?" he asked.

Taking a deep breath, I launched into the story. I was careful to avoid the part about my parents being the Dread Duo, how we'd arrived here in Captain Justice's reality-TV tour bus, and my friends and I being enrolled under fake identities . . . you know, minor details like that.

I carefully moved the sandwich in my backpack and pulled out the slip of paper that we'd gotten off nFinity.

Passing it across the desk I said, "We were hoping maybe you'd know what someone could do with all this stuff."

Dr. Fleming turned away from the window. When his eyes landed on the list, his expression became even more grave.

"Platinum-Sealed Alpha Capacitor, Neutron Flow Reversal Chamber, Oscillating Particle Immobilizer, the Dominion Key . . ." Dr. Fleming's eyes rose until he was staring right at me. "Anyone who brings together these items will be able to rule the earth."

17

All of a sudden, my school tie felt like a noose.

"Each of the items on your list is extremely rare," Dr. Fleming said. "On their own, they pose no threat. But when they're brought together, they create the most powerful weapon on earth."

"What kind of weapon?" Sophie asked.

Dr. Fleming glanced back to the window, at the pouring rain and flashes of lightning. "It's known simply as The Device. When triggered, The Device emits a potent wave of synthetic particulate matter that manipulates human tissue at the cellular level."

"Uh . . ." Milton's eyes looked liked they'd glazed over somewhere in the middle of the last sentence. "What exactly does that mean?"

"The Device brings people under its control," Miranda said. "It can—"

"Turn all of humanity into slaves," Dr. Fleming finished. "Brainless drones forced to do the bidding of a single master."

"Let me see if I've got this straight. This thing—this . . . Device—is possible if someone brings together these four items?" Sophie pointed at nFinity's list.

"I'm afraid so," Dr. Fleming replied.

"Which means there's only one thing standing between Phineas Vex and world domination."

"The Dominion Key," I whispered.

"I know you're into cool weapons and exploding sandwiches," Milton began, "but why would you build the Dominion Key if you knew it could cause so much mayhem?"

"When I learned of The Device, I knew if the Dominion Key fell into the wrong hands, it would spell the end of civilization as we know it. A disaster for humankind. And my invention was essential. The most important piece of the puzzle."

"Please tell me you destroyed it," Sophie said.

Dr. Fleming hunched forward, shaking his head slowly. "I knew I should have. And yet . . . it was my legacy. The product of a decade's research. Tireless work. The thing I shall be remembered for. I couldn't bring myself to destroy it. So instead, I hid it."

"Where?"

"Far from Alabaster. A place only I know about, where it'll be safe."

"It won't be safe for long." Miranda's tone was grave.

"And neither will you. Not if Phineas Vex and his henchmen come looking for you."

"There've been three robberies in the past three days," Sophie said. "Always at night."

I glanced toward the window. The last glimmer of gray light was fading outside.

"In that case, we don't have much time," I said. "We've gotta warn Principal Alabaster. If Grifter and Lunk show up, they'll tear this place apart."

"Very well," Dr. Fleming said. "But before we go, allow me to grab a few things."

He reached under his desk and pulled out a briefcase. With a sharp *click*, he unlatched the case. Then he turned it upside down. Folders and pens and student quizzes spilled out across his desk. I noticed my quiz near the top of the pile. *C–* was written in bold red ink at the top of the page. Maybe if we saved Dr. Fleming's life he'd raise it to a B.

Once his briefcase was empty, Dr. Fleming began filling it with other objects. Sticks of dynamite, time bombs, detonator switches.

The teacher glanced up at us. "Couldn't hurt to have a bit of protection, don't you think?"

When it was full, he lifted a magnet from the side of his filing cabinet. Underneath the magnet was a photograph. A picture of a log cabin surrounded by trees.

Milton pointed at the photo. "What kind of weapon is *that*?"

"It's not a weapon." Dr. Fleming slipped the photo into

his pocket. "Nevertheless, I wouldn't want it to fall into the wrong hands."

I still had no idea why a picture of a log cabin was such a huge deal, but right now we had bigger concerns. Like finding Principal Alabaster and securing the school. My friends and I stumbled back into the hallway. Fleming joined us a moment later.

"Any idea where we can find Principal Alabaster?" Sophie asked.

"His office would be a fair bet," said Dr. Fleming. "He's there most nights. It's on the third floor. Follow me."

We set off in the direction we'd come from. We were halfway to the stuffed tiger when a sound stopped us in our tracks.

CRAAASH!

At first, I assumed it was thunder. But a couple of seconds later, another explosion rang out. And this time, I was sure. It had come from *inside* the school.

"Please tell me that's another one of your experiments," Milton said to Dr. Fleming.

The teacher swallowed hard. "Afraid not."

I raced to the nearest window. It was tough to see anything through the storm. Rain fell in sheets. Wind howled past the stone walls. A burst of lightning exploded across the sky. Suddenly, a shape emerged from the darkness: a charcoal-gray boat tied to the dock, pitching up and down on the waves.

And it definitely wasn't the ferry.

Another blast rang out, even louder than the first two.

There were other noises too—shouts, the clatter of foot-steps, a strange rumble.

"Come on."

Dr. Fleming was already running in the direction of the stairway. My friends and I trailed him. As we hurried down the stairs, the rumbling grew louder and louder.

Milton paused. "What *is* that? Sounds almost like . . . like—"

"Motorcycles." Miranda gripped the banister even tighter, concentrating to focus her Gyft. "Lots of them. They're ransacking the school."

"You mean people *riding* motorcycles?"

"No. I mean—the people *are* the motorcycles."

"Huh?"

Miranda let out an exasperated sigh. "It's complicated. There's too much going on right now. Everything's fuzzy."

"I have a feeling we're going to find out soon enough," Dr. Fleming said. "Whether we want to or not."

He had a point. The sound of revving motorcycles was getting closer. We'd made it to the third-floor landing when a blur of silver appeared at the corner of my vision. Smoke. It quickly transformed into a human shape.

Cassie had joined our group.

Her ivory skin was splotched with red from crying. She looked at us, wide-eyed and worried.

"I'm so glad I found you!" Her words came out in a breathless tumble. "Those things. They're everywhere. At-tacking the school. They—they captured my dad."

"What things?" Sophie asked.

"I don't know. Some kind of monsters. Like nothing I've ever seen before." Cassie grabbed my wrist, her gray eyes wet with tears. "We have to help him!"

"We will." Even with the fear growing inside me, I tried to keep my voice steady and calm. "Tell us where we can find your dad."

"I'll take you there. I know a shortcut."

"You mean like one of your dad's portal thingies?"

"Different kind of shortcut. Come on."

Cassie led us down another stairwell, explosions echoing all around. I was still clueless about what was attacking us. *Motorcycles? Monsters?* I kept expecting to see them around every corner. But all I encountered were students and teachers racing in the other direction. One boy slid up the banister. The purple rabbit we'd seen earlier hopped frantically from one step to the next. This time Milton didn't try to pet her.

At the second floor, Cassie took off at a run. Her silver hair streamed behind her. She skidded to a halt in front of a huge framed painting.

The painting of Herman Alabaster.

But what did a haunted painting have to do with our shortcut?

18

Cassie's great-great-great-grandfather looked just as spooky as ever. His gray eyes followed me everywhere. His frown was buried behind a silver mustache.

"I'm not sure this is the best time to admire the artwork," Milton said.

Ignoring the comment, Cassie placed her hand on the golden nameplate at the bottom of the frame. With a sharp twist, she turned the nameplate upside down. Then she reached under the frame and—

Click!

The painting swung open on hidden hinges. Behind it was a dark tunnel. For a second, I was too stunned to move. The haunted painting was a . . . secret door?

Miranda looked from the tunnel to Dr. Fleming. "Did you know about this?"

The teacher shook his head. "It's news to me."

Cassie climbed onto the ledge of the tunnel and motioned for us to follow. "We've got to hurry!"

Once we were all inside, she pulled the painting closed behind her. As the frame clicked back in place, the last sliver of light vanished, engulfing us in absolute darkness. I felt blind—at least until Cassie flipped on a flashlight.

As the beam of light sliced through the black, tossing around our distorted shadows, I remembered what I'd been told about the ghost of Herman Alabaster. *People claim he lives in the walls. . . . You can sometimes hear him rattling around. . . . He emerges from his painting in the middle of the night to roam the hallways.*

"It's you." I stared at Cassie in amazement. "You're the one walking behind the walls and climbing out of the painting. You're the ghost of Herman Alabaster."

Cassie sighed. "It's true."

Miranda glanced deeper into the tunnel. It stretched a long way, fading into darkness. "What is this place?"

"I know it's not the shortcut you expected," Cassie said. "I'll explain on the way."

She started walking. The rest of us followed, footsteps echoing. The tunnel was just tall enough for us kids, but Dr. Fleming had to hunch to avoid hitting his head. We moved through the narrow space in a single-file line. Every so often, another path would branch off to the right or left, disappearing into the shadows.

Cassie began speaking. "Alabaster Academy was designed by my great-great-great-grandfather—"

"The dude in the painting," Milton said.

"Exactly. Back then, people with special powers weren't superheroes. They weren't celebrities. People saw them differently. As freaks, outcasts, weirdos. For centuries, they'd been put on trial, accused of witchcraft, burned at the stake. With this school, Herman Alabaster wanted to create a safe place for Gyfted kids. So he built this fortress on an island. And as extra security, he designed a network of secret tunnels inside the walls."

Cassie turned a corner. I got the feeling she was glad to have her story to tell. It was an excuse to take her mind off the trouble her dad was facing.

"Herman Alabaster kept these passageways secret," she said. "Only *he* knew they existed. The only people he ever told were his children. Eventually, they told *their* kids. It went on like that. The family secret. And when I was six, my dad took me here for the first time."

"What about the ghost?" Sophie asked.

"That was my grandfather's idea. By the time he was a student at Alabaster, people had been noticing strange noises behind the walls for years. Footsteps. Rattling picture frames. Students and teachers were becoming suspicious. He knew the family secret was at risk. So he came up with a story: the ghost of Herman Alabaster."

Cassie went quiet at the sound of an explosion. Everyone froze. We could hear screams on the other side of the wall, followed by revving engines and squealing tires. Cassie waited until the noise faded, then started walking again at an even faster pace.

"The crazy thing is—it worked." Her voice quivered, but

Cassie kept talking, as if that could make the horrors beyond the tunnel go away. "Any time there's a strange noise, people debate whether it's the ghost of Herman Alabaster. Which means they're *not* debating whether there's a secret tunnel."

"It's quite clever," said Dr. Fleming. "A story gives people something to believe. Even if it's a ghost story."

"My dad loves hanging out in these tunnels," Cassie said. "It's his way of escaping from the responsibilities of being principal. Like he's a kid again. One time, Veronica spotted him climbing out of a painting. He thought for sure the secret was over. But that night all she did was brag about how she'd seen the ghost of Herman Alabaster."

Cassie chuckled, but I didn't have any right to laugh. I'd made the same mistake. The night that I first encountered the painting. At least for a moment, I'd been sure that Principal Alabaster was the ghost of his relative.

"Here it is!"

Cassie aimed her flashlight at the wall, revealing a narrow door, which she pulled open. On the other side was a second door. This one was made of steel and shaped like the outline of a human body; head, shoulders, legs. I was still trying to make sense of the odd sight when Cassie nudged the body-shaped door open a half inch and peered outside.

"All clear," she said. "Let's go!"

We followed Cassie into the hall. Glancing back, I saw what the secret door looked like from the other side. A suit of armor. It was split down the side, so that the front opened like a refrigerator door and the back remained attached to the wall. Once we'd all stepped into the hall, Cassie pushed the door closed and twisted the hilt of the sword, locking it.

From where we were standing, I could hear the revving motors much louder than before. It sounded like a Harley convention was going on around the corner.

Our little group crept toward the classroom where all the noise was coming from. I leaned forward just enough to get a glimpse inside.

What I saw filled me with horror.

19

At the other end of the room, Principal Alabaster was hunched beneath a blackboard. He looked like he'd been on the losing end of a street fight. One eye was swollen shut. His forehead was slashed. Blood flowed into his silver beard.

He was surrounded by a dozen dudes on motorcycles. Each guy looked identical to the next: hulking muscles, shaved heads, stubble. They obviously had a thing for black, because that was the only color they were wearing. Black sunglasses, black leather jacket, black gloves. And yeah, their motorcycles were black too.

And one other thing: where their legs should've been, they had dark pipes that curved and blended into other parts of the engine. A spinning fan for a knee. Gleaming valves instead of thighs.

From the waist up, they looked human. Torso, arms, head. But from the waist *down* . . .

They were attached to their motorcycles.

Sophie yanked me back into the hallway. "Cyclaurs," she whispered. "Half cyborg, half motorcycle. Hundred percent deadly. Straight from the twisted mind of Phineas Vex. My dad fought a bunch of them a few months back. He was lucky to survive."

"What do we do?" Milton asked. "No way can we take those things on."

"We have to do something," Cassie pleaded. "Those monsters are holding my dad hostage!"

From inside the room, one of the Cyclaurs spoke. His voice was a mixture of human and machine sounds, a revving engine that had learned to talk.

"This is your final chance, Alabaster. Tell us where Fleming is."

"I—I told you already." The principal's voice came out weak and desperate. I could barely hear him over the motorcycles. "I don't know where he is."

"This is an insufficient answer."

A sharp crack sounded. Principal Alabaster howled in pain. Glancing into the room, I saw him clutching a bloody lip. Looming over him were two enormous Cyclaurs. One of them reared back. The motorcycle's front headlight glowed a piercing red and released a plasma beam that struck the chalkboard. The explosion sent chalk and stone fragments scattering across the room like shrapnel. When the smoke cleared, all that remained was a crater in the wall.

The Cyclaur's engine voice rattled my chest. *"Next time I aim for your head. Now tell us—where is Fleming?"*

Beside me, Cassie shivered with fear. "Please. We have to save him."

"Not to worry," Dr. Fleming said. "These Cyclaurs clearly have an affection for pyrotechnics. Let's show them what I have to offer."

Dr. Fleming opened his briefcase, bent over, and began fiddling with the contents. He lit the fuse on a stick of dynamite, turned the switch on a time bomb, set some detonators.

And then he stood, clutching explosives in both hands. He took a step into the doorway and cleared his throat.

"Well, hello. I heard someone was asking for me."

All twelve Cyclaurs turned. If it's possible for bionic motorcycle monsters to look surprised, they did. Dr. Fleming tossed his bombs into the room. One flew into the right corner, another slid to the left, and a third skidded straight down the middle.

Fleming's eyes moved from the explosives to Principal Alabaster. "Might be a good moment for a bit of IGF, wouldn't you say, Edwin?"

Principal Alabaster snapped into action. With the Cyclaurs distracted, he brought his hands together. When he pulled them apart, a shimmering portal appeared in front of him. He leaped through the opening just as the first bomb went off.

KA-BOOM!

I dove away from the door. A wave of heat and sound

surged past. For a moment, it felt like the world was ending. When the devastation was finally over, all that was left was a shrill ringing in my ears and a cloud of smoke that hung over everything.

I climbed to my feet and peered through the curtain of smoke and ash. The explosion had obliterated the classroom wall and turned the gang of Cyclaurs into a gruesome junk heap. Bionic body parts were scattered among twisted scraps of metal—half a tire, detached handlebars, an impaled engine.

At least my friends seemed to be okay. Sophie rose, her skin glowing from all the action. Milton and Miranda were wiping dust off their clothes. Dr. Fleming groaned as Cassie helped him up.

"You saved him." Her voice shook with emotion. "Thank you."

Dr. Fleming attempted a weak smile. "Happy to help."

Miranda tilted her head, concentrating. "More bad guys are on their way. We'd better take cover."

"I'm on it." Cassie hurriedly led us back to the suit of armor. She twisted the hilt of the sword and yanked the door open. All of us tumbled through it. Just as she pulled the door closed, I heard two sets of footsteps moving in our direction. One set was small and quick. The other sounded like a cement truck with legs. *BOOM! CRACK! FWUMP!*

Then I heard a familiar voice.

"What the heck happened here?" Grifter asked.

The last time I'd heard her voice, she and her evil friends had been attacking us in the food court. And if she was here, the massive footsteps must've belonged to her concrete pal. Sure enough, a moment later, Lunk spoke in his gravelly drawl.

"Looks like an explosion," he said.

"No duh, rock brains," Grifter spat. "Whoever caused it couldn't have gone far. Come on!"

The two took off running down the hall. Once the sounds had faded, Cassie flipped on her flashlight and turned to face me and my friends. "Okay, seriously? What's going on? Who were those jerks?"

"It's kind of a long story," Milton said.

"Go ahead." Cassie shrugged. "Unless you've got someplace you'd rather be."

An explosion echoed somewhere in the distance. I looked at Sophie, Milton, and Miranda. And in the span of a split second, we came to an unspoken agreement: now that we'd all shared a near-death experience, we might as well tell the truth.

I turned to Cassie and Dr. Fleming. "We're not who we say we are."

I started from the beginning, telling them about how my parents were actually the supervillain team the Dread Duo and Sophie's dad was Captain Justice. And about how Phineas Vex had once abducted my parents and tried to kill Sophie's dad. When I got to the part about being mysteriously recruited to join a superhero group, Cassie interrupted me in a voice that squeaked with excitement.

"You four were in the Alliance of the Impossible!"

"That's right!" Milton said, puffing out his chest proudly.

Cassie beamed at us like she was going to start asking for autographs any second. Dr. Fleming looked less impressed.

"Who—or *what*—was the Alliance of the Impossible?" he asked.

"A team of tween and teen superheroes!" Cassie explained like it was the most obvious thing in the world.

Dr. Fleming rolled his eyes. Not that Cassie noticed. She was too swept up in her enthusiasm.

"They were huge for like five minutes during the summer. Fought Multiplier and his clones in Times Square. Appeared in an episode of *Hangin' with Justice*."

Dr. Fleming only stared at her with a blank look.

Cassie let out an exasperated sigh. Her silver hair whipped around as she turned to face us. "Which one of you was Supersonic?"

Milton's eyes lit up. "That was me!"

Cassie jumped with such excitement that she nearly banged her head on the tunnel's low ceiling. *"OMG!* You were my *favorite!"*

"Really? Me?"

"Definitely! Those rocket shoes! And all the cool gadgets you kept in your utility belt! You were so much cooler than the Nameless Hero."

I should've felt offended to hear the Nameless Hero getting insulted right in front of me. But the weird thing was—I didn't care. My brief stint as a celebrity superhero now seemed like a bizarre dream, like it had all happened to someone else.

Meanwhile, Milton couldn't stop smiling. The whole time we'd been in the Alliance of the Impossible, the Nameless Hero had overshadowed Supersonic. Now it was the other way around. And he clearly liked it.

Sophie, on the other hand, looked offended on my behalf. "You *do* realize that the Nameless Hero is next to you, right?" She pointed at me.

"Oh!" Cassie's eyes widened. "Sorry!"

"No big deal," I said. "Really."

"It was just—the Nameless Hero always seemed so . . . overhyped."

I shrugged. "Can't disagree with you."

"You were, like, really famous for a little while. Then you disappeared." Her forehead wrinkled. "What happened?"

I told Cassie and Dr. Fleming about how nFinity betrayed us and Vex returned from the grave strapped into a ten-foot-tall bionic suit that made him virtually invincible.

"After that, we had to hang up our uniforms," I said. "We went back to our normal lives. And then—just a few days ago—nFinity and a couple of his goons came after us. We had to go into hiding."

"And so we adopted fake identities and came here," Sophie finished. "My dad thought this would be a safe place to hide. Obviously, he was wrong."

"But what are they doing here?" Cassie asked.

"They're here for me." With a heavy sigh, Dr. Fleming told Cassie about the Dominion Key.

"You said you hid the Dominion Key," Sophie pointed out. "So where is it?"

Dr. Fleming considered this question. "You kids told me your secret. The least I can do is return the courtesy."

He reached into his pocket and removed the photo he'd taken with him. The beam of Cassie's flashlight lit up the picture of a log cabin in the woods.

"When I realized the global threat posed by my invention, I resolved to keep it in a safe house. So I built one. All registered under a false name, of course. Completely untraceable." Dr. Fleming ran his thumb across the photo. "I know it may look a little backwoodsy, but on the inside, it's actually quite modern."

"You may think it's safe, but it's not," I said. "Phineas Vex won't stop until he's tracked it down."

"You have to destroy the Dominion Key," Miranda pleaded.

"I know." The flashlight cast deep shadows under Dr. Fleming's eyes, making him look tired and old. "And that's precisely what I intend to do. I just need to find a way to get to it."

"How're you gonna do that?" I asked. "The school is swarming with bad guys."

"And without the ferry, there's no way off this island," Milton pointed out.

All of a sudden, Dr. Fleming's eyes lit up.

"There *is* one other way off . . . ," he said.

When I heard this, it sparked a brief flicker of hope. Maybe we weren't doomed after all. But once Dr. Fleming told us what he had in mind, I felt even worse than before.

There was just one little problem with his plan. It was absolutely nuts.

20

We needed to get up to the roof.

Cassie led us along winding turns and through narrow gaps until she reached her destination: a steel hatch built into the wall. She silenced us with a finger to her lips and listened for Cyclaurs outside. Their engines were barely more than a distant buzz. It sounded like the coast was clear.

"Time to go," Cassie said.

"Thanks for all your help," I said. "We couldn't have made it this far without you. Hopefully, we'll see you again sometime."

I held out my hand for her to shake. Cassie looked down at it like I had string cheese for fingers.

"Save your goodbyes," she snapped. "I'm coming with you."

Now it was my turn to give her a weird look. "The bad

guys are after *us*. Not you. If you come along, you'll just put yourself in danger."

Cassie's determined expression only sharpened. "I've lived my entire life at Alabaster. Do you have any idea what it's like growing up in a school? Stuck on this little island where it never stops raining? Constantly getting teased by the other kids for having generations of principals in the family? Believe me, it gets old."

Cassie's gray eyes moved across the floor of the tunnel.

"With a dad who can transport his family anywhere he wants, you'd think I'd be a world traveler by now, but Dad says Alabaster Academy is a part of who I am. He thinks that if I just spend enough time here, I'll eventually want to follow in his footsteps. But all I've ever wanted was a chance to see the world outside Alabaster. No way I'm passing that up."

I still didn't think it was a good idea. But the sound of Cyclaurs was getting louder and we didn't have time for a debate.

"Fine," I said. "If you really want to skip school that badly."

A smile passed across Cassie's lips. She opened the hatch and cast a glance into the hallway. All clear. She pushed the hatch the rest of the way open and everyone climbed through. Then she closed the door—a framed painting of a silver-haired lady named Alberta Alabaster—and we hurried across the hall.

"The stairs are on the other side of the library." Cassie pointed to a tall wooden door. "This way."

The library had definitely seen better days. Books were strewn everywhere. Skid marks crisscrossed the floors. A wall had been reduced to a smoldering crater.

We'd nearly reached the other end of the library when the door flew open and one of our classmates stepped out.

Winston.

"Goin' somewhere?" He raised his furry eyebrows.

"Out of the way, Winston," Cassie said.

Winston smiled. His fangs glistened.

"I overheard those motorcycle guys sayin' we've got some imposters at Alabaster. Some newbies who showed up a few days ago, lyin' about who they really are." Winston's eyes narrowed as he scanned me and my friends. "And I got a feelin' they're talkin' about you."

"Maybe you're right," I bluffed. "Or maybe your conspiracy theory is just as lousy as your dodgeball skills."

"We'll see."

"Why don't you mind your own business?" Miranda said.

But Winston wasn't budging. He leaned against the doorframe, examining his nails as they slowly grew into claws.

"Teachers are always tellin' me I gotta think about my future." His words came out in something between a normal kid's voice and a growl. "I'm not really the college type. Not even sure I'm cut out for high school. But there's one thing I've always wanted to be when I grow up—"

"Dog food salesman?" Milton guessed.

"Supervillain." Hair was sprouting beneath Winston's

collar. He was becoming a wolf before our eyes. "And if I help out these motorcycle guys, their boss might see my . . . uh—whaddaya call it?—my . . ."

"Potential?" Dr. Fleming said.

"Exactly. My potential as a future supervillain."

"Now, listen here, Winston." Dr. Fleming marched forward. "I insist that you step aside right this—"

"RAAARGH!"

With the kind of quickness you usually only see on the Discovery Channel, Winston swung at Dr. Fleming. His claws ripped at the teacher's shoulder and straight down his chest. Dr. Fleming crumpled to the floor, blood spilling from his wounds.

Winston's mouth foamed—if you could even call it a mouth at this point. Hair sprang up across his face. His nose was elongating into a whiskered snout and his eyes had turned an eerie yellow. Leaping on top of Dr. Fleming, Winston raised his claws to strike again.

It had all happened so quickly. I was still stunned, watching the attack go down like it was a TV show. Milton reacted much more quickly. He surged forward and tackled Winston.

"Get away from him!" Milton screamed.

The two tumbled to the ground. By the time they'd separated, the transformation was complete. There was nothing human about Winston any longer. He'd gone into full wolf mode.

His clothes were lying in a torn heap on the floor. Gray hair stood up along his back. His long, slobbery tongue ran across a row of sharp fangs. With a horrible snarl, the wolf leaped into the air, claws and teeth poised to rip into Milton.

There was no time to think—only to react. Throwing out my hands, I felt a wave of energy ripple across my body. My heart shook. Electrical storms raged through my bloodstream. I flexed my fingers, and all my power channeled down my arms, through my hands . . .

And just like that, everything came to a stop.

Winston froze in midair, inches from Milton. A horror movie on pause.

And he wasn't the only thing stuck in place. Everyone around me was frozen. Dr. Fleming, clinging to his wounded chest. A glowing Sophie in mid-stride, joining the fight. Cassie and Miranda, screaming. All perfectly still.

Even I was unable to move. And yet I could feel the power working inside me, buzzing from my core to the tips of my fingers, where a light had begun to radiate. A shining orb of energy that stretched forward like an illuminated string.

The light snaked toward Winston. Memories flashed through my brain. This wasn't the first time my Gyft had gone haywire. Something like this had happened twice before. Once in Phineas Vex's lair, and again when I was forced to fight a GLOM, a gelatinous green replica of myself (don't ask). Both times had been the same. Time stopped. A string of light. The feeling that I no longer controlled my power, but that my power controlled me.

In other words, all the things I was going through right now.

The last time this happened, I ended up obliterating the GLOM. What if I did the same to Winston? I have to admit, after what he'd done to Dr. Fleming—and what he was about to do to Milton—I wasn't too worried about Winston one way or another. But Milton was right beneath him. Anything that harmed Winston would probably do the same to my best friend.

The light slithered outward, moments away from reaching Winston. Something had shifted in his yellow eyes. All the rage was gone. Now they were filled with fear. He must've been witnessing this too. And so was Milton. I could see recognition in his eyes. As if he could tell that he was moments away from being swallowed up by a glowing blast of pure destruction.

I did everything in my power to focus my mind, clamping down my concentration like a steel trap. Willing myself to stop the light. Every cell in my body straining. Wrestling to regain control.

But none of it worked.

And the light continued to drift.

Closer and closer.

I made one final desperate attempt to rein in my Gyft. And this time something happened. The slightest flicker. I doubled my focus. The effort was like doing a thousand mental push-ups. But it was actually working. The glowing string of energy faded. My fingertips trembled—barely noticeable, yet still a movement. I focused the last ounce of my willpower on pulling back the light, as if playing tug-of-war with my power.

At last, the glow winked away. My head was filled with a sudden rush of noise and motion. The world coming back to life. I didn't have much time to appreciate the moment. The effort of bringing my power back under my control had taken everything out of me. As soon as the world un-froze, I crumpled like a rag doll.

After that, it was lights-out.

21

I woke to see Milton looking down at me.

"Oh, good! You're alive!" He exhaled a relieved breath. "You had me worried there."

I tried to sit up, but the effort sent daggers through my brain. Dropping back to the floor, I blinked up at the ceiling.

"Where's Winston?" I asked in a cracked voice.

"He ran off like a scared puppy. Guess he was freaked out by your special-effects display."

Groaning, I rose to my elbows. The others were huddled close by. Sophie, Miranda, Cassie. And Dr. Fleming. He was staring at me with the strangest expression. Like he was seeing me in a totally different way.

Then he collapsed.

Winston's attack had taken its toll. A bloody gash ran

down Dr. Fleming's chest. His clothes were stained with blood. His face was pale.

Miranda jumped into action mode. "Quick," she said to Milton. "Take your shirt off. We'll use it as a bandage."

Once Milton was down to his T-shirt and khakis, Sophie ripped his button-down shirt into strips that Miranda wrapped around Dr. Fleming's chest. As she worked, the teacher's eyelids flickered and his voice came out in a pained croak.

"I'll never make it to the safe house in this condition," he said. "You'll have to go without me."

"But—"

Dr. Fleming spoke over her protest. "Someone needs to destroy the Dominion Key. It's our only hope. If we don't—"

He broke into a weak cough. But I didn't have any trouble finishing his sentence in my head. *If we don't destroy the Dominion Key, Vex will rule the world.*

We couldn't let that happen.

And so we came up with plan B. Cassie took hold of a brass lamp on the wall and pulled it down like a lever. A nearby bookcase swiveled sideways to reveal another entrance to the secret tunnel.

Helping Dr. Fleming into the tunnel, Sophie said, "You'll be safe in here."

The teacher settled against the stone wall. Cassie handed him the flashlight.

Dr. Fleming reached into his pocket and removed the photograph. His bloody thumbprint was smudged over the picture of the log cabin. With a pen that he pulled from his other pocket, he wrote on the back of the photo.

1 *Noname Rd.*
Bear Creek, MA

"Bear Creek is in western Massachusetts," Dr. Fleming explained. "A tiny little town. Sneeze while you're driving through and you'll miss it. At the edge of town, you'll find a dirt road that seems to go on forever without any sign of civilization. Tall trees and not much else. Just when you're sure the end of the earth is around the next turn, you see it—"

"The safe house," Miranda said.

"Precisely. The location is so remote, the state never bothered to give the road a name." Dr. Fleming pointed at the address. *Noname Rd.* "You could detonate five hundred pounds of heavy artillery in my backyard and nobody would notice. Believe me, I tried it out."

Dr. Fleming pressed the photo into my hand.

"You must find the safe house," he said. "Once Vex's henchmen have vacated the school grounds, I'll figure out another way off this island and meet you there."

"You sure about this?" I asked.

"I'm sure we need to prevent Vex from getting his hands on the Dominion Key. There is nothing more important right now."

Dr. Fleming fixed his gaze on me. And for the second

time, I saw that strange look in his eyes. Like he knew something about me that I didn't.

It lasted for only a second. At the sound of motorcycle engines approaching, he cast a nervous glance toward the library door.

"Now go," he said weakly. "There isn't much time."

"See you soon."

Cassie raised the brass lamp and the bookcase swiveled back into place. We rushed across the ransacked library and back into the hallway. Frightened students peered out at us from their hiding places as we ran toward the door marked NOT AN EXIT. Cassie pushed her way inside and the rest of us followed.

I raced up the stairs, two at a time. Higher and higher. Grasping for the handrails. Up more and more spiraling steps, until we reached our destination.

The lighthouse.

Outside, the storm raged in the darkness. Sheets of rain pounded the glass walls. Inside, the massive lightbulb swiveled slowly. I glanced away as its beam swung in my direction.

At the other end of the glass room, the others were already climbing the ladder to the roof. Cassie pushed the trapdoor open. Rain and wind swept through the opening. As she heaved herself through the hatch and onto the roof, I turned back toward the lighthouse door. I could've sworn I'd heard footsteps pattering up the stairwell.

"Joshua! You coming?" Milton was halfway through the

opening. His wet hair stuck to his forehead as rain fell all around him.

"Be right there!" I called back. "You guys just make sure everything's ready to go!"

Milton nodded and climbed the rest of the way through the hatch. I glanced toward the stairwell again. This time the sound was clear: feet pounding the stairs. I wasn't too excited about saying hi to whoever was approaching. But if we hoped to have any chance of escape, we couldn't risk being followed by the enemy.

I circled back the way I'd come. The banging from the stairwell was louder now. Like a jackhammer getting closer and closer. I reached for the door just as someone thrust it open from the other side.

And all of a sudden, I found myself face to face with Grifter.

"You?" Her features twisted with surprise.

I threw out my arms, spontaneous combustion surging through my veins. Grifter responded with a glance to her side. That was all it took for the telekinetic terror to rip the door off its hinges. The floating steel door swung my way. It would've knocked my head off if I hadn't ducked in the nick of time.

I staggered backward to avoid another swipe—and *another*—until my back was against the glass wall. I waited, every muscle on edge for the next attack. Instead, I heard Grifter's voice.

"Well, well." She walked through the doorway. "Definitely didn't expect to see you here. Our objective was to nab some guy named Fleming. But I doubt Vex is gonna mind if we take you back as well."

Lunk crashed into the room behind her. He was gripping a flamethrower. In his massive cement hands, the weapon looked like a toy. But that didn't make it any less deadly.

When he noticed me, Lunk's huge gray forehead crinkled with confusion. "What's he doin' here?"

"Must've thought he could hide from us on an island of Gyfted preppies," said Grifter. "Am I right?"

Keeping a careful eye on the door floating eerily beside me, I edged an inch closer to the ladder. If I could somehow make it through the trapdoor, maybe I could call my friends for reinforcements. But Grifter guessed what I had in mind. With a flick of her attention toward the trapdoor, she swung it shut and sealed it closed.

Turning her sharp gaze back on me, she said, "Ya know, Vex wasn't too pleased the last time we failed to capture you."

"He called me an oversized cement doofus," Lunk said.

"But once we bring back Nigel Fleming *and* Joshua Dread, he's gonna give us a major promotion. No more taking our orders from nFinity and breaking into science labs. Vex will make us his top lieutenants. We'll be at his side when he rules the world."

Grifter grinned faintly, as if she could already imagine her big promotion.

"So here's how it's gonna go down," she said. "You'll come with us. Tell us where to find Fleming and we won't hurt you too bad before handing you over to Vex. But if you even *think* about putting up a fight, my friend here will show you what third-degree burns feel like."

Lunk hefted his flamethrower in my direction.

My brain churned, but I could see only two options: make a run for the ladder and get burned to a crisp, or surrender to my deadliest enemies.

I wondered which was worse.

22

"**H**urry up, Dread," Grifter called. "We haven't got all day."

She was standing next to the slowly swiveling light. Beside her, Lunk held the flamethrower steady in his cement hands.

The trapdoor rattled. Milton's muffled voice called out, "Joshua, you there? What's going on? This thing's stuck!"

I glanced around the lighthouse, looking for anything I could use as a weapon. With a flamethrower pointed my way and the floating door waiting to bash my brains in, I found it tough to think clearly. Then my eyes landed on the pool of water that had gathered at the foot of the ladder. An idea sparked in my brain.

I turned both hands so that my palms were pressed against the glass. Gritting my teeth, I concentrated my power. Spontaneous combustion rippled through every inch of my body. And then—

CRAAASH!

I stepped away from the glass wall just as it broke into a thousand pieces. At first, it was just the panel behind me. But like dominoes, the other panels shattered one after the other in a circle around the room.

And all of a sudden, we had ourselves an open-air lighthouse.

"Raaarh!" Grifter pointed wildly at the floating door. I jumped aside as it swung my way. The door hurtled past me and vanished into the darkness.

The storm whipped in from all directions. Rain splashed my shoes, drenched my clothes. But I wasn't the only one exposed to the elements. A wave of wind and rain slammed against Lunk. And like in the food court, the water had an instantaneous effect on the concrete giant. His gray skin melted away. It pooled around his feet and washed over the sides of the lighthouse.

All that was left was a wimpy teenager in his boxer shorts.

His flamethrower clattered to the ground. I made a move for it, but Grifter was too quick. The flamethrower rose into the air like it was dangling from invisible string. In an instant, it was aimed right at me.

"That was a neat trick, Dread," Grifter spat. "But it's too little, too late."

She flexed her finger. Even though the flamethrower was five feet away, drifting in the air, the trigger pulled. Fire burst across the lighthouse. I dove sideways and slid across the wet floor.

The flames barely missed me. But I was sprawled on my stomach now, surrounded by shards of broken glass, unable to flee any farther. The flamethrower swiveled in the air, pointing straight at me.

In my peripheral vision I could see the massive light making its slow rotation.

Grifter grinned triumphantly. "I'm gonna enjoy watching you burn, Dread."

"Before you do, you might want to take a look at *that*." I pointed at the enormous light just as it swiveled toward her.

Confused, Grifter snapped her head sideways . . .

And found herself staring at a ten-foot-tall lightbulb.

Dr. Fleming's words from this morning flickered through my brain. *You may want to avert your eyes as the light passes by,* he'd warned. *Otherwise you'll be seeing stars for the next week.*

"Aaagh!"

Grifter clutched at her face like she'd just been splashed with acid. The flamethrower fell to the ground. Above me, I heard the trapdoor swing open. And when I looked up, I saw Milton staring down at me.

"Finally!" he said. "What took you so—"

His jaw dropped when he noticed the scene beneath him. The lighthouse had been transformed into a wind tunnel. Rain splashed over shattered glass. A flamethrower lay in a pool of water. One of our enemies clutched at her eyes and stumbled across the floor, mumbling, "Can't see, can't see." The other henchman had just shed about six hundred pounds of concrete. His bony knees trembled. He did his best to cover his boxer shorts with his hands.

"What'd I miss?" Milton asked.

"I'll explain on the roof."

I climbed the ladder and heaved myself through the trapdoor. On the roof, Sophie ran toward me. Her glowing skin was reflected in the water that splashed all around.

"What happened?" she yelled over the storm. "Milton said the trapdoor was stuck."

"Grifter and Lunk!" I hollered back. No need for further explanation. "But I took care of them. Is everything ready?"

"Just about."

Behind Sophie, Miranda was standing next to Daisy's cage. The metal door had been ripped open (thanks to Sophie) and Cassie was already inside, climbing up the back of the gigantic robotic duck.

This was all part of Dr. Fleming's plan. Back in the tunnel, he'd explained it to us. *Get to the roof of the lighthouse tower,* he'd instructed. *There's a control panel built into the back of the robot's neck.*

At the time, we'd all stared at him, thinking the same thing: *You want us to fly out of here on the back of a humongous robotic duck?*

And yet here we were.

Cassie pulled open the control panel and reached inside. Whatever she did, it must've worked. The metal bird suddenly snapped to life. The duck's eyes lit up with an orange glow and she ruffled its wings. With Cassie holding tight, Daisy stepped out of its cage.

"Climb aboard!" Cassie called. "There are places to secure your hands and feet."

I joined the others at the duck's side. Sophie climbed on, followed by Miranda and Milton.

I wiped the rain from my eyes and reached for Daisy's wing, finding a groove in the metal that made a perfect handhold. After clambering up the wing and onto the robot's back, I located slots for my hands and feet.

Daisy was big enough for each of us to take a spot. Cassie was close to the bird's neck. Miranda was beside me. Milton and Sophie were behind us, their feet lodged into grooves just above the duck's tail feathers.

Cassie guided Daisy to the edge of the roof. "Everyone ready?" she asked.

I looked down at the jagged rocks and tumbling waves far below. Beyond them, the ocean stretched in every direction. Rain blanketed the churning mass of dark water. Not the most welcoming thing to see just before taking Daisy for a ride. But we hadn't ventured to the rooftop for a view, and there was no chance of going back down.

It was now or never.

Cassie reached for the control panel in the duck's armor. She pressed a button that caused Daisy's wings to start flapping. The massive wings beat up and down with a steady *fwump-fwump*.

A burst of noise below us clawed at my attention. It was the sound of a plasma cannon firing. A section of the roof crumbled and a red beam shot through. When I glanced into the opening, fear knotted my stomach.

Three Cyclaurs were inside the lighthouse.

One of the monsters reared back, performing a wheelie. Its headlights glowed red and another blast of plasma rocketed upward. More of the roof fell away, missing us by less than a foot.

Perched on the roof, waiting for Daisy to take flight, we were a sitting duck. Literally.

"We've gotta get out of here!" I screamed over the sound of the storm and the blasting cannons.

"But Daisy's not ready yet!" Cassie screamed back. "I just need a little more time!"

"That's not an option!" Another explosion shook underneath us. A plasma beam whizzed past. "The whole roof's gonna collapse any second!"

Cassie's eyes were wide with fear. "Everybody hold on tight!"

She flicked the joystick and the duck shot forward. As the robot's long, webbed feet left the edge of the building, the rest of the roof collapsed. Daisy tumbled into the air in a chaos of flapping wings. For a moment, I was sure we were actually flying. But it turned out I was slightly mistaken.

We were falling.

Daisy let out a long electronic *QUAAACK!* and gravity yanked us downward with a lurch. Wind and rain slammed my face. I gripped the handholds with all my strength. The rocky shore rushed closer and closer.

I clenched my eyes shut, bracing for the impact. Instead, I felt a forward rush. When I opened my eyes, I saw the ocean streaking beneath us.

We'd taken flight.

Cassie pulled back on the joystick and Daisy soared upward. I felt a surge of immense relief that lasted a total of two seconds before I realized we hadn't escaped danger just yet.

A detonation sounded somewhere behind us and a red plasma beam streaked past, grazing Daisy's wing. Sparks exploded. Everything shook. The robot spun out of control and the world became a blur of motion and screams.

In a flash, I saw Miranda lose her grip. She slid across the bird's wet metallic side, straining for something to grab on to. Holding on with one hand, I thrust out my other. For a split second, I grasped her hand. But the robot jolted sideways.

Miranda's fingers slipped through mine.

She fell away.

Panic shot through every cell of my body. Miranda tumbled downward. In the next moment, she was gone.

23

As soon as Cassie regained control, she guided Daisy close to the water where we'd seen Miranda fall. We scanned the tumble of dark waves, searching for our friend, but there was no sign of her.

The storm raged around us. Plasma beams shot from the lighthouse tower, where the Cyclaurs were treating us like target practice.

"We've gotta get out of here!" Cassie screamed after a blast of plasma barely missed us. "If Daisy takes one more hit, we're all going down!"

I knew she was right. But that didn't make it any easier to leave Miranda behind. As we veered away from Alabaster, I looked back across the vast ocean.

Miranda was nowhere to be seen.

We flew for a long time in silence. Nobody was willing to say what was going through our heads. Miranda was gone.

I held tight to Daisy's back, wind and rain hitting my face as the ocean rushed past beneath us. Memories kept flashing through my mind. Miranda falling. Her fingers slipping out of my grip.

We flew on, the rain mixing with tears on my cheeks.

As we neared the shore, the rain fizzled into fog. Soon enough, all signs of the storm had vanished. Overhead the moon shone pale and silver at the edges of clouds. Below us were the shimmering lights of cars and buildings. Cassie guided Daisy higher so that people on the ground wouldn't wonder why a humongous metal duck was soaring overhead with four kids hanging on to its back.

I tried to call my parents, but my phone refused to work. Like everything else, it was soaked from the storm. The others tried their phones with the same result. Nothing.

"We need a place to land this thing." Cassie glanced nervously at Daisy's wing. The tip had been blasted away, leaving a charred section of twisted metal. "The damage could've been a lot worse, considering. But flying with a damaged wing takes extra power, and the batteries are nearly drained."

"So no chance Daisy will last till Bear Creek?" I asked.

Cassie shook her head, looking at the control panel. "We're lucky we even made it to shore. I'd say we have another hour of battery life. At the most."

"Anyone know a place where we can recharge a giant robotic duck?" Milton asked.

Nobody answered. We were too far from Sheepsdale to make it home. Turning around and heading back to Alabaster wasn't an option either.

Just as I was starting to lose hope entirely, Sophie spoke up.

"I might know a place."

❦

Following Sophie's directions, Cassie navigated the duck to an isolated farmhouse at the end of a long dirt road. Judging by the condition Daisy was in, we'd arrived just in time. The robot's glowing eyes flickered. It wheezed one last *Quaaa-ack* before its eyes turned dark and its wings stopped flapping. We crash-landed in a field, taking out a few rows of zucchini in the process.

Milton climbed to his feet, pulling a chunk of vegetation out of his hair. "Where exactly are we?"

"I know the people who live here," Sophie said. "Family friends."

Somewhere behind us, a twig cracked. I whirled around to see two men emerge from the darkness. Their faces were hidden in shadows, but I could plainly make out a rifle in one of the men's hands.

Beside me, Cassie gulped. "They don't *look* like friends."

The two men stepped closer. In the moonlight, I caught a glimpse of their faces. The first thing I noticed was that they were . . . old. They must've been in their seventies or eighties. The shorter of the two was bald, with a pair of wire-frame spectacles perched on the end of his nose. The other had a full head of wavy, white hair. They both looked weirdly familiar, although I had no idea why.

The taller of the two raised his rifle. "Is there a reason why you kids are trespassing on private property?"

"Or why your pet chicken just destroyed half our crop?" said the other.

"Actually, it's a duck," Milton clarified.

He went quiet when the taller guy cocked his gun.

Sophie took a step toward the men, her hands raised high in the air. "Marvin, Gus—it's me. Sophie. These are my friends."

When they heard Sophie's name, the men's attitudes immediately changed. The tall one lowered his rifle. The other guy adjusted his glasses and peered at her in utter disbelief.

"Sophie?" said the guy with the gun. His tone had gone from Cranky Old Man to Concerned Grandpa in no time flat. "What're you doing here? You're soaking wet. Is everything okay?"

"Actually, we could use some help," Sophie said.

The two men nodded. "Of course, of course," said the taller one.

"Let's get you into something dry," said the other. His eyes flashed back to Daisy. "You're welcome in the house, but the chicken stays outside."

We trudged across the wet soil, between rows of vegetables. Along the way, Sophie told the men how we'd ended up there and explained that we needed to get to

Bear Creek as soon as possible. I was still clueless about who these guys were and why they looked so familiar, but with Sophie in the middle of her story and one of the men still gripping his rifle, I figured it wasn't the best time to interrupt.

We piled our muddy shoes and wet socks on the front doorstep and followed the men into the farmhouse. When I reached the doorway, I froze. The living room was a serious case of sensory overload. On the walls were framed photos, paintings, taxidermied fish, clocks, collector's edition spoons, and about a million other things. An unruly mob of knickknacks crowded on the mantel. Eight different rugs overlapped across the hardwood floor.

Once I stepped into the room, though, certain things began to stand out. A faded poster showing a superhero and his sidekick in old-fashioned uniforms. Black-and-white pictures of the same heroic duo shaking hands with long-ago presidents and foreign dignitaries. A framed issue of *Super Scoop* that looked like it had been on the newsstands around the time that dinosaurs went extinct.

Milton's wide-eyed gaze moved from the figures on the magazine to the two men standing in front of us. "The people on the cover," he breathed. "They're you! I mean, you're them! I mean . . . you two are . . ."

"Mr. Marvelous and Whiz Kid!" Cassie finished, sounding just as amazed.

That was why they looked so familiar! Mr. Marvelous was the original celebrity superhero. He'd become famous for flying around the world, fighting evil, punching dictators. He was joined everywhere by his trusty sidekick, Whiz Kid.

Of course, that was a very long time ago. Nowadays, you only saw Mr. Marvelous and Whiz Kid in vintage comic books and old newsreel footage. To be honest, I'd forgotten they were still around.

And yet here they were. The guy with the white hair who'd pulled a gun on us—he was obviously Mr. Marvelous. He'd put on about fifty pounds—and fifty *years*—since his heyday. But there was no mistaking his wavy hair and square jaw. The smaller man with glasses was Whiz Kid. Although now, Whiz *Geezer* was more appropriate. Or maybe Whiz Senior Citizen.

"I can't believe I'm standing in the same living room as Mr. Marvelous and Whiz Kid!" Milton gushed. "Just wait till I tell my grandmother! She used to have such a crush on you guys!"

"That's very nice to hear." Mr. Marvelous chuckled. "Although we retired a few years ago—"

"More like a few decades," Whiz Kid cut in.

"These days, we go by our real names. You can call me Marvin."

"And I'm Gus," said his former sidekick.

Cassie turned to Sophie. "Where do *you* come into all this?"

"Remember what I said about my dad being Captain Justice?" Sophie asked.

"Uh . . . yeah." Cassie shot Sophie a *no duh* look. "Not the kind of thing you forget."

169

It's been a few decades since Mr. Marvelous and Whiz Kid were the most famous superheroes on the planet. Nowadays, they're better known as Marvin and Gus. But these two retirees can still kick some supervillainous butt when duty calls.

"Well, when my dad was just starting his career, he appeared at the Superhero Spirit Awards with Mr. Marvelous and Whiz Kid."

"He won Newcomer of the Year," said Marvin.

"And we were there to receive the Lifetime Achievement Award," Gus added.

"We got to know each other over the years," Marvin said. "Captain Justice was on his way in, we were on our way out. He was looking for guidance, advice—"

"He was looking for mentors," Gus said.

"And we knew from the moment we first met him that Captain Justice was the future of superheroism. A new generation. We wanted to pass the mantle."

"Plus he had much cooler gadgets." Gus's eyes crinkled behind his glasses as he smiled. "And when Sophie was born, Justice asked us to be her godfathers."

"Once we left the superhero business, we moved out to this farm, looking for a little privacy after fifty years in the public eye," Marvin said. "I guess you could say we don't save the world too often anymore."

"It's hard enough finding the car keys when we want to go grocery shopping," Gus said.

"But it's always a highlight whenever our goddaughter comes to visit." Marvin patted Sophie on her shoulder, raising one eyebrow. "Even if those visits usually come with a little more advance notice."

"Sorry to show up so unexpectedly," Sophie said. "We didn't know where else to go."

"You can drop in on us anytime." Gus laughed at his own joke. "Now let's find you kids some dry clothes."

Sophie had a few spare outfits at the house that she and Cassie could wear. And Gus let Milton and me borrow some of his old T-shirts and shorts. His clothes were a couple of sizes too large, and my T-shirt read SUPER SENIORS CARIBBEAN CRUISE. At least they were dry.

Cassie called her dad on the landline to let him know she was okay but that Miranda had gone missing just beyond the island shore. Her distressed voice mingled with the background noise of our soaked clothes tumbling in the dryer.

The rest of us settled around the living room. Gus handed each of us a bowl of steaming soup. I burned my tongue while eating it but was so hungry I hardly noticed.

Marvin and Gus tried to lighten the mood by showing off some of the gadgets they'd once used.

"Today's superheroes act like big shots with all their fancy devices," Gus said, "but in our day, we had some impressive technology too. Like my patented Whiz-Watch."

Gus rolled up his sleeve to show off the biggest watch I'd ever seen.

"This watch comes equipped with all kinds of tools that a superhero might need," he went on. "There's a compass, a calculator, a thermometer, glow-in-the-dark functionality, and a tape recorder—*all* built into a single watch!"

Gus's proud grin faded a little when Milton pointed out that his Captain Justice–themed watch could do all those things too.

"And I got it for free after buying ten boxes of Frosted Fuel Flakes!" Milton added.

While Gus grumbled, Marvin picked a clunky aluminum cylinder up off the coffee table.

"Well, you won't be getting *this* with any boxes of cereal." Marvin clasped the bulky device around his forearm like a cast. "The one-of-a-kind, patented Marvelous-Grab. Still comes in handy around the house. Like when I realize I left my tea on the counter and don't feel like getting out of my chair."

Raising the arm that was shrouded in the Marvelous-Grab, Marvin pressed a big red button. The gadget let out a metallic *splink*, a rusty *groooan*, a sharp *ping*, and then . . . nothing happened.

"Darn thing gets jammed sometimes."

Marvin banged on the device a few times with the palm of his hand. The third time he clobbered it, the Marvelous-Grab burst open and a metallic claw on an extendable spring shot across the room. It missed his tea mug by about ten feet, and instead knocked a stuffed fish off the wall.

"Well, you get the idea," Marvin muttered, once the claw zoomed back into the Marvelous-Grab.

When Cassie was through talking to her dad, I got up to call my parents. But before I reached the phone, lights flickered in the darkness outside the windows. We were out in the middle of nowhere—no other houses or paved roads for miles. As the lights grew nearer, fear gripped my chest and I heard the familiar rumble of motorcycles getting louder.

"Uh, guys . . ." My voice shook. "We've got company."

24

For a second, nobody moved. Then the realization hit the living room like a bomb.

The Cyclaurs were headed our way.

Everyone snapped into motion.

"Come with me." Marvin tossed the Marvelous-Grab to the ground and rose from his chair. "We can go out the back door."

"Then what?" Sophie asked. "We can't outrun those guys."

Marvin answered without slowing down. "I know a way to get you kids out of here."

We were nearly to the back door when Milton called out, "What about our shoes?"

"I'll get them." Gus turned and raced across the house at a speed that seemed impossible for a guy his age—or *any* age. He shot to the front door like a bolt of lightning.

Seeing him move like that brought back to mind a news story I'd seen a few years ago, a tribute to Mr. Marvelous and his sidekick, who got the name Whiz Kid because of his power to whiz from point A to point B at remarkable speeds. Of course, halfway through the show, my parents made me turn it off. "You know we don't allow this kind of thing in our house!" Mom had snapped. Grabbing the remote, Dad had shut the TV off, saying something about how "good guys are a bad influence." After that, I'd forgotten about Whiz Kid and his superspeed.

Until now.

By the time we reached the back door, Gus came rocketing across the room, a pile of shoes bundled in his arms. While my friends and I laced up, Gus leaned forward with his hands on his knees, red-faced and wheezing as he caught his breath.

"Been a long time since I moved like that," he said.

Out the door, we hurried through the darkness until reaching a barn. The entire structure looked tilted and ramshackle. Clumps of weeds grew out of the storm drain, and paint peeled from the walls. It made me wonder what was hidden inside and whether it would really do us any good in our escape.

"Just need to find the key," Marvin muttered, jangling through keys of all different sizes and shapes. "It's gotta be one of these."

"Need some extra light?" Sophie held out one glowing hand.

In the background, the roar of Cyclaurs was getting louder and louder. Marvin's trembling fingers flicked through the keys as he shook his head in frustration.

"Ah, forget it," he said finally. He shoved the keys into his pocket and grabbed the door. With a single pull of the handle, the lock burst apart and the door flew off its hinges, landing about fifteen feet behind us.

All I could see was darkness. The growl of motorcycles sounded like it was coming from right behind us.

"Time's running out," Gus said. "Everyone inside."

I trailed the others into the barn, Sophie's glow lighting the way. Along the walls of the barn, tables and workbenches were covered in tools and equipment. But it was the center of the space that caught my attention. In front of us was a car. And not just any car either. It was . . .

"The MarvelousMobile!" Milton exclaimed. "I can't believe it still exists!"

Neither could I. The car looked like something that should've been in a museum. It had a long front end, with bulky, rusted fenders and M-shaped headlights. A jet turbine bulged from the rear, with two enormous tail fins on either side of it. The entire thing had been painted red, white, and blue.

The MarvelousMobile was the car that Mr. Marvelous and Whiz Kid had used to save the world too many times to count. Of course, that had been many, many years ago.

"Does this thing even *work* anymore?" Cassie stared skeptically at the old-fashioned car.

"Of course!" Marvin said in a defensive tone.

"Except when it breaks down," Gus added. "Which is pretty often."

"Don't listen to him. I've spent the last decade fixing up the MarvelousMobile. Replacing the engine, retooling the jet boosters. This beauty's as good as new." Marvin gave the rear bumper an affectionate pat. The rear bumper groaned and fell onto the floor in a heap of metal. "Well, *almost* new."

I was having some serious doubts about our getaway. But with the sound of the Cyclaurs getting louder with each passing second, we didn't really have a lot of other options.

Reaching under the car, Marvin removed a key and unlocked the driver's-side door. "There's only room for four. You kids will have to go on without us."

"What do you mean?" I asked. "We can't leave you here."

"We'll be fine," Gus said.

Marvin cast a glance toward the approaching headlights. His jaw flexed and his eyes narrowed with certainty. "I can't wait to make those young whippersnappers pay for trespassing on private property."

Maybe it was the dim light of the barn or the knowledge that they already had a few decades of experience fighting bad guys under their belt, but at that moment, the two men looked a whole lot like the superheroes on the vintage posters and in the black-and-white photos.

"Uh . . . if you aren't coming, then who's gonna drive?" Milton looked questioningly at Marvin and Gus. "I don't know how it was when you guys were kids, but today, they don't hand out driver's licenses to twelve-year-olds."

"I can drive." Sophie slid into the seat. When she saw the surprised looks the rest of us were giving her, she shrugged. "Marvin and Gus used to bring me along on rides. And sometimes they let me take the wheel."

"Use these." Gus handed her a pair of wooden blocks that he'd grabbed off a workbench. "They'll help you reach the pedals."

This didn't exactly fill me with confidence, but right now we had bigger worries. Milton and Cassie climbed into the cramped backseat, while I got in the passenger seat. Sophie turned the key and the engine burbled, letting out a series of groans and clanks. When the engine refused to start, Sophie pressed down on the block, pumping the gas pedal as she turned the key again. Still no luck.

I couldn't believe it, but I was actually starting to miss Daisy.

Sophie took a deep breath. The illumination coming off her skin filled the interior of the car with light. Closing her eyes, she whispered, "Please, please, please," and gave the key another turn.

25

The engine roared to life. I wanted to cheer. At least until I remembered we were seconds away from being surrounded by Cyclaurs.

"Thank you so much!" Sophie said. "We'll call you once our lives aren't in danger anymore."

Shifting the MarvelousMobile into reverse, she pulled out of the barn. As soon as we were outside, the windows flashed with the headlights of Cyclaurs roaring in our direction. Sophie jammed the stick shift and we shot forward.

I caught a glimpse of Marvin grabbing an anvil and heaving it at one of the Cyclaurs. The anvil smashed into the robot, ripping its bionic top off the motorcycle. The other Cyclaurs must've realized these old dudes were a lot tougher than they looked, and skidded to follow us instead.

Tires kicked up a wave of dirt. Headlights flashed and bounced across a wilderness of trees and tall grass. Sophie spun the wheel and we hit a bump that sent the Marvelous-Mobile airborne.

We landed hard on a dirt road. Cyclaurs were all around us. One pulled steady with the passenger window. His bald head glistened in the moonlight. His dark eyes glared down at me. With a swing of his fist, he smashed the window. He looked like he was about to do the same to my skull when Sophie swerved the car to the side, slamming him into a tangle of bushes.

But there were plenty more. Behind us, a Cyclaur ripped one of the tail fins loose. The scream of their engines echoed in my brain.

"Let's see how well those guys follow us with a smoke screen blocking their vision," Sophie said.

She hit a button on the dashboard. I turned in my seat, expecting to see the air behind us fill with smoke. Instead, a tiny cloud puffed out of the car's backside and immediately vanished in the wind.

Milton groaned. "That was disappointing."

"Marvin must've forgotten to refill the smoke-screen formula," Sophie said through gritted teeth. "Looks like we'll have to go with the backup plan—*oil slick*."

She pushed another button. I guess slippery oil was supposed to shoot out from the car's rear, but all that happened was the windshield wipers started flapping back and forth.

"Stupid car!" Sophie banged her palm against the steering wheel. The impact must've triggered something, because there was a loud *FWOOOSH!* All of a sudden, the MarvelousMobile blasted forward like someone had just hit the fast-forward button. As I gripped the edges of my seat, my eyes flashed to the rearview mirror.

A flame was streaking from the turbine engine. Sophie had turned on the jet boosters.

We left the Cyclaurs in our dust. That was the good news. The bad news was we were rocketing down a dark dirt road at about three hundred miles an hour, being driven by someone who could barely see above the steering wheel.

"WAAAHH!" Milton and Cassie screamed from the back-seat.

A jumble of shapes blurred in the windshield, appearing and disappearing in the shaky headlights. The frame of the ancient car trembled.

Cassie called out, "Watch out for the—*OOF!*" She winced when we hit a massive bump. "Too late."

I pointed at a dark form that had appeared in front of us. "Tree, tree, tree!"

Sophie swerved just in time to avoid slamming into the tree. But this set her on course to collide with a—

"Ditch, ditch, ditch!"

Sophie spun the wheel in the other direction and managed to straighten the vehicle out on the dirt road again.

"Gotta turn off the jet boosters!" she hollered over the roaring engines.

"How?" I yelled back.

"There has to be a button."

"Yeah, but—which one?"

Sophie jolted the steering wheel and a twisted log shot

past my shattered window, missing us by an inch. "I can't keep this going much longer! Just try anything!"

I flipped a switch in the center of the dashboard. Suddenly, the roof launched into the air.

Great. I'd just turned the MarvelousMobile into a convertible.

With the wind howling all around us, I hit a different button. This one turned on the radio, which was blaring an old-timey bluegrass song.

"I'll never find the right one!" I screamed.

Then my eyes landed on the steering wheel. I leaned over and pounded the same spot that Sophie had hit before. And it actually worked! The jet engines spluttered out and the vehicle lurched to a more manageable speed.

Sophie breathed a sigh of relief. Spinning in my seat, I gazed through the back window. No sign of headlights. Only darkness.

"The jet booster gave us a jump on the Cyclaurs," Cassie said.

"Even if it *did* nearly get us killed," Sophie added.

Milton leaned forward, patting Sophie on the shoulder. "Nice driving skills. I'm calling you next time I need a ride."

A few minutes later, the dirt road became a paved one that led to the highway. There were hardly any other cars at such a late hour. And in the middle of the night, the MarvelousMobile blended into the darkness well. Which was probably a good thing, since a sixty-year-old superhero car with a twelve-year-old behind the wheel might draw some unwanted attention.

"Now we just need to figure out how to get to Bear Creek," Cassie said.

Milton leaned forward from the backseat. "I'm guessing this thing doesn't come equipped with GPS."

Keeping one hand on the wheel, Sophie pointed with the other. "Check the glove compartment."

I undid the latch and the glove compartment swung open. The inside was crammed: Cape repair kit. Bottle of zombie-bite antibiotics that had expired in 1982. Pair of reading glasses. The usual stuff you expect to find in the glove compartment of a car owned by two elderly super-heroes.

Near the back, I located a Massachusetts state map. The thing looked like it had been printed sometime before my parents were born. The brittle paper cracked at the edges as I unfolded it. Once it was spread out in front of me, the map took up the entire passenger side.

"Okay . . . now what?"

In the dim interior light of the MarvelousMobile, my eyes searched the map. Squiggly lines in all different colors. Clusters of city names and random numbers. For all I could tell, it might've been a map of the moon.

The stiff paper crinkled in my hand. "Anyone know how to use one of these?"

Sophie shook her head.

"I only use Google Maps," Milton said from the backseat.

"Same here," Cassie said.

We could face down motorcycle monsters and super-powered henchmen, but apparently reading an old-fashioned map was too much.

I squinted at the enormous page, turning it one way, then the other. How did anyone ever find what they were looking for with these things? You can't zoom in or enter the address. It won't tell you what direction you're going in.

"Dr. Fleming mentioned that Bear Creek's in western Massachusetts," Sophie said, not taking her eyes off the road.

"That's right," Cassie said. "And it's a really small town. So I bet the name is written in really small font."

I could work with that. Focusing on the left side of the state, I ignored any cities that were printed in bold letters, instead searching the names of towns that were written in such faint, faded letters that I could barely read them. It took a while, but eventually I found it.

Bear Creek.

"Looks like the town's close to a highway." I carefully ran my finger along the red line that was thicker than all the other lines around it until I spotted a number. "Highway Ninety."

"That's the highway we're on!" At the next sign, Sophie pointed. And sure enough, 90w was reflected in the MarvelousMobile's headlights.

"That means we're going west," Milton said.

We were on our way to Bear Creek.

ᛋ

After an hour of driving, Milton had conked out in the backseat. Beside him, Cassie was asleep with her head on his shoulder.

I was exhausted too, but every time I closed my eyes, I saw Miranda. Her face slick with rain. Her hand reaching out. Her fingers slipping through mine. Her mouth open in a silent scream as she fell.

I opened my eyes, trying to shake away the memory.

"You okay?" Sophie asked. Even though her eyes were focused on the road, it felt like she was looking right at me.

I didn't answer her question for a long time, just stared at the highway that stretched into the darkness. Finally I spoke in a voice that was barely loud enough to be heard over the howling wind.

"I could've saved her."

Sophie gripped the steering wheel tighter. "You can't blame yourself. You did everything you could."

I shook my head. "If I'd held on just a little tighter, she wouldn't have . . ."

I couldn't say any more. But the words filled my mind anyway. *Wouldn't have slipped. Wouldn't have fallen. Wouldn't have died.*

"You can't save everyone, Joshua."

Keeping one hand on the steering wheel, Sophie reached out with the other and took my hand. Our fingers looped together. Normally that kind of thing would've made both of us really awkward, but in that moment it actually made me feel better.

Neither of us spoke. The wind howled, whipping our hair around like crazy.

Right then, I wished we could drive the rest of the way like that. But I guess driver's safety is more important because a couple of seconds later, Sophie let go and brought her hand back to the steering wheel.

"Sorry." She let out a nervous chuckle. Was it my imagination, or had she started glowing—just a little—around the eyes? "I just thought . . . you know—"

"No. It was nice. I mean—not *that* kind of nice." Suddenly my palms were sweaty. I wiped them against my shorts.

Remember how I said it *wasn't* awkward? Well, never mind about that. Suddenly, there was enough awkwardness inside the MarvelousMobile to fill a football stadium.

We drove nearly the rest of the way in silence.

🔥

The sun was just beginning to peer over the treetops when we reached Bear Creek. The town was just like Dr. Fleming had described. Not much to it. Not even a traffic light. We passed a diner, a church, a hardware store. A few other shops with boarded-up windows. A couple of streets led to small homes with overgrown lawns. And that was pretty much it.

I glanced around warily. With the sun coming up, a vintage red, white, and blue superhero car with four kids inside was a lot more noticeable. Luckily, it was still early. The streets and sidewalks were empty.

Like Dr. Fleming had said, at the edge of town was a street sign with the words we were looking for:

NONAME RD.

Sophie turned onto the dirt road. When we bumped over a pothole, Milton jolted awake. Blinking drowsily, he seemed surprised to find Cassie sleeping peacefully on his shoulder. As he shifted in his seat, Cassie's eyes flickered open. Pushing back her silver hair, she rose to an upright position.

"Hope I didn't drool on your shoulder," she mumbled.

"No big deal," Milton said. "I can handle a little drool."

"We're getting close." Sophie guided the car over another pothole. The MarvelousMobile lurched and groaned. "Safe house should be coming up."

I remembered what Dr. Fleming had said. *A dirt road that seems to go on forever without any sign of civilization.* It was starting to feel that way. Trees, trees, bump in the road, more trees. At least we wouldn't be spotted by anyone. But the isolation also gave me a weird nervous feeling. What if something happened out here? Something unexpected? Something bad?

I pushed the thought from my head. We were on our way to a safe house. And a safe house is supposed to be *safe,* right?

"We're here!"

As we rounded a curve in the dirt road, I saw it. The log cabin. It looked exactly like the photograph. Sophie pulled the MarvelousMobile to the side of the road and we climbed out.

As we approached, I noticed that a few of the trees had been rigged with security cameras. A laser sensor poked up from the grass to scan our movements. If it weren't for the fact that we had the exact same model on our own front lawn, I probably would've mistaken it for a sprinkler.

When we reached the front door, I looked around uncertainly.

"Uh . . . should we knock, or just—"

I went silent when I heard a sound.

Click.

The door swung open.

26

Dr. Fleming was standing in the doorway. I stared in amazement. Last we'd seen him, he'd been pale and weak from Winston's attack, hunched inside the library with nothing but Milton's shirt to stop the bleeding. Now he looked as healthy as ever.

"Welcome!" he said. "So glad you could make it!"

After another second or two of disbelief, our questions came tumbling out all at once.

"When'd you get here?"

"How'd you make it out of the school?"

"What about your injury?"

"Can I use your bathroom?"

The last question came from Milton. He was hopping from one foot to the other. Sophie shot him a look.

"What?" Milton shrugged. "It was a long car ride."

"I'll explain everything in due time," Dr. Fleming said. "For now, please, come inside. Make yourselves at home."

Once all of us had a chance to use the restroom and wash up, Dr. Fleming showed us to the dining room. On the way, I gaped at my surroundings. The outside of his safe house looked like the kind of place Abraham Lincoln might've grown up in, but the inside was more like a high-tech home of the future. Voice-activated appliances, a couch that slid across the floor depending on where you wanted to sit. An entire wall was lined with LCD monitors, showing high-definition security footage of the grounds outside.

When we reached the dining room, Dr. Fleming ran a finger across a touch-screen pad on the wall. A blank section of the floor flipped open and out popped a dining room table and six chairs. The table was already set with bowls and cereal.

"Sorry there's no milk," Dr. Fleming said. "Didn't have a chance to stop by the market on the—" He went silent when he noticed for the first time who was missing. "What happened to Miranda?"

My eyes dropped to the floor. "She . . . didn't make it."

Dr. Fleming lowered himself slowly into a chair. "Oh, dear. I'm so sorry."

Choking back tears, Cassie told him about how Daisy twisted out of control, how Miranda lost her grip and dropped into the darkness.

"We didn't see what happened after that," Sophie said.

"For all we know, Miranda survived the fall and swam to shore."

I tried to find hope in her words, but all I could think about was the dark, slashing rain. The crashing waves. The tall, sharp rocks that lined Alabaster Island. How could anyone survive that?

Even though all I'd had to eat in the last twelve hours was half a bowl of soup, talking about Miranda had caused my appetite to shrivel. I forced down a few bites of cereal as Dr. Fleming told us his side of the story.

"I waited inside the tunnel, pain searing my chest and shoulder, until I heard two voices on the other side of the shelf. One unmistakably belonged to that bratty girl we'd heard earlier. She kept screaming about how she'd gone blind—"

"Grifter," I said. "She had a little run-in with a gigantic lightbulb."

"The other voice was harder to place. A teenage boy complaining that all he had on were boxer shorts."

"That would be Lunk. He doesn't react well with water."

"In any case, I overheard the girl say that you'd made it off the island. Unfortunately, this bit of good news was matched by some rather unfortunate news. According to the boy in boxer shorts, there were more Cyclaurs waiting on shore. I heard the static of a walkie-talkie. The girl alerted the Cyclaurs that their target would be riding a giant robotic duck. 'Follow them!' she commanded."

"Yeah, they caught up with us a little later," Sophie said.

"Luckily, we managed to escape in the Marvelous-Mobile," Milton added.

Dr. Fleming wrinkled his brow. "The *what*?"

"We'll tell you later. What happened next?"

"Grifter and Lunk assumed I'd made it off the island as well. They gathered up the remaining Cyclaurs and headed in the direction of their boat. Once I was sure they were gone, I climbed out of the tunnel. Fortunately, it was a short walk to the office of Bernadette Oakley, the school nurse. Under most circumstances, I would've spent the next week in the hospital recovering. With Nurse Oakley, it took only an hour."

"Nurse Oakley's the best," Cassie said. "She has the power of healing. When I broke my arm in the third grade, it was completely better by that night."

"So then what happened?" Sophie set down her spoon, turning back to Dr. Fleming. "How'd you get here?"

"After Nurse Oakley patched me up, I hurried back to my office. I could scarcely believe what I saw on the way there. Alabaster Academy looked like a war zone. Children were in shock. So were teachers. I wanted to help, but I knew there were more important matters at hand. In my office, I dusted off the old hover scooter that I keep in the closet. A few minutes later, I was on my way."

"But what about the Dominion Key?" I asked.

"Ah yes." Dr. Fleming fixed me with an odd gaze. It reminded me of the looks he had given me at Alabaster. Like he knew something about me that even I didn't know. "If you're finished with your breakfast, I'll be glad to fill you in on every last detail."

I pushed away my bowl and stood from the table. "I'm ready."

Milton took one last bite of his cereal. Still chewing, he said, "Me too."

"Very well," Dr. Fleming said. "Come with me."

We followed him out of the dining room, up a flight of stairs, and through an open doorway. The room was nearly empty—no furniture, no windows—except for a built-in touch screen and a large silver ring that dangled from a hook.

Dr. Fleming plucked the ring off the wall and placed it over his forehead.

"What's up with the headband?" Cassie asked.

"Oh, this?" Dr. Fleming adjusted the silver band. "You'll find out in a moment."

There was something strange about his tone. But I didn't have a lot of time to wonder about it. Because right then, Dr. Fleming tapped the touch screen and the lights dimmed. In the center of the room, a 3-D holographic image appeared, a blue cluster slowly rotating halfway between the floor and the ceiling.

Dr. Fleming tapped the screen again. The image expanded. Then it broke apart into three different holograms, each bigger than me, that drifted around us like blue planets. They seemed to be diagrams. Technological designs, surrounded by equations and labels.

It was like being inside a science textbook.

I approached one of the holograms, reading the bold label that floated above it. *Platinum-Sealed Alpha Capacitor.* The same words I'd seen on nFinity's list. The same object that Grifter and Lunk stole a few days earlier. The other two diagrams matched as well. *Oscillating Particle Immobilizer. Neutron Flow Reversal Chamber.*

"These are the objects that Phineas Vex has stolen so far." Dr. Fleming gestured to the holograms. "All in his effort to build The Device. A weapon that can freeze time and space. That can turn every human on the planet into a perfectly still, helpless being. Like a mannequin in a department store. Armies toppled. The most secure bank vaults plundered. Entire continents falling under a single person's control."

"But where's the Dominion Key?" Sophie asked. "Did you already destroy it?"

"Not exactly." Dr. Fleming was standing inside one of the huge 3-D holograms. As the blue cloud swiveled around him, his features seemed to change, turning eerie and cold. The silver headband glimmered in the strange light. "You see, I couldn't destroy the Dominion Key."

Milton scrunched his brow. "What do you mean?"

"Yeah! What if Vex shows up?" Cassie asked.

"The truth is, I never possessed the Dominion Key." The blue holographic cloud swirled and shifted around him. "Not until now."

I was still trying to make sense of Dr. Fleming's words when he tapped the touch screen again. The holograms vanished and the door beside him snapped shut.

DR. NIGEL FLEMING

If you take Dr. Fleming's class in high-grade weaponry, you're guaranteed to have a blast. Literally. But his greatest achievement could result in the destruction of the entire world.

Without the hazy blue veil over his face, I could see his expression clearly now. And it sent a chill down my spine.

"I truly am sorry about this," he said. "But I had no other choice."

Dr. Fleming tapped another key on his touch screen. All at once, I realized—coming here had been a huge mistake.

27

Before I could react, an invisible force knocked me off my feet. I felt myself snap backward as if I were flicked across the room by the world's biggest rubber band. An instant later, my back slammed against the wall. Pain erupted through my entire body.

I was pinned to the wall. Unable to move. My arms and legs were spread like jumping jacks on pause. My head was tilted slightly to one side, so I could see the same had happened to my friends. They were sprawled out across different parts of the wall, each frozen in their own crazy poses. Cassie had hit the wall sideways. Even her hair was attached, spread around her head like a silver fan. Sophie was beside her. One arm above her head, the other close to her waist. Nearest to me was Milton. His eyes—the only part of his body he could move—darted back and forth.

We were stuck like insects in a spiderweb.

Only Dr. Fleming was left standing where he'd been before. His hand hovered over the touch screen. Light glinted off his silver headband.

"What's going on?" Sophie's skin glowed as she struggled to pull herself free. But even her superstrength was powerless against the unseen force. "What is this?"

"I call this my antimagnet room," Dr. Fleming said. "I devised the technology myself. It works like a heavy-duty electromagnet. Except instead of attracting metallic objects, the wall attracts everything that *isn't* metal. Like *you*, for example."

Dr. Fleming loosened his sleeve and pulled it back. Silver gleamed underneath. He was wearing a metallic undershirt. He bent down and rolled up the bottoms of his pants. Same thing. Silver underneath.

All of a sudden, I understood why he'd put on the silver headband when we entered the room. It was to match the rest of the metallic outfit he had on under his regular clothes.

The magnetized gear was keeping him from sticking to the wall like the rest of us.

Meanwhile, my friends and I were pinned to the edges of the room like magnets against a fridge.

I concentrated on summoning my Gyft. Spontaneous combustion quivered through my veins, but it didn't make any difference. I couldn't move.

There was no point in screaming. We were in the middle

of nowhere. *You could detonate five hundred pounds of heavy artillery in my backyard and nobody would notice.* That was what Fleming had said about his safe house yesterday.

We were completely alone.

"Have you lost your mind?" Cassie narrowed her eyes at Dr. Fleming. "Why are you doing this?"

"It's quite simple, really." A creepy smile spread across Dr. Fleming's lips. "I saw an opportunity I couldn't pass up. A chance to finally possess the Dominion Key."

"What're you talking about?" Milton asked. "I thought you already built it."

"Not exactly. You see, my invention isn't technically the Dominion Key. It's actually"—Dr. Fleming squinted, searching for the right words—"an apparatus for harnessing the power of the Dominion Key. More like a big electrical socket. And the thing you plug into this socket—well, *that's* the Dominion Key."

"So why don't you get something else to plug into your stupid socket?" Sophie said.

"It's not that easy. The Dominion Key cannot be constructed of metal and circuitry. It's not like the other parts of The Device at all. In fact, it's right here in this room."

Cassie glanced frantically at the blank walls and floor. "What do you mean? What is it?"

"Not what. *Who.*" Dr. Fleming's gaze focused on me, and I felt every inch of my body turn to ice. "Joshua Dread— you *are* the Dominion Key."

200

28

I felt like I'd just swallowed a hand grenade. Everything inside me shattered. Burst to pieces. And I was left with . . .

A memory.

Dr. Fleming's words catapulted my brain to the last time I was face to face with Phineas Vex. Or maybe I should say face to *knee*. Vex had towered over me in his indestructible bionic suit. He was enormous. His booming voice had rattled my skull.

The only reason I'm sparing your life is because I have something much bigger in store for you.

The memory fast-forwarded past other events. The confrontation with nFinity and his goons in the food court. The attack on Alabaster. All along, I'd been unable to figure out why Vex was going to so much trouble to capture me. Vex wasn't a guy who ordinarily valued human life. So why spare mine?

What did he want with me?

The question had been hanging over me for months. And finally, I had an answer. The reason Vex would stop at nothing to track me down and keep me alive.

I was the Dominion Key.

I was the one thing that could deliver Phineas Vex world domination.

Dr. Fleming was looking at me with a gleam in his eyes, as if he enjoyed watching me put it all together.

"And then yesterday, you kids came into my office with tales of rare components getting stolen from high-security labs," he said. "Phineas Vex was after The Device. Naturally, I was afraid. I knew that my invention was essential to harnessing the Dominion Key. Which meant Vex would be coming after me. And then came our encounter with your wolfy classmate, Winston. At that moment, I recognized who you really are."

After Winston's attack, Dr. Fleming had stared at me in the strangest way. As if he knew something about me that I didn't. Now I understood why.

"The power of spontaneous combustion is extremely rare, extremely volatile," Dr. Fleming said. "And it comes with a little-known side effect called TPIS. Temporary Particle Immobilization Syndrome. The ability to freeze time and space. Usually accompanied by an illuminated string of pure energy capable of destruction on a massive scale."

TPIS. Was it supposed to make me feel any better that my freaky condition came with its own scientific name?

"You, Joshua Dread, are capable of freezing time and space. Which is precisely what The Device does. Except on a much, *much* bigger scale. That's why Vex has been chasing you all this time. Somehow, he must've witnessed your power in action."

Suddenly, I remembered the first time I fought Phineas Vex. In his underground lair. It was also the first time my Gyft went haywire. The world stopped. My power took control. And Vex was front and center for the display. He'd been trying to capture me ever since.

Dr. Fleming stepped toward me.

"It was only a matter of time until Vex tracked me down," he said. "I would've never been safe. Even here. But now I have something Vex needs. Something he's been looking for all this time. I have you."

Dr. Fleming was standing close enough now that I could've reached out and strangled him if it weren't for the antimagnetized wall. I strained every muscle, trying to free myself, but it was useless.

"You're insane." My voice shook with rage. "Phineas Vex will never bargain with you."

"That's where you're wrong. With my unique expertise in high-grade weaponry, I'd make a wonderful asset for any evil billionaire with an interest in world domination. In fact, Vex has already promised to make me his chief adviser. He's on his way now. Should be arriving any minute."

My heart skipped a beat. The situation was bad now,

but once Vex arrived, things would only get worse. Much worse.

Dr. Fleming walked to the other end of the room. He fiddled with the touch screen until a surveillance video showing the front of his house appeared. Still no sign of Vex. Or anyone else.

As Fleming cycled through more surveillance footage, I glanced at my friends. I could see my own fear reflected in their expressions. Then I caught Milton's eye. He wasn't speaking, but I could tell right away that he was trying to say something to me. His eyes flicked down to the pocket of his shorts. Just barely poking out was a corner of plastic.

It took me another moment to recognize what I was seeing. The sealed plastic bag Dr. Fleming had given us yesterday. And inside was—

The peanut butter and jelly sandwich.

Correction: the *exploding* peanut butter and jelly sandwich.

The way Milton was stuck against the wall, there was no way he could reach it. But one of my hands was less than an inch from his pocket. If I could move just a little, I might be able to crack the seal open.

I strained, flexing the entire left side of my body. Shoulder, arm, fingers—anything that would bring me a little closer to the bag. But nothing happened. It was like I was glued to the wall.

I could see Dr. Fleming out of the corner of my eye, still inspecting the screen. Turning my attention back to the sandwich in Milton's pocket, I focused my Gyft. I concentrated all my energy on my left hand. Spontaneous combustion surged through my chest and crackled down my arm.

And it worked! The blast was powerful enough to knock my hand free of the wall. It wasn't much, but it did the job. A split second later, the antimagnetism yanked my hand back. My palm smacked the wall with a *FWUMP!*

Dr. Fleming whirled. "What was that?"

He scanned the four of us. I did my best to look innocent. Then Dr. Fleming's eyes narrowed. He was looking right at the spot where my left hand had just been. In my peripheral vision, I could barely make out what he'd spotted.

My charred handprint on the wall. A leftover of spontaneous combustion.

Luckily, Dr. Fleming was too distracted by the burned wall to notice where my hand had landed. My fingertips were at the edge of the plastic bag. If I could wiggle them a little bit, then maybe, just maybe . . .

Dr. Fleming made a *tsk-tsk* noise. As if we were back in first period and I'd just flunked a quiz. "I understand you're upset, Joshua," he said. "But really—*must* you leave marks on my wall?"

He calmly walked toward us. His shoes clicked on the floor.

"Your spontaneous combustion won't do any good here," he said. "The antimagnetic force is far too strong."

"We'll see about that." Gritting my teeth, I set off

another pulse of spontaneous combustion. This time, as my hand blasted away from the wall, I squeezed the plastic between my fingers. Just like the last time, my hand shot outward . . . and was immediately pulled back again.

My knuckles collided with the wall. I winced, pain shooting up my hand.

"What did I tell you?" Dr. Fleming took another step my way. "You're just hurting yourself now. So why don't you act like a good little hostage and wait patiently until—"

He went quiet suddenly. His eyes widened. And I knew exactly what had caught his attention. I'd managed to pull the sandwich free from Milton's pocket. It was lying on the floor at Dr. Fleming's feet. The seal was ripped open.

I looked from the sandwich to Dr. Fleming. "Hope you're in the mood for peanut butter and jelly."

Dr. Fleming tried to turn, but he was too late. In the next instant, the sandwich exploded. Peanut butter and jelly flew everywhere. A bunch of it got on Milton and me. But most of the brown and purple goo blasted across Dr. Fleming.

His clothes, his face, his hair—he was covered in PB&J.

With Fleming distracted, Cassie vanished into smoke. The force of the antimagnet didn't seem to affect her in that form. The wisp of silver streaked across the air and transformed back into Cassie. As soon as she was herself again, the invisible force yanked her toward the wall—but not before she knocked the silver headband off Fleming's head.

Without the band, Dr. Fleming was suddenly vulnerable

to the antimagnet. He surged forward. His arms flailed. Peanut butter splattered all over the place. And—

WHAM!

He head-butted the wall.

The impact caused his body to go limp. His eyes rolled to the back of his head. His tongue lolled out of his mouth.

"Nice job, guys," Sophie said. "Now we just need to find a way off this wall."

"I'll take care of that." Cassie transformed herself again. The smoke whipped across the room. When it reached the touch screen, a finger emerged from the cloud. It looked half human, half smoke. The vaporous pale finger seemed to struggle against the pull of the antimagnet. But because she wasn't fully formed, Cassie could resist enough to tap the screen.

It was kind of like watching a ghost play with an iPad. Soon enough, she managed to disengage the antimagnet. All at once, the force vanished. My friends and I collapsed to the floor. So did Dr. Fleming. Sophie rushed to him. She ran a hand along his wrist. After a second, she glanced up.

"He's alive," she said. "Should we tie him up?"

"No time." Cassie was in full human form again, staring worriedly at the screen. Dark shapes moved across the surveillance video. "Looks like Vex has nearly reached the safe house. And he brought an army with him."

29

We raced through the futuristic house. Down the stairs, into the hall, across the dining room. Empty bowls and cereal boxes were still scattered across the table. Less than an hour had passed since the last time we were here. The world had completely changed since breakfast.

"They'll be pulling up soon," Sophie said. "Maybe we can escape out the back door."

Sophie skidded around a corner into a sleek white kitchen. She was halfway across the room when the door on the opposite side blew off its hinges.

Standing in the obliterated doorway was nFinity.

"Hey, Soph." His voice came out casual, as if he'd just bumped into a friend after school. But in his eyes, I saw murder. "I was wondering when we'd get the chance to hang out again."

Sophie returned his greeting by reaching for the silver refrigerator beside her. With remarkable ease, she wrenched it from the wall. Pipes burst; steel scraped against marble. And in the next moment, Sophie thrust the fridge nFinity's way.

Our former teammate sidestepped the attack. The refrigerator smashed through the wall.

"Is that any way to say hello?"

nFinity ran a hand through his floppy brown hair. He might have acted all calm and confident, but he looked even worse than he had in the food court: Dark rings under his eyes. Splotchy, pale skin.

The four of us—Sophie, Milton, Cassie, and I—were crowded at the other end of the kitchen.

Sophie made a move for the stove, but nFinity was ready this time. He thrust out an arm and unleashed a blast of fire that was bigger than Sophie. Flames tore through the air. Sophie stumbled backward.

nFinity snapped his hand shut. The fire went out at once.

"There's no need for this to get violent," he said. "Give yourselves up and I'll talk to Vex. Ask him to go easy on you. He listens to me."

"He's *using* you!" Sophie spat back.

"News flash: that's the way the world works. You think it was any different when I was a superhero? As long as you're making money and bringing in commercial deals, everyone treats you like a rock star. But that all ends the second something new comes along."

nFinity flashed a dirty look my way. Obviously, he was still ticked about being upstaged by the Nameless Hero.

"At least with Phineas Vex, I know exactly what he stands for." Flames swirled in the palms of nFinity's hands. "He doesn't hide who he is. If he wants something, he steals it. No lies, no hidden motives. Not like Gavin Garland. Or your friend Nigel Fleming. Where is Fleming, anyway?" nFinity glanced around. "Ah well, I guess it doesn't matter. We have what we're looking for."

nFinity's eyes fixed on me.

I clenched my jaw. Any minute, Vex would arrive. And I really didn't want to be here when he did. I lurched to my side and grabbed the first thing I could get my hands on. Which happened to be . . . a spatula. Not exactly the world's best weapon. But with a little spontaneous combustion, it would do.

Energy surged inside me. I reared back and threw the spatula with all my power. By the time it left my hand, it was blazing. But nFinity was ready. He lifted both hands, surrounding himself with a wall of fire. It was like a shield, incinerating anything that came close before it could harm him.

As he rose, the flames rose with him, transforming before my eyes into an eight-foot-tall dragon made entirely of fire. Flames curved into sharp teeth and a long lizard tongue. A blazing pair of wings flapped up and down, sending sparks scattering. Burning talons slashed at the air. A red and orange tail whipped from side to side. On either side of the dragon's head, two white-hot eyes flickered.

I desperately reached for anything I could find on the counter—a spice rack, a salad bowl, a toaster. One after the other, I charged the objects with spontaneous combustion and tossed them nFinity's way.

The dragon snapped its fiery teeth and slashed with its flaming claws, turning my "weapons" into ash before they could cause any damage.

It was clear that I wouldn't have much success fighting an enormous fire dragon with kitchen utensils. Time to move on to another strategy.

Run.

My friends and I staggered into the dining room. The dragon chased us, leaving fire in its wake. Flames danced across the walls. The table was a red blaze. In the living room, Milton pointed at a back window. "Sophie, can you break the glass?"

"No problem." Sophie grabbed a large-screen TV off the wall and tossed it through the window like a giant Frisbee. Glass shattered, giving us an opening.

But before we could set off for the broken window, a spark hit the rug in front of Cassie. Flames rose, taking the form of the dragon's claws. They slashed at Cassie. For one horrible moment, I thought she was a goner. But by the time the fiery claws swung, Cassie had vanished. A wisp of silver smoke rippled across the living room. When it reached my side, the smoke transformed back into Cassie.

"Any other ideas?" she asked.

I cast a glance back the way we'd come. nFinity was standing in the dining room. Or what used to be the dining room. Now it was an inferno. Fire roared all around him. Orange and red blazed in his eyes.

"It's hopeless, Dread," he snarled. "Give yourself up."

Sophie grabbed my arm. "Don't listen to him!"

She pulled me toward a hall. Milton and Cassie ran after us. The fire spread on all sides, shifting and changing around us, taking on awful forms. The dragon's head—huge and horrifying—snapped its fiery jaws. The tail swung down from the ceiling. A claw slashed the air.

Heat seared my skin. Everywhere we turned, another flaming obstacle stood in our way. My friends and I huddled at the edge of the living room as the blazing red dragon circled us, closer and closer and—

Then it vanished. And so did the rest of the fire. The forest of flames winked out like a light.

I whirled around to see nFinity lying on the floor, unconscious. Mom was standing over him, gripping a frying pan.

"Didn't your parents ever tell you not to play with fire?" she said (even though I doubt nFinity heard her).

Dad stepped into the charred dining room beside her. The two of them weren't dressed like Dr. Dread and the Botanist. More like a suburban couple. But the way they glared at nFinity was pure supervillain. A hundred different emotions well up inside my throat: relief, love, excitement. . . . But most of all, I was confused.

"Where . . . What . . ." I swallowed. "How'd you find us?"

"We received a call from Edwin Alabaster," Mom said.

I'd never been so happy to find out the principal had

called my parents. I rushed across the room on shaky legs. As I hugged my mom and dad, they updated me on the rest of the story.

"Alabaster told us about how the school was attacked," Dad said.

"And that you kids managed to get off the island," Mom added.

"It must've been a bad connection, because it sounded like he said you escaped on a giant duck—"

"We assumed he was trying to say 'truck'—"

I chuckled. "Actually, you had it right the first time."

"Anyway," Mom went on, "Alabaster informed us that he'd just received a call from his daughter, who said you were all on your way to a safe house of some kind. He gave us the address and we came straight here."

"Just in time, by the looks of it." Dad's eyes were magnified behind the thick glasses he wore whenever he wasn't dressed up as Dr. Dread. He examined the charbroiled interior of Dr. Fleming's house. "What exactly happened here?"

"The explanations are going to have to wait." Sophie was standing at a window, peering outside. "There's an evil army in the front yard."

Milton rushed to the shattered back window. "There are more bad guys out here too!"

Sophie clenched her glowing jaw. "They've got us surrounded."

Looking out the window, I saw Vex's minions everywhere. Hundreds of Cyclaurs guarded the perimeter of the house. The morning sun gleamed off their bald heads and motorcycle parts.

And from the sky, their leader emerged.

The figure was a colossus of impenetrable titanium and horrible gadgetry, with hulking arms and legs and chest. Jet boosters flamed from the palms of his hands and the soles of his feet as he drifted closer and closer to the ground. I could just barely see the clear window in the head of the bionic body. The scarred face of a nightmare peering down at us.

Phineas Vex had arrived.

30

"This is bad," Sophie muttered.

Milton turned from the broken window, his features pale with worry. "This is *worse* than bad. This is the end of the world."

Fear buzzed in my chest like a hive of angry hornets. The Cyclaurs revved their engines, as if to cheer on the arrival of Vex. My brain was a screaming match of differing opinions about what to do next. *Run for your life! No, stand and fight! No, pee your pants and cry like a baby!*

I was getting dangerously close to going with option #3 when an astonishing sight appeared over the tree line.

Daisy.

Her broken wing had been repaired. The enormous robotic duck swept over the enemy lines. And riding on Daisy's back were two superheroes making their first public appearance in a *very* long time.

Mr. Marvelous and Whiz Kid.

Somehow they'd managed to squeeze into their old uniforms—although the *M* logo had completely faded from Mr. Marvelous's chest and the fabric of Whiz Kid's one-piece was stretched so tightly across his paunch that it looked ready to burst.

We watched through the window, amazed. The duck angled low over the yard, grabbing hold of a Cyclaur in each of its webbed feet. The tattooed motorcycle dudes looked a little surprised that they were suddenly in the grasp of the world's largest waterfowl . . . and even more surprised when Daisy flung them at a couple of trees. The Cyclaurs smashed into a mass of bionic body parts and twisted metal.

Other Cyclaurs turned their headlights on the huge duck. But by the time they fired, Marvin and Gus had navigated Daisy high into the air. Flying over the Cyclaurs, the bird released a series of egg bombs, one after the other.

BOOM!

POWWW!

KABLOOOEY!

The ring of Cyclaurs was consumed by explosions. A wave of fire was followed by a storm of shattered motorcycle parts and shrapnel.

"Nice try, but nothing will stop me this time." Vex's voice boomed across the front yard. The window frame rattled.

All around him was a scene of pure chaos. The wreckage of demolished Cyclaurs was scattered everywhere. Craters had formed in the earth where Daisy's eggs had crashed. Fire raged in the trees.

But Vex was unharmed. He began walking toward the house, each step shaking the floor beneath our feet. Flames were reflected in the window that shielded his scarred face. A red glow danced in his good eye. The other eye was white and unseeing. His lips curled into a horrible leer.

In the sky, Daisy veered toward him. Marvin and Gus were still perched on the duck's back, their expressions sharp with determination. Without slowing his pace, Vex raised a hulking arm. A bolt of lightning formed in the clear blue sky and struck Daisy's wing. The robot rocked sideways and crashed into a stretch of trees.

I lost sight of Marvin and Gus. I could only hope they'd survived.

"You really think a couple of washed-up superheroes and a robotic duck can do anything against me?" Vex's terrible scowl deepened. "I am invincible. And once I have captured you, Joshua Dread, I will possess the key to ultimate world domination."

My head filled with horrible visions of Phineas Vex using The Device—*and me*—to bring the world to its knees. Entire armies unable to defend themselves. Governments crumbling. People living in fear, slaves to the wishes of an evil overlord.

Then something else appeared. Something so unexpected—so unbelievable—that for a moment, I was sure I was hallucinating.

Miranda.

I blinked, taking another look. It was really her. She was alive!

She emerged from a bend in the road, racing in our direction. And she'd brought most of Alabaster Academy with her. Students ranging from sixth graders to high schoolers, rushing forward like an attacking army—except for the fact that they were wearing school uniforms. And it wasn't just students either. A bunch of teachers were in the crowd. I recognized Coach Stillwell with his bristling mustache and undersized shorts. Above him, gripping the handlebars of a hover scooter, his silver hair whipping in the wind, was Principal Alabaster himself.

They must've raided Dr. Fleming's supply of high-grade weaponry. Older kids had plasma cannons and rocket launchers. Middle schoolers were equipped with explosives the size of baseballs. Many of the teachers held glowing spears. Most of the crowd was on foot, but those with the Gyft of flight soared alongside some students and teachers who were outfitted with jet packs and hover vehicles.

The sight of them made my heart jump. Especially Miranda. Ever since I'd watched her fall, fear had settled in the pit of my stomach. The fear that she was gone. That she was dead. I'd never been happier to be wrong. She'd survived. And by the looks of it, she was leading the charge to save us.

My exultant mood lasted for about half a second. Then reality crashed in. There was just one thing standing between us. And that one thing happened to be huge. Invincible. Unstoppable.

Phineas Vex turned to face the students and teachers. Two hatches opened in his shoulders and a duo of guns emerged, each taking aim at the group.

"Engage Machine Guns of Animosity!" bellowed Vex.

A rapid-fire string of blasts echoed and the guns released a spray of glowing red bullets—holograms with the deadliness of real ammunition.

Horror clawed me from the inside out. Our classmates and teachers had come here to rescue us, but instead they were running full speed toward their death. And there was nothing any of us could do. I'd already watched Miranda come close to dying once. Now I had the very bad feeling that I was about to witness the real thing.

But Miranda had something else in mind. Before Vex had even begun firing his hologram machine gun, she motioned to a tall, older girl beside her.

"Brittany—NOW!" she commanded.

The girl stepped in front of the group. I'd seen her once or twice in the rec room back at Alabaster. Now she spread her arms and a pure white field of energy formed in front of her, a wall of illumination that spanned the width of the road and was several times her height.

"Get behind it!" Miranda called out.

The rest of the group obeyed her command, crowding together so the wall of light shielded them. It all went down with such speed—such precision—that it could've only been orchestrated by a Senser, someone who knows what's going to happen moments before it takes place.

In other words, someone like Miranda.

I gasped. The spray of bullets hit the energy shield with a raucous clatter. But the wall of light stood. And everyone behind it was unharmed.

For the time being, at least. Unfortunately, Vex had a lot more deadly tricks up his bionic sleeves.

His next move was straight from my mom's set of skills. All at once, the tall trees on either side of the road jolted forward and began plucking people from the ground with their leafy branches.

"SPEARS!" Miranda hollered, and about a dozen teachers on hover scooters veered close to the trees, slashing at the branches with glowing spears before anyone was lifted more than a few feet off the ground.

For every attack that Vex sent the group's way, Miranda was waiting with a countermove. A gaping hole opened in the earth in front of them, but Miranda was already guiding everyone to one side. As they raced safely around the edge of the hole, Vex flung out his arms, sending a wave of ice crashing toward the group.

At the exact same moment, Miranda yelled, "Ronny, Johnny—GO!"

A pair of teenage twins emerged from the crowd, their eyes glowing green. For a moment, it looked like they were wearing radioactive contact lenses. And then a blast of green energy shot out of their eyes and collided with the tidal wave of ice, turning it into a giant slushie that rained down harmlessly over the students and teachers.

The group made steady progress, advancing closer and

closer to Vex between attacks. Miranda led the front line like a general.

When they were no more than twenty-five feet from Vex, Miranda brought the group to a halt. Raising one hand, she hollered, "Ready!"

The group prepared their weapons, raising plasma cannons and heaving rocket launchers onto their shoulders.

"Aim!"

Miranda's voice echoed across the yard. The army of students and teachers waited for her signal. And then . . .

"Fire!"

The noise that followed was deafening. Fifty simultaneous blasts. Plasma beams and rockets hurtling forward. Glowing spears arching through the air. Baseball-sized explosives raining down. Those without weapons used their powers. A sonic shriek. Another round of green energy from the radioactive twins. And all of it—a massive storm of weaponry and superpowers, unleashed at the exact same moment—was aimed at a single target.

Vex.

His huge bionic form was consumed in a fiery cloud. The impact bloomed like an exploding star.

I staggered backward, shielding my eyes. A tremor shook the earth and a wave of heat washed over me.

Once the roar faded, I was left with a buzzing in my ears. I turned and squinted through the smoke. All that was left of the spot where Vex had been standing was a massive crater. Fires raged at the edges of the hole in the earth.

A twinge of hope flickered inside me. Nothing could've survived that kind of devastation. . . . Right?

Wrong.

I was still peering through the wall of gray smoke and flaming ashes when something moved. A dark shape, rising from the crater.

31

Phineas Vex appeared from the smoke, propelled out of the hole in the earth by jet boosters that flamed from his hands and feet. Shock ran through every cell of my body. Vex had been bombarded with enough firepower to bring down a small army. But you'd never have known that by looking at him. His bionic suit was still in mint condition. There wasn't a single dent in his armor. Not even a scratch.

Vex landed at the edge of the crater with a crashing *thud*. "Your puny weapons cannot stop me." His voice thundered across the devastated landscape. "*Nothing* can stop me. And soon the world will cower under my control. But first, I must take what I came for."

Vex turned and thrust out his armored hand. Energy rippled from his fingertips, and the wall of Dr. Fleming's house disintegrated. Wood and plaster were transformed into ash. Glass melted inside the window frame. A hole formed in the wall—a crumbled opening that looked out on the obliterated front yard. And Vex.

Now that there was nothing standing between us, my thoughts converged into a terrible realization: Vex was right. There *was* no stopping him. The students and teachers from Alabaster had unleashed all their ammunition, all their powers . . . yet he was still alive. Unharmed. And soon he would rule the earth.

But for some strange reason, my friends and family weren't going down without a fight. Sophie stared at me, her blue-gray eyes peering from her glowing face. She put a hand on my shoulder.

"We won't let him take you," she whispered.

"Yeah." Milton placed his hand on my other shoulder. I could see the fear in his face, but his voice was firm. "I don't care how big he is; nobody messes with my best friend."

Beside him, Cassie and my parents stepped forward. Their hands came to rest on my shoulders as well.

"We love you, Son," Dad said.

"We're here for you," Mom said.

"All the way," Cassie added.

My voice rose in sudden desperation. "You can't do this. It's me he wants. Not you. There's still time. Run. Get as far from here as possible. Please." I tried to say more, but my throat went dry and my voice cracked.

Not that my words did any good. No matter how hopeless the situation seemed, my friends and family were sticking by me.

There in Dr. Fleming's living room, we lined up side by side. The ground shook with Vex's approach. More sections of the wall crumbled around us. With each step Vex took in our direction, his demented grin widened.

He was less than twenty feet away when something flickered through the smoke behind him. A blur. There and then gone. I was just beginning to convince myself it was nothing when I saw the movement again. A human form weaving through the air on a hover scooter. As the figure got closer, I saw it more clearly.

Principal Alabaster had separated from the group and was speeding toward Vex. Not that Vex noticed. All his twisted attention was on me. Which meant he was unaware when Alabaster came to a halt a few feet behind him and brought his hands together . . . unaware when the principal pulled his hands apart, creating an opening in the universe . . . unaware when Alabaster navigated his scooter up, then down, then side to side, so that the rip in space grew taller and wider . . . unaware that behind him was a portal to another place entirely.

It looked sort of like Principal Alabaster had pulled apart a curtain behind Vex, revealing a view of endless white and cloudless sky—right in the middle of the smoke and ash of Fleming's yard.

The opening was bigger than what I'd seen Principal Alabaster create back at school. Much bigger. Maybe even big enough to transport one humongous bionic supervillain . . .

And that was when I knew what needed to be done.

I stepped forward, clenching my hands into fists. Spontaneous combustion crackled in my veins. But I was going to need more than spontaneous combustion this time. I was going to need a power that I'd never harnessed before. At least, not intentionally.

Summoning all my concentration, I thrust my arms forward, as if I were shoving an invisible force in front of me. Energy throbbed in my chest, swirling across my arms and legs. And . . .

Nothing happened.

Dr. Fleming had said that spontaneous combustion came with the ability to freeze time and space. Temporary Particle Immobilization Syndrome, he'd called it. His words scrolled across my mind. *Usually accompanied by an illuminated string of pure energy capable of destruction on a massive scale.*

If there was ever a time when a little Temporary Particle Immobilization Syndrome would come in handy, this was it. But who was I kidding? The power had only popped up on a few rare occasions in my life, and never when I'd actually seen it coming. So what made me think I could just whip it up now?

My hands sank to my sides. Vex obviously knew what I'd tried—and failed—to do. He narrowed his one good eye at me.

"Give it up, Joshua Dread," he boomed. "The power you seek is not yours to command. The truth is, you need me just as much as I need you. The Device will grant you the full extent of your abilities."

Behind him, the portal shimmered. He was still unaware that he was standing in front of a window to another place. Not that it mattered, since there was no way of getting him through it.

"Face it, Dread." His amplified voice made my stomach curl. "Without my help, without The Device, you'll always be the one who makes things blow up. A nice party trick, perhaps. But you can be so much more."

I couldn't bear to listen to another word. A flurry of rage and horror and hatred blocked out everything but the sight of Vex. Without even my realizing it, my arms were suddenly in front of me again—every muscle tensed, every tendon straining. A rush of energy surged through me. The air around me shook with pure power.

For the flash of a moment, I saw Vex's expression change. From sadistic glee to something else . . .

Fear.

It was a look you don't get from Vex too often. Which made it even more incredible when his face froze that way. Every feature locked into place. And his body too. His armor-plated arms and legs, his bionic suit—all suspended, unmoving, perfectly still.

The world around him had also come to a stop. Behind Vex, Principal Alabaster was perched motionless on his hover scooter. In the background, I caught sight of the others from Alabaster. Miranda was positioned in front of her army of students and teachers, all as still as figures in the most amazing wax museum on earth.

The only movement came from a ribbon of light that

stretched out from my hands, across the yard, past frozen clouds of smoke and unmoving scraps of ash. Closer and closer to Vex.

When the string of illumination made contact with Vex's heavily armored chest, it was like someone had pressed the play button on a remote. The world clicked into motion again.

Vex exploded backward, his massive arms and legs flailing. At the same time, a force pulled me in the opposite direction, as if I'd been hooked to a bungee cord that yanked my feet off the ground.

A vision flashed in front of my eyes: Phineas Vex flying through the portal that Principal Alabaster had created, vanishing into another place entirely. Endless white and cloudless sky.

"Nooo!" Vex's shriek came through the opening.

In a flash, Alabaster pulled the seam in the universe closed. The portal was gone. And so was Vex.

Unfortunately, I didn't really get much of a chance to enjoy the moment. Because the force that had knocked me off my feet threw me across Fleming's living room.

A jolt of pain shot through me. And then I collided with something that turned my world to black.

32

*I*t was all a dream.

The attack at the food court, the sudden move to Alabaster, the face-off with Phineas Vex . . . it was all so bizarre and disturbing. There was no other explanation. I was asleep right now, snoozing peacefully, and none of the things that had gone down over the past week had really happened.

Any second now, I was going to wake up in my usual bed in Sheepsdale. Go downstairs to see my parents waiting for me with my usual breakfast. Micus would throw his usual clump of soil at my face.

Everything would be back to normal.

But when my eyes flickered open, the scenery above looked nothing like the ceiling of my bedroom. And if all that was only a dream, then why did my body feel like it had just been used as a punching bag?

My back was stiff as a board. Pain shot down every inch of my arms and legs. I couldn't even turn my neck to look around. About the only thing I *could* do was let out a weak, gurgling moan. So that was what I did.

"Oh my gosh, he's awake!"

Sophie appeared above me. Her face broke into a relieved grin. Her hair hung down around me like a blond tent. Her eyes looked red from crying.

"Joshua—I was so worried," she whispered in a trembling voice.

She leaned toward me. If I could've moved, I'm sure I would've squirmed awkwardly at being so close. At least I didn't let out another pitiful gurgle-moan.

Sophie's face was only a few inches from mine when I heard another voice.

"Careful not to touch him!" said a woman I couldn't see.

I felt a strange rush of disappointment when Sophie pulled away. Another face replaced hers in my field of vision—that of a middle-aged woman with short gray hair and a worried expression.

"Any sudden movements could worsen the injury," she said. "Just keep perfectly still."

"That shouldn't be a problem," I croaked.

"I'm Bernadette Oakley," said the woman in a gruff voice. "I'm here to help you get better."

"You're in good hands, Joshua," came a voice that I recognized as Principal Alabaster's. I couldn't see him—only hear him. "Nurse Oakley is exceptionally qualified for this kind of situation."

Through the clouds in my head, I remembered Cassie and Dr. Fleming mentioning the name Oakley. The school nurse with the power of healing. And if there was one thing I could use right now, it was some superpowered healing.

"Do you remember what happened before your injury?" Nurse Oakley asked.

"Yeah," I whispered. "There was an explosion. Knocked me backward. Then I hit something."

"No memory loss. That's a good sign."

I wasn't so sure about that. After the experience I'd just been through, there were a few things I would've been glad to wipe from my memory forever.

"Vex?" I said. "Is he . . . I mean, did he—"

"He's gone," said Alabaster. "Vanished into an interspatial gateway."

"But where'd he go? What if he—"

"Don't concern yourself with that right now," the nurse said. "At the moment, the priority is making sure you get better."

There was so much more I wanted to know. Where did Phineas Vex get transported to? What happened to everyone else? Were there any other injuries? But I was already feeling so weak, and the strain of speaking had taken its toll. When I opened my mouth, all I managed to get out was a groan that sounded like *"Bluuurphh!"*

"Just relax." Nurse Oakley gently placed a hand on my chest. "I'm going to begin the healing procedure. And just a warning—this might sting a little."

The nurse's hand pressed into my chest. An instant later, a bolt of pure pain surged through my entire body. Then I lost consciousness again.

ꙮ

Nurse Oakley had a twisted idea of "healing." While I was out, I dreamed of pitchforks and blankets made of fire ants. When I finally awoke, I heard people talking somewhere out of my line of sight.

". . . sure he's okay?" asked Milton. "Looks like he's hurting pretty bad."

"That's part of the process," Nurse Oakley replied. "In order to heal him, I first have to extract the injuries from his body all at once. Sort of like pulling a tooth. Ordinarily, his recovery would be slow and painful. Instead, it's very fast and very painful."

"I'm just glad he survived," said Cassie. "The way he hit the wall, that was—"

"Awesome, right?" Milton guessed.

"Actually, I was going to say deadly."

"Oh, right. That too," Milton said. "But I wasn't worried. Joshua and I have been in *tons* of deadly situations." He made it sound like something to brag about.

Another voice joined the conversation. My mom's. "How long until he's fully recovered?" she asked.

"Tough to say," said Nurse Oakley. "Couple of hours, most likely. Maybe longer."

"The portal that you opened back there?" Dad began. "Where *was* that?"

"Antarctica," the principal replied. "We took a family vacation there a few years back—"

Cassie interrupted her dad with a groan. "Worst. Vacation. Ever."

"It was an opportunity to witness a completely unique ecosystem firsthand," Alabaster said, before adding: "Although I *will* admit, it did get rather tedious after a while. Now it's where I send anything that I never want to see again. Like Vex."

I thought of the gateway Alabaster had pulled open. The endless white landscape and cloudless blue sky. I imagined Vex suddenly appearing there. No doubt he would find his way back to civilization eventually. But by then we would be long gone.

The only question was . . . *where would we go?*

I didn't have much time to wonder about this, though, because right then I felt Nurse Oakley bring a hand down on my chest again. Another burst of pain shocked my system and I blinked out like a light.

🔥

When I came to, Marvin and Gus were looking down at me. Marvin had a grisly cut running along his forehead and Gus's faded uniform was ripped and burned in about twelve different places, but at least they were okay. They seemed surprised to see me open my eyes. And even more surprised when I spoke.

"Thanks for letting us borrow your car," I managed to wheeze.

The two elderly superheroes grinned.

"How ya feeling?" Gus asked.

"Been better." The words came out in a slow, weak voice. "Sorry that . . . we got you involved in all this."

"You kidding?" Marvin's smile widened. "This has been the most fun we've had in thirty years!"

Gus nodded eagerly. "We'd been out of the superhero business so long, we'd forgotten what a thrill it is to kick some supervillainous butt."

"How's Daisy?" I asked.

"Wrecked," Marvin replied. "After Vex's lightning strike, she crashed hard. Wing's all busted up. Tail's out of whack."

"But since your former teacher won't be able to take care of her any longer, we've decided to adopt the old bird. We can have her all repaired and in flying condition again in six months."

The "former teacher" comment sent my thoughts hurtling in another direction. "Dr. Fleming?" I asked. "Where is he?"

"We found him unconscious upstairs. Sophie told us everything. How he lured you here. Took you kids hostage. Summoned Vex."

Gus shook his head sadly. "When Fleming woke up, he confessed to all of it."

234

"What's going to happen to him?" I asked.

"I'd say there's a good chance he'll have his teacher's certificate revoked." Gus smirked.

"And that he'll spend the next couple of decades in Graavenskall," Marvin added.

Graavenskall. The maximum-security prison for supervillains. It's where the world's baddest bad guys get sent when their schemes go awry.

"What about nFinity?" I asked.

From the look that Gus and Marvin exchanged, I knew they wouldn't have good news. "Unfortunately, nFinity escaped." Gus let out a heavy sigh. "By the time the authorities got to the house, he was gone."

"The police are searching the woods," Marvin said. "If he's anywhere within a twenty-mile radius, they'll find him."

I wasn't holding my breath. By now, nFinity would be long gone.

At least for the time being. Soon enough, he'd be back again. And that was a reunion I definitely *wasn't* looking forward to.

Marvin glanced sideways and his forehead wrinkled. "Uh-oh. Looks like the school nurse just noticed you're awake."

I heard Nurse Oakley's voice in the distance. "What're you two doing talking to my patient? He needs to rest!"

Marvin turned back to me. "Take care of yourself, Joshua Dread. What you did back there was truly heroic."

Coming from Mr. Marvelous, this was a pretty big compliment.

My view of the superheroes was replaced by that of Nurse Oakley. I could see from her expression that she was gearing up for another round of her torturous "healing."

"Do we really need any more of the whole pain-extraction thing?" I asked in a quavering voice. "I'm actually feeling a lot better. Really—I'm practically—"

Her hands came down on my chest. A fresh wave of agony blanketed my body.

🦂

The next time I opened my eyes, I felt a million times better. Nurse Oakley's methods might've been unusual, but they seemed to have worked wonders. I was wide awake and bursting with energy.

Rising to a sitting position, I blinked at my surroundings. Dr. Fleming's safe house looked like a disaster zone. Charred furniture. Ashes littered across the floor. A gaping hole in the wall revealing a view of even worse chaos outside. A scarred landscape of motorcycle parts and mangled trees.

And crossing this scenery toward me was Miranda. "I can't believe you survived," she said.

"I had the exact same thought when I saw you," I said.

Miranda gave a half shrug. "I guess we're both lucky to be here."

"But what happened? How'd you—"

"Make it out alive?" Miranda finished. "After I fell, I eventually washed up on the shore of Alabaster Island. I must've passed out, because the next thing I remember is hearing people calling my name. It was a search party of students and teachers. Principal Alabaster was with them. Once I was back inside the school, there was an assembly of everyone at Alabaster. I knew exactly where you guys were headed. And I had a hunch that Vex and his foot soldiers might end up there too. By the end of the assembly, we'd made up our minds—we had to get to Bear Creek. We packed a few hover buses with students, teachers, and a whole lot of deadly weapons. And, well, you know the rest."

"You saved our lives. If you hadn't shown up when you did . . ." I shivered just thinking how close we'd come to complete catastrophe. Death, imprisonment, world domination.

Not exactly my idea of a good time.

Miranda's dark eyes considered me for a moment like she'd just gotten a glimpse of my future. "Hey, Joshua," she said. "One last thing . . ."

"Yeah?"

Her face broke into a grin. "You're about to get run over by a trash can."

I blinked. "Huh?"

Our conversation was interrupted by a screeching electronic voice. *"JOSHUAAA!"*

I turned just in time to see a silver blur rushing in my

direction. A squat shape that *did* look a lot like a dumpy metal trash can. Except I knew at once what it really was.

"Ellio—"

Before I could get the rest out, the robot butler knocked me onto my back with his "hug." All of a sudden, I had a feeling I might need another visit from Nurse Oakley.

33

"**H**ow wuuuzzz your new schoool?"

Elliot's squeal rang in my ears. I climbed to my feet, wiping the dirt off my tattered clothes even as the robot's protractible arms wrapped tightly around me.

"Not so great, actually," I admitted.

"I misssed youuu!"

"I—uh . . . missed you too." I wriggled free of Elliot's grasp. "How'd you get here?"

My dad stepped forward with an explanation. "Your mother and I decided to bring him with us. He rode on the back of my hover scooter."

"I ooonly felll off onccce!"

"We parked the scooters in the bushes," Mom said. "Elliot waited there until we were sure you were okay."

"But we've already filled him in on what he missed," Dad said.

"Baaad man got zapped tooo North Pole!" Elliot chimed in.

"Actually, Antarctica is the *South* Pole," Dad corrected. His eyes turned to me. "You showed great courage back there, Son."

The memories flickered in my brain. The world coming to a sudden standstill. Nothing moving but a string of light. Vex flying backward through the gateway.

I shook my head, as if that would rid me of the thoughts. "I don't even know how I made it happen."

"You're getting stronger," Mom said. "More powerful."

"Yeah, and thanks to that power, the whole world is gonna suffer if Vex ever *does* get his hands on me."

Dad's magnified eyes didn't blink. "Then we'll make sure that doesn't happen."

"Unfortunately, that means you won't be able to return to Alabaster," Mom said. "Now that Vex knows you were there, it wouldn't be safe any longer."

Our conversation was interrupted by a sound outside. A steady *thwump*ing that grew louder and louder. My family and I rushed to the front yard. Gazing up at the sky, we saw a bright red helicopter coming in for a landing. Stanley was in the pilot's seat. Squeezed into the cockpit beside him were Captain Justice and Scarlett Flame.

The spinning propellers blew away broken branches and loose chunks of earth. By the time the helicopter had touched down, a mob of excited students and teachers had gathered close by.

Captain Justice kicked open the door to the helicopter and leaped outside. Ignoring the screaming students around him, he scanned the swarm of faces until he saw who he was looking for.

"Sophie!"

The superhero rushed forward and wrapped his muscular arms around his daughter. A wave of whispers passed through the crowd of classmates.

"Oh my gosh!"

"The newbie knows Captain Justice!"

"I'm jealous!"

Captain Justice held Sophie by the shoulders, gazing at her. "Scarlett and I came as soon as we heard. Are you all right?"

"I'm fine, Dad," Sophie said.

Scarlett Flame approached, sunlight glistening across her golden body armor. She placed one manicured hand on Captain Justice's shoulder and the other on Sophie's. "We were so worried that we canceled the rest of our publicity tour."

Sophie glanced up at her dad's girlfriend. I could see a hundred snarky thoughts pass across her face. But instead, Sophie swallowed. And all she said was "I'm glad you guys came."

"We're just sorry it couldn't have been sooner." Captain Justice gazed at the destruction all around: A massive crater in the ground. Scorched trees. A log cabin with half its front wall missing. "Looks like we missed all the fun."

Milton pushed through the crowd of onlookers and

wrapped his arms around the two newly arrived super-heroes.

"Group hug!"

"Yes—uh . . . it's nice to see you as well, Marlon," said Captain Justice.

As the sun gradually rose higher in the clear blue sky, Captain Justice and Scarlett Flame signed autographs for everyone. Eventually, Principal Alabaster separated from the group and approached my parents. "Delightful seeing you again after all these years," he said. "I'd love to stay and catch up, but I'm afraid we've got to get back."

"We truly appreciate everything you did to keep our son and his friends safe," Dad said.

"Just doing my job." Principal Alabaster's twinkling gray eyes moved from me to my parents. "You know, your twenty-five-year class reunion is coming up. Perhaps I'll see you there?"

A half smile appeared on my mom's face as she replied, "Not a chance."

"That's what I thought you'd say." Principal Alabaster turned back to the excited mob. "Okay, everyone. Autograph time's over. Back to school."

The crowd let out a disappointed groan. Principal Alabaster pulled open another seam in the universe. By the looks of it, this portal led directly into the stone entrance of Alabaster Academy. As the principal ushered students and teachers through the gateway, I stood to the side with Sophie, Milton, my parents, and Elliot, saying our goodbyes.

Cassie emerged from the group. "Too bad you guys can't

come back to school." She pushed a strand of silver hair from her forehead and her eyes landed on Milton. "I'll miss hanging out with you."

"Me too," Milton said at once. "I'll let you know where we end up. Maybe your dad can teleport you there on weekends."

Cassie smiled. "That'd be nice. And you can show me your Supersonic uniform."

Milton nodded eagerly. "My jet-boots still fit!"

Cassie let out an excited chirp. She rushed forward and kissed Milton on the cheek. When she hopped backward again, Milton's face had gone red all over.

"See ya!" Cassie waved as she vanished through the portal.

For a few moments, Milton stood there with a goofy grin on his face—until Miranda knocked him out of his daze with a punch to the shoulder.

"Snap out of it, lover boy." She chuckled, turning to the rest of us. "Well, I guess this is goodbye."

"What do you mean?" I knitted my brow. "Aren't you coming with us?"

I knew at once from the look on Miranda's face that she wasn't. I guess it shouldn't have come as such a surprise. Out of the four of us, she'd done the best at Alabaster. She'd excelled in everything—from defusing bombs to avoiding dodgeballs. She was obviously meant for a place like Alabaster.

But none of that meant I was happy to see her go. Miranda had become one of my best friends over the summer. I had no idea where I'd end up, but knowing she wouldn't be there really bummed me out.

One glimpse at Sophie and Milton was all it took to let me know that Miranda had already broken the news to them. Probably while I was unconscious.

"My mom and I have spent the past two years traveling the country, trying to improve my Gyft and get noticed," Miranda said. "Along the way, I've lost every friend I've ever had. But at Alabaster . . ." She couldn't help grinning. "It's the best of both worlds. I'll be able to train my powers without switching schools every few months. There's only one downside—I'll miss you guys."

"We'll miss you too," I said.

Miranda hugged Sophie, Milton, and me, then turned and skipped through the portal, into the entry hall of Alabaster Academy, where a large group of Gyfted kids were waiting for her.

Principal Alabaster gave us one final wave. Then he stepped into the entry hall, closing the interspatial gateway behind him as if he were zipping up a tent.

🜍

There was enough room in Scarlett's helicopter for three additional passengers. Since my parents' hover scooters were parked close by, they would travel separately with Elliot, while Milton, Sophie, and I would hitch a ride with the superheroes.

"I call shotgun!" Milton raced excitedly to the helicopter door.

Captain Justice and Scarlett Flame followed him, holding hands.

"Ugh." Sophie made a face. "They better not make out the whole way."

As Sophie trailed them, I waited behind with my parents and Elliot.

"What'll we do now?" I asked.

Dad shook his head. "We're not entirely sure. At the moment, we don't even know whether we can call ourselves supervillains. I mean, just *look* at us. These days, we spend most of our time with Captain Justice."

"Don't forget his girlfriend and her solid-gold swimsuit," Mom grumbled.

"Maybe it's time we get back out there. Show the world we're still capable of awful treachery." Dad's expression filled with sudden purpose. "After all, it's been nearly a year since our last wicked plot."

I shuddered. That's just what I needed in my life—*more* wicked plots.

"First things first," Mom said. "We'll all meet up again in Sheepsdale. We figure we have less than twenty-four hours to vacate the house before Vex regroups and comes looking for us. Wherever we end up, we need to make sure we can bring the zombies. And Micus."

"Don't forget about Elliot," Dad said.

"Yeaaahhh! Donnn't forrrget meee!"

"And as for you"—Mom ruffled my hair—"we've got to ensure that you get a good education."

"And that you remain safe," Dad added.

"Maybe we'll try homeschooling."

My head filled with dreary thoughts of never leaving the house, enduring lessons interrupted by the groans of hungry zombies, with nobody to hang out with but two supervillains, a dysfunctional robot butler, and a murderous mutant houseplant.

Now, that *would* be a wicked plot.

I hugged my parents and Elliot goodbye. Once they took off in the direction of their hover scooters, I climbed into the back. My shoulder pressed up against Sophie's as I settled into the cramped cabin.

Stanley started the engine. I heard the *whoosh* of propellers beginning to swirl above us. Soon, the helicopter lifted off. We were on our way.

Acknowledgments

Joshua Dread began as a Microsoft Word file on my computer, and it would've stayed that way were it not for the intelligence and efforts of my agent, Sarah Burnes. Thank you for your excellent guidance over three books now. Many thanks also to Logan Garrison, who spotted Joshua in her crowded slush pile and got this whole thing started. Rebecca Gardner and Will Roberts have done an extraordinary job of sharing this series with the world and setting Joshua Dread up with all his different aliases: Joshua Schreck, Lucas D., Jack Vandal, and more to come. Thank you to everyone at the Gernert Company. Without a doubt, the best agency a guy could ever want!

A HUGE thank you goes out to my editor, Wendy Loggia, for your insight, wisdom, and advocacy on behalf of this series. And for making me a better writer.

Thank you, Mary Van Akin. I truly appreciate your publicity expertise, patience, and dedication over the last year. And thanks to Nicole Banholzer for taking the torch from Mary and offering your enthusiasm and ideas from day one.

I am so fortunate to have the support of Delacorte Press/ Random House Children's Books. In particular, and in no particular order: Krista Vitola, Trish Parcell, Bobbie Ford, Adrienne Waintraub, Lisa McClatchy, Brenda Conway, and Beverly Horowitz. This series would not have been possible without all of your commitment, attention, emails, calls, contacts, expertise, experience, and a million other little things that helped get Joshua Dread onto bookshelves (both real and virtual) and into readers' hands.

Thank you to the copy editors who have worked behind the scenes on all three books. You make me seem much more intelligent and observant than I actually am.

My gratitude goes out to the terrific folks at the Random House Audio/Listening Library imprint—Dan Zitt, Laura Duane, Jodie Cohen, Katherine Fleming, and Catherine Bucaria—for bringing Joshua Dread to life. And to Maxwell Glick, for playing all the parts so well.

Thank you to Brandon Dorman. Your covers keep getting better.

Cathy Berner at the Blue Willow Bookshop in Houston has been a wonderful advocate for this series from the beginning. I owe you some Jacques Torres, Cathy.

When I was writing the acknowledgments for the first Joshua Dread, I had no idea what an enormous role librarians and teachers would play. Traveling to schools and libraries across the country, I've seen firsthand what a difference you make in the lives of your students. I am truly encouraged by your passion and dedication to reading, writing, curiosity, and creativity.

The following educators are among those who invited me into their schools and offered me an opportunity to share my story with their students: Tim Jones, Debra Yocum, Michael Kandel, Margaret Mary Ryan, Jami Ryan, Sarah Murphy, Phoebe Search, Beth McGregor, Vikki Terrile, Tiffany Nienow, Cheryl Patrick, Cindy Kunz, Diana Hood, Sue McDowell, Sydnie Kleinhenz, Kim Warwick, Alicia Vandenbroek, Margaret Garrett, Kay Almquist, Ashley Wagon, Noland Harmon, Brandee Smith, Marilyn Fowler, Jeanette Dow, Babette Vandervert, Erica Briscoe, Kim Logue, and Leigh Collazo. THANK YOU!

A number of people were generous enough to let me stay at their homes while I was on the road promoting this series.

Thank you to Debi Thompson Campbell, Chris and Lee Daniels, and Bob and Mia Leland.

I am so grateful for the support from my family throughout the years. Doug, Sherilyn, and Kim Svien. Erin and Dennis Sissell. Mike, Carla, and Cody Owens. Layla Price. Stephen and Claudia Greek. Amy and Stephen Snell. Lauren and Travis Trull. Caitlyn and John Moore. Kristy Fowler Compton.

My greatest appreciation goes to my grandparents James and Sue Greek, to whom this book is dedicated.

Ein ganz herzliches Dankeschön auch an meine Schwiegereltern, Michael und Irmtrud Schlör, ebenso wie an Karin Schlör, Kalle Geis und Zenta Englert. Ich bin so dankbar, ein Teil eurer Familie zu sein.

Thank you to my brother, Evan Bacon. I might be able to invent robots on the page, but you build them in real life. And to Laura Cattani and the entire Cattani family, who generously open their home for ranch Thanksgivings and reggae parties.

Words cannot express my gratitude for my parents, Terry and Jamie Bacon. Thank you for everything. (And sorry for making Joshua's parents horrible supervillains. It's a total coincidence, I swear.)

And my final thank you goes to Eva. My wife and best friend, walking companion and translation consultant, social coordinator, and the person I want to do everything with. Always and forever. None of this would've been possible without you.

You are the Key.

Miriam Berkley

LEE BACON grew up in Texas with parents who never once tried to destroy the world (at least, not that he knew of). He is the author of the Joshua Dread series and lives in Brooklyn, New York. Visit him at leebaconbooks.com.